200
NOTABLE DAYS

SENATE STORIES · 1787 TO 2002

RICHARD A. BAKER, *Senate Historian*

Prepared under the direction of Emily J. Reynolds, Secretary of the Senate

U.S. GOVERNMENT PRINTING OFFICE
WASHINGTON, DC

Library of Congress Cataloging-in-Publication Data

Baker, Richard A.
 200 notable days : Senate stories, 1787 to 2002 / Richard A. Baker.
  p. cm.
 Includes bibliographical references and index.
 ISBN 0-16-076331-2 (alk. paper)
 1. United States. Congress. Senate—History. 2. United States. Congress.
Senate—History—Anecdotes. 3. Legislative bodies—United States—History. 4.
Legislative bodies—United States—History—Anecdotes. I. Title. II. Title:
Two hundred notable days.

JK1161.B313 2006
328.73'071—dc22

                                                        2006046631

For sale by the Superintendent of Documents, U.S. Government Printing Office
Internet: bookstore.gpo.gov Phone: toll free (866) 512-1800; DC area (202) 512-1800
Fax: (202) 512-2250 Mail: Stop IDCC, Washington, DC 20402-0001

ISBN 0-16-076331-2

CONTENTS

INTRODUCTION

I t is impossible to walk through the busy corridors of the United States Capitol without hearing stories. The building's marble and sandstone halls echo with loud stories, whispered stories, stories told in English and in a multitude of other languages. Members of Congress tell stories to colleagues and constituents. Red-jacketed Capitol tour guides spend long days as professional storytellers, and serve as models for the many congressional staff, seasonal interns, and even legislative pages called on to help introduce the Capitol and Congress to the millions who flock annually to Washington, D. C. Knowing that individual visitors may come to Capitol Hill only once in a lifetime, these hosts rely on historical vignettes to enliven the experience. Years later, many of those visitors will recount to family and friends, in letter-perfect detail, the stories they heard on their first visit to the United States Capitol.

Over the past 30 years as Senate Historian, I have prepared countless historical narratives to inform senators, staff, constituents, and others who are curious about the traditions, personalities, and legislative landmarks of the "World's Greatest Deliberative Body." More recently, I have reshaped many of these stories into brief sketches for those who have a strong interest in the subject but lack the time to explore extended historical essays. From hundreds of Senate anecdotes, I have selected the 200 that appear in this volume. Each includes references for further reading.

There are stories reflecting all areas of Senate activity, from its important constitutional prerogatives—such as confirmation of presidential nominations—to historical milestones of decidedly less importance. An example of the latter occurred in 1930 as senators confronted the choice of continuing with traditional operator-assisted telephones or accepting a daunting new product of communications technology—the dial phone.

From the well-known and notorious, to the unusual and even whimsical, these stories are presented to enlighten, inspire, amuse, and inform. Each story amplifies the narratives that precede and follow it. Read collectively, they provide clear impressions about the forces, events, and personalities that have shaped the Senate of the 21st century.

Richard A. Baker, Senate Historian

CHAPTER I

FORMATIVE YEARS
OF THE SENATE
1787-1800

State Houses Will Elect Senators

Who should elect United States senators? When the framers of the Constitution convened in Philadelphia in 1787, they struggled over three possible answers to this question.

Under one plan, each state legislature would send a list of candidates to the U.S. House of Representatives so that the House could make the selections. Yet this would have made the Senate dependent upon the House, ignoring James Madison's advice that the best way to protect against tyrannical governments was to balance the ambitions of one branch against those of a corresponding branch. Madison and his constitution-writing colleagues had in mind a system in which the Senate keeps an eye on the House, while the House watches the Senate.

Or perhaps the people could elect their own senators. This had the disadvantage, as far as city dwellers and those with commercial interests were concerned, of favoring the nation's larger agricultural population. Connecticut's Roger Sherman warned against direct election. "The people should have as little to do as may be about the government. They lack information and are constantly liable to be misled."

On June 7, 1787, the framers settled on a third option. They decided that state legislatures should select senators, without any involvement by the House of Representatives. The state legislatures, they argued, would provide the necessary "filtration" to produce better senators—the elect of the elected. The framers hoped that this arrangement would give state political leaders a sense of participation, calming their fears about the dangers of a strong centralized government. The advantage of this plan, they believed, was that all laws would be passed by a "dual constituency" composed of a body elected directly by the people (or at least the white males entitled to vote for members of their state legislatures) and one chosen by the elected representatives of individual states.

After several decades, as service in the Senate became more highly prized and political parties gained wider influence in directing state legislative operations, this system of indirect election began to break down. When separate parties controlled a legislature's two houses, deadlocks frequently deprived states of their full Senate representation.

A plan for direct popular election lingered for decades. Finally, a campaign to make governmental institutions more responsive to the people propelled the measure to ratification in 1913 as the Constitution's 17th Amendment.

Fifty-five delegates met in Philadelphia during the hot summer of 1787 to frame a new constitution for the United States.

Further Reading

Ahmar, Akhil Reed. *America's Constitution: A Biography.* New York: Random House, 2005.

Crook, Sara Brandes, and John R. Hibbing. "A Not-so-Distant Mirror: The 17th Amendment and Congressional Change." *American Political Science Review 91* (December 1997): 845-853.

June 19, 1787

Seven-Year Senate Terms?

On June 19, 1787, the framers of the U.S. Constitution decided that the term of a senator should run for seven years. They also tentatively agreed that House members should serve three years, that Congress should elect the president, that the president should serve for a term equal to that of a senator, and that the Senate should appoint Supreme Court justices. Obviously, the framers had a lot of work ahead of them over the following three months to shape the delicately balanced Constitution we know today.

Why a seven-year term for senators? Members of the existing Congress under the Articles of Confederation—a unicameral body—served one-year terms. In deciding to create a bicameral congress to replace that moribund institution, the Constitution's framers recognized that the Senate, chosen by state legislatures, would be a smaller body than the popularly elected House. To avoid being unduly threatened by public opinion, or overwhelmed by the House's larger membership, senators would need the protection of longer terms.

The framers looked to the various state legislatures for models. Although the majority of states set one-year terms for both legislative bodies, several established longer tenures for upper house members. Delaware had three-year terms with one-third of its senate's nine members up for election each year. New York and Virginia state senators served four-year terms. Only Maryland's aristocratic senate featured five-year terms, making this legislative body the focus of the Constitutional Convention's Senate term debates.

Framers either praised Maryland's long terms for checking the lower house's populist impulses, or feared them for the same reason. Some convention delegates believed that even five-year U.S. Senate terms were too short to counteract the dangerous notions likely to emerge from the House of Representatives.

James Madison first supported the seven-year term but then raised it to nine, so that one-third of the Senate seats could be renewed every three years. Others thought that was too long. On June 26, the convention compromised on the six-year term, with a two-year renewal cycle. None of this pleased New York Delegate Alexander Hamilton, who believed that the only protection for senators against the "amazing violence and turbulence of the democratic spirit" would be terms lasting a lifetime.

The framers of the Constitution met in Philadelphia at the Pennsylvania State House, now known as Independence Hall.

Further Reading

Haynes, George H. *The Election of Senators.* New York: Henry Holt and Company, 1906.

Madison, James. *Notes of Debates in the Federal Convention of 1787.* Athens, Ohio: Ohio University Press, 1984.

Story, Joseph. *Commentaries on the Constitution of the United States.* Boston: Hillard, Gray, 1833.

July 16, 1787

Framers Reach a "Great Compromise"

An excerpt from the Journal of the Constitutional Convention showing the "Great Compromise."

July 16, 1987, began with a light breeze, a cloudless sky, and a spirit of celebration. On that day, 200 senators and representatives boarded a special train for a journey to Philadelphia to celebrate a singular congressional anniversary. Exactly 200 years earlier, the framers of the U.S. Constitution, meeting at the Pennsylvania State House (now known as Independence Hall) in Philadelphia, had reached a supremely important agreement. Their so-called Great Compromise (or Connecticut Compromise in honor of its architects, Connecticut delegates Roger Sherman and Oliver Ellsworth) provided a dual system of congressional representation. In the House of Representatives each state would be assigned a number of seats in proportion to its population. In the Senate, all states would have the same number of seats. Today, we take this arrangement for granted; in the wilting-hot summer of 1787, it was a new idea.

In the weeks before July 16, 1787, the framers had made several important decisions about the Senate's structure. They turned aside a proposal to have the House of Representatives elect senators from lists submitted by the individual state legislatures and agreed that those legislatures should elect their own senators.

By July 16, the convention had already set the minimum age for senators at 30 and the term length at 6 years, as opposed to 25 for House members, with 2-year terms. James Madison explained that these distinctions, based on "the nature of the senatorial trust, which requires greater extent of information and stability of character," would allow the Senate "to proceed with more coolness, with more system, and with more wisdom than the popular[ly elected] branch."

The issue of representation, however, threatened to destroy the seven-week-old convention. Delegates from the large states believed that because their states contributed proportionally more to the nation's financial and defensive resources, they should enjoy proportionally greater representation in the Senate as well as in the House. Small-state delegates demanded, with comparable intensity, that all states be equally represented in both houses. When Sherman proposed the compromise, Benjamin Franklin agreed that each state should have an equal vote in the Senate in all matters—except those involving money.

Over the Fourth of July holiday, delegates worked out a compromise plan that sidetracked Franklin's proposal. On July 16, voting by states, the convention adopted the Great Compromise by a heart-stopping margin of one vote. As the 1987 celebrants duly noted, without that vote, there would likely have been no Constitution.

Further Reading

Farrand, Max. *The Framing of the Constitution of the United States.* New Haven: Yale University Press, 1913. Chapter 7.

Rossiter, Clinton. *1787: The Grand Convention.* New York: Macmillan, 1966. Chapter 10.

September 30, 1788

First Two Senators—an Odd Couple

When the necessary ninth state ratified the U.S. Constitution in June 1788, the Congress under the Articles of Confederation began planning the transition to the new federal government. On September 13, 1788, that soon-to-expire Congress issued an ordinance giving states authority to begin conducting elections for their senators and representatives.

Less than three weeks later, on September 30, Pennsylvania became the first state to elect its two United States senators. By a vote of 66 to 1, its legislature accorded William Maclay the distinction of being the first person elected to the Senate and, by the closer margin of 37 to 31, gave the second seat to the more controversial Robert Morris. The two men stood at polar extremes from one another. Robert Morris was a wealthy Philadelphia merchant who distrusted governments based on popular choice. By contrast, Maclay was an agrarian "small d" democrat from upstate Harrisburg who distrusted Philadelphia aristocrats in general and Morris in particular. Each man savagely undercut the other, for example, in campaigns to have their respective cities chosen as the national capital.

Of William Maclay, one biographer has written that he was "reserved, pessimistic about human nature, and Calvinistic in his morality. Analytical and introspective, he was also self-assured, proud, self-conscious, and quick to take offense." Maclay vigor-ously fought what he considered to be the Senate's willingness to strengthen the presidency and soon became an outspoken anti-administration senator. Perhaps as an outlet to his growing frustrations, he kept a diary of Senate proceedings, which in his day were conducted entirely behind closed doors. Although Maclay served for only two years, his diary is indispensable for understanding the early Senate.

In the early 1780s, Robert Morris had served as superintendent of finance, making him the chief administrator of the Confederation government and the nation's second most powerful figure after George Washington. He had nominated Washington to serve as president of the Constitutional Convention and later loaned him the use of his finely appointed Philadelphia mansion when Washington resided in that city. One of the nation's richest men, Morris saw nothing wrong with using privileged government information to shape his personal investment strategy. While a senator, he became entangled in disastrous land speculation schemes, which led to his financial ruin. Several years after leaving the Senate in 1795, he entered into another term of service—three years in a debtors' prison.

Robert Morris, senator from Pennsylvania (1789-1795).

William Maclay, senator from Pennsylvania (1789-1791).

Further Reading

Bowling, Kenneth R. and Helen E. Veit, eds. *The Diary of William Maclay and other Notes on Senate Debates.* Baltimore: Johns Hopkins Press, 1988.
Ver Steeg, Clarence L. *Robert Morris: Revolutionary Era Financier.* New York: Octagon, 1972.

March 4, 1789

First Senators Arrive for Session

On March 4, 1789, eight conscientious senators overcame difficult late winter travel conditions to reach the nation's temporary capital in New York City. Eleven states had by then ratified the Constitution. Out of the 22 eligible senators, the Senate needed 12 present to achieve a quorum to conduct business.

At the appointed hour for the new government to begin, the eight senators-elect climbed the stairs of New York's old city hall. Hoping to convince Congress to make New York the nation's permanent capital, city leaders had recently named that building Federal Hall and tripled its size. When the eight senators reached their elegant chamber on the building's top story, the Senate literally became the "upper house."

All eight were men of distinction in government and politics. Most had served in their state legislatures and the Continental Congress. Six were framers of the Constitution.

New Hampshire's John Langdon would become the Senate's first president pro tempore. Connecticut sent William Samuel Johnson and Oliver Ellsworth. As a senator, Johnson would continue in his other job—president of nearby Columbia College. Oliver Ellsworth was best known for his proposal at the Constitutional Convention creating the Senate as a body that represented the states equally—the so-called Connecticut Compromise.

Pennsylvania sent William Maclay, who would keep the only detailed record of what happened behind the Senate's closed doors during the precedent-setting First Congress. His Pennsylvania colleague was Robert Morris. One of the nation's wealthiest men, Morris had helped to finance the American Revolution and signed both the Declaration of Independence and the Constitution.

Without a quorum, the eight senators wrote to their missing colleagues "earnest[ly] requesting that you will be so obliging as to attend as soon as possible." Two weeks passed before William Paterson ambled over from New Jersey and Richard Bassett arrived from Delaware. This left the Senate two members short of a quorum, as the House of Representatives waited impatiently on the floor below. Finally, on April 6, the necessary 12th member arrived. The Senate then turned to its first order of business—certifying the election of George Washington—five weeks after his presidential term had officially begun.

In January 1790, at the start of the second session, a more experienced Senate reduced its convening delay to only two days. Finally, at the beginning of the third session in December 1790, the necessary quorum appeared on time and the Senate got down to business as planned. The House of Representatives experienced similar delays for all three First Congress sessions.

Federal Hall in New York City (as it appeared in 1797) where Congress met from 1789-1790.

Further Reading
U.S. Congress. Senate. *The Senate, 1789-1989,* Volume 1, by Robert C. Byrd. 100th Congress, 1st sess., 1988. S. Doc.100-20. Chapter 1.

Senate Doorkeeper Elected

James Mathers did not know exactly how old he was in 1789, but he guessed that he was close to 45. He knew for sure that he had been born in Ireland and that his family had moved to New York before the Revolutionary War. As a young man, he enlisted in the Continental army, served throughout the long conflict, and suffered a serious wound that would trouble him for the rest of his life.

After the war, with a large family to support, Mathers took a job as a clerk for the Continental Congress. In 1788, this one-chambered national legislature, then located in New York City, appointed Mathers to be its principal doorkeeper. He assumed those duties just as that body was about to go out of existence to make way for the Congress established under the newly ratified Constitution of 1787.

The Senate of the First Congress achieved a quorum for business on April 6, 1789. The following day, it elected Mathers as its doorkeeper. The post of doorkeeper was particularly important for a legislature that intended to conduct all its sessions in secret, just as the Continental Congress had.

With one assistant, Mathers tended the chamber door, maintained the Senate's two horses, and purchased firewood.

In May 1790, as Congress prepared to move to Philadelphia for a 10-year residence, while the new national capital was being constructed in Washington, D.C., he supervised shipment of the Senate's records and furnishings. When the Senate decided to open its sessions to the public in 1795, Mathers became responsible for enforcing order in the galleries. Three years later, on the eve of the Senate's first impeachment trial, members realized that they needed an officer with the police powers necessary to arrest any who refused an order to appear before that proceeding. Consequently, Mathers took on the expanded title of "sergeant at arms and doorkeeper."

When the Senate finally moved to Washington in 1800, Mathers helped establish the Senate's new quarters and remained on the job until 1811, when he died after falling down a flight of stairs. This Irish immigrant of humble origins maintains the distinction of holding the post of Senate sergeant at arms longer than any of his 36 successors. He is truly one of the Senate's "founding fathers."

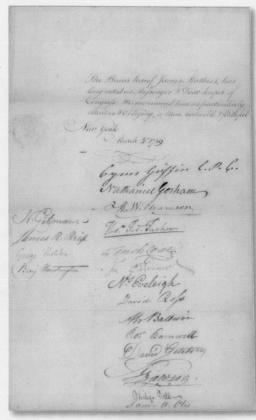

Petition to recommend James Mathers for the position of Senate Doorkeeper.

Further Reading

National Intelligencer (Washington, D.C.), September 5, 1811.

April 8, 1789

Help Wanted

Here is a job posting that could have appeared in the spring of 1789. "Newly established legislative body seeks experienced public administrator. Successful candidate must be able to maintain confidence of demanding individuals holding diverse political views. Specific duties include journal-keeping, bill management, payroll preparation, and stationery acquisition. Administrator must be able to supervise two clerks, keep secrets, and write neatly. Salary: $1,500."

On April 8, 1789, the Senate filled that position by electing Samuel Otis to be the first secretary of the Senate. A protégé of Vice President John Adams, the 48-year-old Otis was well qualified for the job. He had been quartermaster of the Continental army during the Revolutionary War, speaker of the Massachusetts house of representatives, and a member of the Congress under the Articles of Confederation.

Otis' early duties combined substance with symbolism. In addition to engaging the many tasks associated with establishing a new institution, he had the high honor of holding the Bible as George Washington took his presidential oath of office. As the Senate set down its legislative procedures and carefully negotiated relations with the House and President Washington, Otis became a key player. At a time when senators spent less than half of each year on the job in the nation's capital, Otis was on the job year round.

During the 12 years that John Adams served as vice president and then president, Otis enjoyed great job security. The situation changed, however, in 1801, when control of the Senate shifted from the Adams Federalists to the Jeffersonian Republicans. When John Quincy Adams became a senator in 1803, he reported to his father that Otis "is much alarmed at the prospect of being removed from office." Through the considerable political turbulence in the years ahead, Samuel Otis held on as secretary, despite occasional complaints from senators about the Senate's journals not being kept up to date or records being kept in a "blind confused manner."

During his 25 years in office, a service record never likely to be broken, Secretary Otis never missed a day on the job. To the very end of his life, he remained intensely devoted to the Senate. Suffering from "excessive fatigue" early in 1814, he held on until April, when the Senate completed its work for the session. Only then did he die.

Samuel A. Otis, first secretary of the Senate (1789-1814).

Further Reading

National Cyclopaedia of American Biography, Vol. 2. New York: James T. White & Company, 1921.

Morison, Samuel Eliot. *The Life and Letters of Harrison Gray Otis.* Boston: Houghton Mifflin, 1913. Vol 1.

April 27, 1789

The Senate Prepares for a President

On April 27, 1789, confusion and frustration dominated the Senate's proceedings. President-elect George Washington would arrive at New York City's Federal Hall in three days to take his oath. The Senate was not prepared. Questions had to be answered. By what title should he be addressed? In which chamber would the ceremonies take place? Should members receive his address standing or seated? Where would the post-inaugural religious service be held?

Since its first meeting, three weeks earlier, the Senate had been deeply absorbed with matters of protocol and procedure. Behind many contentious debates lay the Senate's desire to ensure its equal—if not superior—status relative to the House of Representatives. For example, the Senate devised a plan for delivering messages between the two chambers. The Senate provided that its secretary would take legislation and other documents to the House. For traffic coming in the other direction, however, the Senate expected no fewer than two House members to carry legislation. For other messages, one member would be sufficient. The House greeted the Senate's proposal with laughter and sent its clerk. A similar response awaited a Senate plan to pay its members a dollar a day more than House members.

John Adams, who had taken his vice-presidential oath six days earlier, worried about the protocol of titles. Should the House Speaker be addressed as "Honorable"? The Senate voted

no. What about the president? How about "His Highness the President of the United States of America and Protector of their Liberties"? A Senate majority thought that was fine. When the House later disagreed, a compromise produced the current simplified title. Should Adams act as president of the Senate or vice president of the United States? No one had an answer.

On April 30, as the Senate debated these issues, the House of Representatives filed into the Senate Chamber. Because someone had forgotten to send out the presidential escort committee, members waited another hour. Finally, Washington arrived. After a fumbled greeting from Adams, the president-elect took his oath and delivered his address in a halting and nervous manner. Following the church service, senators returned to their chamber to plan a formal reply. Protocol issues continued to preoccupy the Senate throughout that First Congress—and beyond.

In this Currier and Ives depiction, made in the 1870s, George Washington takes the presidential oath of office, while Samuel Otis, the secretary of the Senate, holds the Bible.

Further Reading

U.S. Congress. Senate. *The Senate, 1789-1989*, Volume 1, by Robert C. Byrd. 100th Cong., 1st sess., 1988. S. Doc.100-20. Chapter 1.

Senators Receive Class Assignments

On the morning of May 15, 1789, Tristram Dalton climbed the steep stairs to the Senate Chamber in New York City's Federal Hall. At a few minutes after 11 a.m., the recently elected Massachusetts senator placed his hand into a small wooden box. With Vice President John Adams presiding and 12 of the Senate's 20 members looking on, Dalton grasped a small slip of paper and lifted it for all to see. He then read its brief notation: "Number One." With that ritual act, seven senators became members of "Class One" and learned that their terms of office would expire within two years.

A day earlier, a special committee had assigned each of the 20 senators to one of three as yet unnumbered classes. (Although the Senate was meeting in the nation's temporary capital of New York City, New York would not get around to selecting its senators for another two months. Rhode Island and North Carolina, among the original 13 states, had yet to ratify the Constitution.) Assignment of senators to classes was done in such a way that each class would

A rendition of the Senate Chamber in New York's Federal Hall, where the Senate met from 1789 to 1790.

contain members drawn from all sections of the country but no more than one senator from any state. The Senate had then designated three senators—one from each class—to draw lots from a box on behalf of their respective classes.

The brief ceremony was repeated twice more that morning, although we do not know in what order the slips were drawn. The designee of a second group of seven senators drew the number two, thereby placing those members in "Class Two" with a term of four years. The remaining six senators won the Class Three identification and a full six-year term. The Senate had thereby set into operation its constitutionally required "class system," in which one-third of that body's seats would be subject to election every two years.

Since 1789, the Senate has placed senators from newly admitted states into classes in such a way as to keep those classes nearly equal in size. When Hawaii, the most recently admitted state, sent its first two senators in 1959, the wooden box contained numbers one and three. Repeating Tristram Dalton's long-ago gesture, Senator Hiram Fong drew Class One, while Oren Long entered Class Three, thus setting the current 33-33-34 arrangement among the three classes.

Further Reading
U.S. Congress. *Senate Journal.* 1st Cong, 1st sess., May15, 1789.

July 17, 1789

Senator Ellsworth's Judiciary Act

When the Senate first convened in 1789, many expected it to be a fairly passive body, similar to the state senates on which it was partly modeled. Aside from acting on nominations and treaties, the Senate's principal job was seen as reviewing legislation crafted in the House of Representatives. Although this anticipation proved fairly accurate for the first several decades, there are notable exceptions. The Judiciary Act of 1789, almost exclusively the Senate's handiwork, profoundly influenced the nation's judicial and constitutional development to the present day.

On April 7, 1789, the day after achieving its first quorum, the Senate appointed a committee, composed of one senator from each of the 10 states then represented in that body, to draft legislation to shape the national judiciary. As Connecticut's Oliver Ellsworth received the most votes for that assignment, he became the panel's chairman.

The Constitution barely mentions the judiciary's structure beyond providing for a supreme court and any lower courts that Congress might wish to establish. It is silent on the Supreme Court's size and frequency of sessions as well as judges' qualifications and compensation.

Oliver Ellsworth was ideally suited to serve as principal author of the Judiciary Act. He had shaped the Constitution's first draft and its crucial "Connecticut Compromise," which produced a bicameral Congress with the states equally represented in the Senate. His Senate colleagues had also selected him to chair a committee to draft the chamber's rules of procedure. Ellsworth quickly won wide respect for his diligence, or, as one biographer has put it, "his recognition of the fact that in the senatorial office drudging spadework was even more important than speeches and votes."

On July 17, 1789, the Senate enacted its version of this landmark statute. With House revisions, it became law two months later. Oliver Ellsworth remained a highly effective senator until 1796, when he moved to the Supreme Court as chief justice of the United States. Although Ellsworth, more than any other, shaped the federal judicial system, his strengths as a legislative craftsman failed to translate to success as a jurist. Deteriorating health forced his resignation within four years.

Today, constitutional scholars remember Oliver Ellsworth's Judiciary Act as "the keystone of American federalism" and they note John Adams' assessment that, in the federal government's earliest years, he was its "firmest pillar."

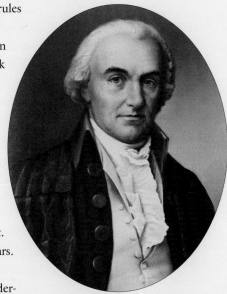

Oliver Ellsworth, senator from Connecticut (1789-1796), chief justice of the United States (1796-1800).

Further Reading

Casto, William R. *Oliver Ellsworth and the Creation of the Federal Republic.* New York: Second Circuit Committee on History and Commemorative Events, 1997.

Irritating the President

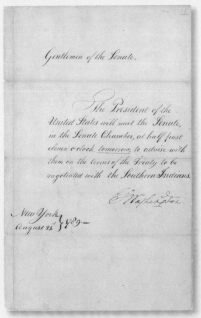

President Washington's visit to the Senate regarding a proposed treaty with the southern Indians proved so unsatisfactory that he never again sought the Senate's advice in person.

The Senate spent most of its first year setting precedents. During the month of August 1789, it established two precedents that particularly irritated President George Washington.

On August 5, for the first time, the Senate refused to confirm a presidential appointee. Ignoring the budding concept of "senatorial courtesy," President George Washington had failed to consult with Georgia's two senators before he nominated Benjamin Fishbourn to the post of naval officer for the Port of Savannah. One of those senators, James Gunn, favored another candidate who was a close political ally. Gunn promptly engineered the Senate rejection of Fishbourn.

From late in the 18th century until the early 1930s, senators occasionally derailed nominations for positions wholly within their states simply by proclaiming them "personally obnoxious." No further explanation was required or expected.

On the day after the Fishbourn rejection, President Washington angrily drafted a letter to the Senate. The overly formal style of the message failed to hide the chief executive's irritation. He began by noting that the Senate must have had its own good reasons for turning down his nominee. Then his frustration burst through. "Permit me to submit to your consideration whether on occasions where the propriety of Nominations appear questionable to you, it would not be expedient to communicate that circumstance to me, and thereby avail yourselves of the information which led me to make them, and which I would with pleasure lay before you." He explained his own close association with Fishbourn, whom he considered brave, loyal, experienced, and—pointedly—popular among the political leaders of his state. The president then nominated a candidate acceptable to Senator Gunn.

Three weeks later, on August 22, 1789, the president visited the Senate to receive its advice and consent for an Indian treaty. He occupied the presiding officer's chair while Senate President John Adams sat at the desk assigned to the Senate's secretary. Intimidated by Washington's presence, senators found it difficult to concentrate on the treaty's provisions as Adams read them aloud. After hearing the contents of several supporting documents, members decided they needed more time. An angry president spoke for the first time during the proceedings: "This defeats every purpose of my being here!" Although he returned two days later to observe additional debate and the treaty's approval, he conducted all further treaty business with the Senate in writing.

Further Reading

Josephy, Alvin M., Jr. *The American Heritage History of the Congress of the United States.* New York: American Heritage, 1975. Chapter 2.

U.S. Congress. Senate. *The United States Senate, 1787-1801: A Dissertation on the First Fourteen Years of the Upper Legislative Body,* by Roy Swanstrom. 100th Cong., 1st sess., 1988 (originally published as a Senate document in 1962). S. Doc. 100-31. Chapters 7-8.

September 11, 1789

First Cabinet Confirmation

On September 11, 1789, the new federal government under the Constitution took a large step forward. On that day, the president of the United States sent his first cabinet nomination to the Senate for its "advice and consent." Minutes later, perhaps even before the messenger returned to the president's office, senators approved unanimously the appointment of Alexander Hamilton to be secretary of the treasury.

At the Constitutional Convention in 1787, and in the subsequent campaign to ensure the Constitution's ratification, Hamilton vigorously supported provisions that divided responsibility for appointing government officials between the president and the Senate. He believed that a role for the Senate in the filling of key government positions would prevent the president from selecting friends, neighbors, relatives, or other "unfit characters" to jobs for which they lacked necessary skills, temperament, or experience.

Aside from the appointment process, the Constitution included only a passing reference to the operation of executive branch agencies. The framers assumed that the Congress would draft suitable legislation to allow the executive to manage the basic governmental functions of finance, foreign relations, and defense.

In establishing the first cabinet departments, Congress considered Treasury to be the most important. Legislators spelled out its responsibilities in great detail and provided staff resources greater than all other government agencies combined.

Alexander Hamilton campaigned actively for the position of treasury secretary, even though friends had advised him to avoid that job at a time when the nation's finances were in a "deep, dark, and dreary chaos." They urged him, instead, to seek nomination as chief justice of the United States or to run for a seat in the Senate.

Robert Morris, the Pennsylvania senator and financier, counseled President George Washington to nominate the 34-year-old Hamilton, whom he described as "damned sharp." Nine days after the president signed legislation creating the Treasury Department, he dispatched his messenger to the Senate with Hamilton's nomination.

Alexander Hamilton's intense ambition, his passion for order and efficiency, together with his tendency to meddle in the operations of other cabinet agencies, made him the administrative architect of the new government. The combination of special congressional powers vested in the Treasury Department and the president's relative inexperience in financial affairs allowed the secretary to pursue a course of his own choosing. One member of Congress commented, "Congress may go home. Mr. Hamilton is all-powerful and fails in nothing that he attempts."

George Washington, far right, chose as members of his first cabinet, left to right, Henry Knox, Thomas Jefferson, Edmund Randolph, and Alexander Hamilton.

Further Reading
Chernow, Ron. *Alexander Hamilton*. New York: Penguin Press, 2004.

August 12, 1790

Farewell to New York

When Congress convened a special ceremonial session at Federal Hall in New York City on September 6, 2002, to honor the victims and heroes of the September 11, 2001, terrorist attacks, participants were reminded that 212 years had passed since Congress last met in that city.

New York had hosted the Congress that operated under the Articles of Confederation from 1785 to 1789. When the new federal government was launched with the 1788 ratification of the U.S. Constitution, New York City continued as the nation's temporary capital. Hoping to convince the new Congress to make their city the permanent seat of government, local business interests contributed funding for a major expansion of the city hall.

When Congress convened for the first time on March 4, 1789, the old building had been converted into a splendid capitol, optimistically renamed Federal Hall. The Senate Chamber occupied a richly carpeted 40-by-30-foot-long room on the building's second floor. The chamber's most striking features were its high arched ceiling, tall windows curtained in crimson damask, fireplace mantels in handsomely polished marble, and a presiding officer's chair elevated three feet from the floor and placed under a crimson canopy. Noticeably absent from the lavishly ornate chamber was a spectators' gallery—a sign that Senate deliberations were to be closed to the public.

The precedent-setting first and second sessions of the First Congress proved highly productive. The second session, which concluded on August 12, 1790, enacted legislation that put the nation on a firm financial foundation, authorized the first census of population, established a government for the western territories south of the Ohio River, and—in the Residence Act of 1790—provided a location for the first permanent seat of government. Under that plan, the government would abandon New York in favor of Philadelphia, which would serve as the temporary capital city for 10 years. In 1800, the government would again move, this time to its permanent location in Washington, D.C.

As its final action on August 12, the Senate adopted a resolution thanking New York for its generous hospitality. Soon after Congress departed, Federal Hall again became the local city hall, until it was demolished in 1812. In 1842, the Federal Hall in which the 2002 ceremonial session took place was erected on part of the original site and is now designated a National Memorial.

This cartoon provides a cynical view of the profit opportunity that Congress's temporary move presented for Philadelphians.

Further Reading

Josephy, Alvin M., Jr. *The American Heritage History of the Congress of the United States.* New York: American Heritage, 1975. Chapter 2.

December 6, 1790

The Senate Moves to Philadelphia

On a cold Monday in December, the Senate convened for the first time in Philadelphia. The Residence Act of 1790 settled Congress in that city until 1800, when the entire government would move to the District of Columbia.

As Pennsylvania's capital and the nation's largest city, Philadelphia in 1790 was rapidly developing as a prosperous commercial center, with well-paved and regularly laid-out streets. As one newly arrived member observed, Philadelphians "believe themselves to be the first people in America as well in manners as in arts, and like Englishmen, they are at no pains to disguise this opinion."

Fifteen of the Senate's 26 members attended that initial session in Congress Hall. This imposing two-story Georgian brick building, designed to complement the State House—Independence Hall—directly to its east, had been completed only the year before. In the Senate's elegantly outfitted second-floor chamber, senators found two semicircular rows of mahogany writing desks and a canopied dais for the presiding officer. A specially woven Axminster carpet, featuring the Great Seal of the United States, covered the plain board floor. The chamber's 13 windows, hung with green wooden Venetian blinds and crimson damask curtains, provided added daytime illumination, while candles placed on members' desks lit the chamber for rare late afternoon and evening sessions.

The members who inaugurated this chamber were an experienced lot. More than three-quarters had served in the Continental Congresses and in state legislatures. Ten had participated in the Constitutional Convention. Nearly half were college graduates; two-thirds had some legal training.

Despite Philadelphia's attractions, senators encountered significant hardships, among them the high cost of living, the greater attractiveness of state legislative service, and the difficulty of a six-year absence from one's livelihood. While most members attended faithfully in the early months of a session, some tended to slip away in the spring and early summer. During the 1790s, in the final weeks of each Congress' first session, fully a quarter of the Senate's members failed to participate in votes. Senators also resigned at a high rate. Of the 86 who served in the Senate during its 10-year Philadelphia residence, one-third departed before their terms expired. It was not uncommon for as many as four senators to successively fill one seat over the course of a six-year term. Only three senators served all ten years in Philadelphia!

Congress met in the Philadelphia County Court House, now known as Congress Hall, from 1790 until 1800.

Further Reading

Baker, Richard A. "The United States Senate in Philadelphia." *In The House and Senate in the 1790s: Petitioning, Lobbying, and Institutional Development*, edited by Kenneth R. Bowling and Donald R. Kennon. Athens, Ohio: Ohio University Press, 2002.

Presidential Succession

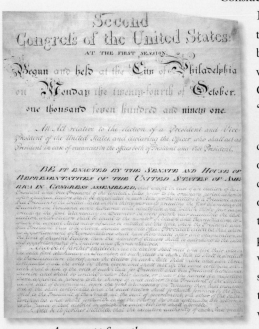

An excerpt from the Presidential Succession Act of 1792.

The framers of the Constitution left Congress with considerable responsibility for resolving questions about the new government's structure and operations. Considering the high rates of serious illness and early death in late 18th-century America, one of the most pressing among those questions was, "Who would become president if both the president and vice president died or were otherwise unavailable to serve during their terms of office?" The Constitution provides only that Congress may pass a law "declaring what Officer shall then act as President."

In 1791, a House committee recommended that this duty fall to the cabinet's senior member—the secretary of state. Federalist senators objected because they had no desire to see Secretary of State Thomas Jefferson, leader of the growing Antifederalist opposition, placed so close to the presidency. Others proposed the Senate's president pro tempore, reasoning that as this official succeeded the vice president in presiding over the Senate, he should also succeed the vice president in performing the duties of the presidency. This plan attracted opposition from those who assumed the president pro tempore would remain a senator while temporarily performing duties of the presidency and feared the arrangement would upset the balance of powers between the two branches. Others suggested the chief justice of the United States or the Speaker of the House of Representatives. At an impasse, Congress adjourned for nine months, thereby risking governmental paralysis in the event of presidential and vice-presidential vacancies.

Early in the Second Congress, on February 20, 1792, the Senate joined the House in passing the Presidential Succession Act—a compromise measure that placed in the line of succession its president pro tempore, followed by the House Speaker.

Years later, in 1886, Congress responded to longstanding uneasiness with this arrangement by removing its two officers from the line of succession and substituting the president's cabinet members, by rank, beginning with the secretary of state. This troublesome issue received yet another revision in 1947, when Congress inserted the House speaker and Senate president pro tempore, in that order, ahead of the president's cabinet.

Further Reading

Feerick, John D. *From Falling Hands: The Story of Presidential Succession*. New York: Fordham University Press, 1965.

December 2, 1793

The First Monday in December

The first Monday in December! In recent times, these five words conjure up images of members rushing to wrap up last-minute legislative business in order to return home for end-of-year holidays. Immediately after World War II, to ensure that members would be long gone by December, Congress enacted legislation requiring both houses to adjourn no later than July 30 of each year.

Such concerns would surely have amazed the 18th-century framers of the U.S. Constitution. Tied to an agriculturally based economy, with its cycle of planting, growing, and harvesting, these farmer-statesmen considered the dormant month of December as a particularly good time for members of Congress to begin, rather than end, their legislative sessions.

Accordingly, they provided in Article I, Section 4 of the Constitution that "The Congress shall assemble at least once in every year, and such meeting shall be on the first Monday in December, unless they shall by law appoint a different day." In September 1788, after the necessary three-quarters of the states ratified the Constitution, the existing Congress, under the Articles of Confederation, passed such a law, setting March 4, 1789, as the convening date of the First Congress. March 4 thereby became the starting point for members' terms of office, while future legislative sessions would begin in early December.

In its closing days, however, the First Congress provided that the Second Congress would convene several weeks early,

on October 24, 1791. Not until the Third Congress met on December 2, 1793, did a first session begin according to the Constitution's "First Monday in December" timetable. For the next 140 years, Congress generally followed this pattern, although presidents, facing national emergencies or other "extraordinary occasions" exercised their constitutional prerogative to "convene both Houses, or either of them," at other times.

Outgoing presidents routinely used this provision to issue proclamations that called the Senate into a brief session at the March 4 start of their successor's term to confirm cabinet and other key executive nominations.

With the 1933 adoption of the Constitution's 20th Amendment, setting January 3 as the annual meeting date, the first Monday in December became just another relic of the nation's 18th-century agrarian society.

From 1946 until 1990, when Congress repealed the "mandatory" July 30 adjournment as an unattainable goal, members found themselves still in session in December during 19 of those 44 years.

The Senate Chamber inside Congress Hall, where the Senate met from 1790 to 1800.

Further Reading

Kyvig, David. *Explicit and Authentic Acts: Amending the U.S. Constitution, 1776-1995.* Lawrence, KS: University Press of Kansas, 1996. Chapter 12.

Madison, James. *Notes of Debates in the Federal Convention of 1787.* Athens, OH: Ohio University Press, 1984. [August 7, 1787]

Uproar over Senate Approval of Jay Treaty

John Jay, chief justice of the United States (1789-1795).

A howling, stone-throwing mob marched on the Philadelphia home of Pennsylvania Senator William Bingham. In Frankfort, Kentucky, the state legislature denounced Senator Humphrey Marshall and demanded that the Constitution be amended to allow for the recall of United States senators. So angry were his constituents, as one writer observed, that Marshall was "burned in effigy, vilified in print, and stoned in Frankfort." Many of the other senators who, on June 24, 1795, had provided the exact 20-to-10 two-thirds majority necessary to ratify John Jay's treaty with Great Britain experienced similar popular outrage.

A year earlier, at President George Washington's request, Chief Justice of the United States John Jay sailed to London to negotiate a reduction of tensions between the two nations. The president wanted Great Britain to withdraw its troops from the United States' northwestern territories, to compensate slaveholders for slaves British soldiers had abducted during the Revolutionary War, to pay ship owners for trading vessels seized by its navy, and to allow free trade with the British West Indies. Jay achieved only a limited success, however, gaining the withdrawal of troops and compensation to American merchants. He failed to obtain protections for American shipping or reimbursement for stolen slaves, and he prematurely conceded American responsibility to pay British merchants for pre-Revolutionary War debts.

Jay's treaty contained provisions that many considered humiliating to the United States, but President Washington sent it to the Senate for formal approval. The president and his supporters argued that Jay had obtained the best possible deal and that the nation could ill afford another war with Britain. The treaty's opponents, members of the Senate's anti-administration Democratic-Republican minority, demanded that the treaty be renegotiated because—among other reasons—it failed to protect America's trading agreements with France. The president's allies among the Senate's Federalist majority rejected this proposal and narrowly approved the treaty.

When the text of the treaty became public, mobs took to the streets to condemn George Washington, John Jay, and the United States Senate. Even John Rutledge, Washington's recess appointee to replace Jay as chief justice, criticized ratification of the treaty as a sellout. When the Senate reconvened in December 1795, it retaliated by immediately rejecting the imprudent Rutledge's pending nomination. Although debate over the flawed pact deepened the nation's political divisions and destroyed relations with France, its ratification likely saved the still-fragile republic from a potentially disastrous new war with Britain.

Further Reading

Combs, Jerald A. *The Jay Treaty: Political Battleground of the Founding Fathers.* Berkeley: University of California Press, 1970.

Estes, Todd. *The Jay Treaty Debate, Public Opinion, and the Evolution of Early American Political Culture.* Amherst, MA: University of Massachusetts Press, 2006.

October 24, 1795

Constituents Tell Senator How to Vote

The presumed right of the people to instruct their elected representatives extends back to colonial times. In drafting the Bill of Rights in 1789, the House of Representatives briefly considered recognizing such a right, but then overwhelmingly rejected it. The House response underscored representatives' traditional desire to temper their constituents' views with their own knowledge and opinions.

This issue hit the early Senate with special force. Unlike the House, whose members were elected by a diffused constituency of individual citizens, senators came to their seats through the choice of their state legislatures—bodies skilled in framing expressions of opinion. Soon after the Senate first convened in 1789, its members began receiving letters of instruction. In 1791, the Virginia legislature directed its two senators to vote to end the Senate's practice of meeting behind closed doors—the better to keep senators accountable. When senators received instructions with which they agreed, some made a great show of following them. When they disagreed, however, they faced a choice: they could ignore the instructions, or they could resign.

On October 24, 1795, the *Kentucky Gazette* printed a petition from the inhabitants of Clark County to that state's legislature. The petitioners angrily denounced U.S. Senator Humphrey Marshall for his vote in favor of ratifying the Jay Treaty. The citizens urged the legislature to instruct Marshall to oppose the treaty if it should come before the Senate again.

Noting that Marshall had five years remaining in his term, others traced the problem to the length of senators' terms. Six-year terms endangered "the liberties of America," they argued, by destroying senators' sense of responsibility and enabling "them to carry into execution schemes pregnant with the greatest evils." These petitioners requested their state legislature to instruct both of Kentucky's senators to propose a constitutional amendment permitting a state legislature to recall senators by a two-thirds vote.

A Federalist facing a hostile Jeffersonian-Republican legislature, Humphrey Marshall appealed directly to the people through a series of articles explaining his ratification vote. He asserted that as a senator he was less interested in winning popularity contests than in doing his duty to the nation—"according to my own judgment."

Shortly afterwards, a mob dragged Marshall from his house. Only by seconds did this skilled orator talk the crowd out of throwing him into the Kentucky River. Stoned by angry citizens in the state capital, he kept a low profile for the remainder of his term.

Humphrey Marshall, senator from Kentucky (1795-1801).

Further Reading

Quisenberry, Anderson C. *The Life and Times of Hon. Humphrey Marshall.* Winchester, Ky.: Sun Publishing, 1892.

The Senate Opens its Doors

Question: Who was the first employee hired by the Senate? Answer: The doorkeeper. His job was particularly important to the Senate of 1789 because members intended to conduct all their sessions behind closed doors. The doorkeeper's orders: No public; no House members!

The framers of the Constitution assumed that the Senate would follow their own practice, as well as that of the Continental Congress, of meeting in secret. They believed that occasional publication of an official journal, with information on how members voted on legislative matters, would be sufficient to keep the public informed. In the Senate, defenders of secrecy looked with disdain on the House where members were tempted to play to a gallery of hissing and cheering onlookers. In an era before reliable shorthand reporting, press accounts of House activity were notoriously incomplete and distorted along partisan lines.

Opposition to the closed-door policy increased steadily over the first five years of the Senate's existence. At a time when senators owed their election to state legislatures, those bodies loudly complained that they could not effectively assess their senators' behavior from outside a closed door. Eventually, individual senators recognized that their legislative positions could more easily win popular support if publicly aired. The growing notion of the Senate as a "lurking hole" in which conspiracies were hatched against the public interest had to be put to rest. Additionally, press coverage of the House helped popularize that body's role and the public began to use the words "House" and "Congress" interchangeably. The Senate was in danger of becoming the forgotten chamber.

The opportunity for change arrived with a dispute over the seating of Pennsylvania's controversial Senator-elect Albert Gallatin. Senators, then meeting in Philadelphia, realized the delicacy of the situation in which they were questioning the action of the Pennsylvania legislature, which at that time met in the building next door. Wishing to avoid the charges of "Star Chamber" that would surely follow a secret vote to reject Gallatin, the Federalist majority agreed to open Senate doors just for that occasion. Several weeks after denying Gallatin his seat, the Senate decided to open its proceedings permanently as soon as a suitable gallery could be constructed. After an initial eruption of curiosity when that gallery opened in December 1795, however, the press showed little sustained interest in covering Senate debates, which lacked the fire and drama of those in the other body.

Albert Gallatin of Pennsylvania failed to meet the citizenship requirement for a seat in the U.S. Senate.

Further Reading

U.S. Congress. Senate. *The United States Senate, 1787-1801: A Dissertation on the First Fourteen Years of the Upper Legislative Body*, by Roy Swanstrom. 100th Cong., 1st sess., 1988 (originally published as a Senate document in 1962). S. Doc. 100-31. Chapter 14.

December 15, 1795

A Chief Justice Nomination Rejected

On December 15, 1795, the Senate administered a stinging blow to one of the nation's most distinguished "founding fathers." By a vote of 10 to 14, it rejected President George Washington's nomination of South Carolinian John Rutledge to be chief justice of the United States.

Born to one of Charleston's elite families, John Rutledge rapidly gained political and judicial distinction during the American Revolution. At an early age, he represented South Carolina in the Stamp Act Congress and in the Continental Congress. In 1775, he helped draft the constitution for the newly formed "Republic of South Carolina," and a year later he became that republic's president. When British troops captured Charleston in 1779, the state legislature elected Rutledge governor and handed him virtually absolute power. After the war, he served as chief judge of a state court and, in 1787, played a major role in drafting the U.S. Constitution.

In recognition of these contributions, President George Washington nominated—and the Senate quickly confirmed—Rutledge as the first U.S. Supreme Court's senior associate justice. Although Rutledge accepted his commission, he failed to attend the Court's meetings and resigned in 1791 to become chief justice of a South Carolina court.

In June 1795, Rutledge offered President Washington his services as a replacement for the soon-to-retire Chief Justice John

Jay. Washington readily agreed and, with the Senate in recess, promised to give Rutledge a temporary commission upon his arrival at the August session of the Supreme Court.

Several weeks after learning this, however, Rutledge complicated his confirmation chances by delivering a speech vehemently attacking the controversial Jay Treaty, which he believed to be excessively pro-British. Rutledge seemed blind to the fact that the president had supported—and the Senate had recently consented to—that difficult treaty. Many administration supporters cited this ill-timed speech as evidence of Rutledge's advancing mental incapacity. Rutledge ignored the escalating criticism and took his seat on the high court.

When the Senate convened in December, it promptly voted down his nomination. Rutledge thus became the first rejected Supreme Court nominee and the only one among the 15 who would gain their offices through recess appointments not to be subsequently confirmed. In turning down Rutledge, the Senate made it clear that an examination of a nominee's qualifications would include his political views. Those who differed substantively from the majority of senators could expect rough going.

President Washington quickly calmed the rough waters by nominating to the Court one of the Senate's own members, the author of the 1789 Judiciary Act, Connecticut's Oliver Ellsworth.

John Rutledge of South Carolina became the first Supreme Court nominee rejected by the Senate.

Further Reading
Barry, Richard. *Mr. Rutledge of South Carolina*. Salem, NH: Ayer, 1993.
Combs, Jerald A. *The Jay Treaty: Political Battleground of the Founding Fathers*. Berkeley: University of California Press, 1970.
Haw, James. *John & Edward Rutledge of South Carolina*. Athens: University of Georgia Press, 1997.

February 15, 1797

John Adams' Senate Farewell

Thanks to best-selling biographies by historians David McCullough and Joseph Ellis, Americans have rediscovered John Adams. As the nation's first vice president, and therefore the Senate's first president, Adams significantly influenced the formation of early Senate procedures and precedents. He also arranged for his Massachusetts political protégé Samuel Otis to become secretary of the Senate—an office from which Otis shaped the Senate's administrative operations for a quarter century.

When Adams began his duties in 1789, he privately complained that while he was "Not wholly without experience in public assemblies," he was "more accustomed to take a share in their debates than to preside in their deliberations." Although he promised to refrain from interjecting his own views, he soon forgot that promise. In office for only a month, he entered an extended debate over what title to use in addressing the nation's chief executive. The House had proposed "Mr. President." Believing that titles inspire respect, Adams hoped the Senate would recommend something like

"His Majesty the President." Ultimately, the Senate agreed to the House version, but word of Adams' seemingly aristocratic attitude leaked out of the closed Senate sessions and earned him considerable public scorn.

Senators quickly began to resent Adams' pedantic lectures. His friend John Trumbull warned that "he who mingles in debate subjects himself to frequent retorts from his opposers, places himself on the same ground with his inferiors in rank, appears too much like the leader of a party, and renders it more difficult for him to support the dignity of the chair and to preserve order and regularity in debate." Stung by this criticism, Adams told Trumbull, "I have no desire ever to open my mouth again upon any question." And, for the remainder of his term, he seldom did.

On February 15, 1797, as he prepared for his own presidential inauguration, Adams appeared before the Senate for the last time as its presiding officer. In his farewell address, he assured members that he had abandoned his earlier notion that the office of senator should be a hereditary one. The "eloquence, patriotism, and independence" that he had witnessed during his eight years there convinced him "no council more permanent than this will be necessary to defend the rights, liberties, and properties of the people, and to protect the Constitution of the United States."

John Adams served as the first vice president of the United States, and therefore as the Senate's first president.

Further Reading

Ellis, Joseph. *Passionate Sage: The Character and Legacy of John Adams.* New York: W. W. Norton, 2001.

McCullough, David. *John Adams.* New York: Simon & Schuster, 2001.

Thompson, C. Bradley. *John Adams & The Spirit of Liberty.* Lawrence: University Press of Kansas, 1998.

February 5, 1798

To Arrest an Impeached Senator

When barely nine years old, the Senate confronted a crisis of authority. An impeached senator refused to attend his trial in the Senate Chamber. Unlike the House of Representatives, or the British House of Commons, the Senate lacked a sergeant at arms to enforce its orders. On February 5, 1798, the Senate expanded the duties, title, and salary of its doorkeeper to create the post of sergeant at arms. It then directed that officer to arrest the fugitive senator—the Honorable William Blount.

A signer of the U.S. Constitution, William Blount in 1796 had become one of Tennessee's first two senators. A year later President John Adams notified Congress that his administration had uncovered a conspiracy involving several American citizens who had offered to assist Great Britain in an improbable scheme to take possession of the Spanish-controlled territories of Louisiana and the Floridas. Blount was among the named conspirators. He had apparently devised the plot to prevent Spain from ceding its territories to France, a transaction that would have depressed the value of his extensive southwestern landholdings.

On July 7, 1797, while the Senate pondered what to do about Blount, the House of Representatives, for the first time in history, voted a bill of impeachment. The following day, the Senate expelled Blount—its first use of that constitutional power—and adjourned until November. Prior to adjourning, the Senate ordered Blount to answer impeachment charges before a select committee that would meet during the recess. Blount failed to appear. He had departed for Tennessee with no intention of returning.

On February 5, 1798, as the Senate prepared for his trial—uncertain whether a senator, or former senator, was even liable for impeachment—it issued the arrest order. The sergeant at arms ultimately failed in his first mission, however, as Blount refused to be taken from Tennessee.

The Senate also adopted its first impeachment rule, which provided for the respectful reception of the House's impeachment articles. Several days later, the Senate adopted an oath, as required by the Constitution, binding members to "do impartial justice, according to law." Congress then adjourned for 10 months.

When the Senate reconvened in December 1798, it adopted additional impeachment rules. Drawn from British parliamentary and American colonial and state practice, these rules serve as the earliest foundation for those in effect today. A year later, the Senate dismissed the impeachment case against Blount for lack of jurisdiction.

William Blount, senator from Tennessee (1796-1797).

Further Reading

Melton, Buckner F., Jr. *The First Impeachment: The Constitution's Framers and the Case of Senator William Blount*. Macon, GA: Mercer University Press, 1998.

June 25, 1798

The Senate Enforces Attendance

The framers of the Constitution feared that members of Congress could strangle the government by simply failing to attend legislative sessions. Without a quorum, the Senate or House would be powerless to act. Accordingly, the Constitution writers provided that each body could "compel the Attendance of absent Members, in such Manner, and under such Penalties as each House may provide."

On June 25, 1798, the Senate adopted a rule specifying its manner and penalties for enforcing senators' attendance. As spring gave way to summer, more than one-third of the Senate's membership failed to show up for individual votes. Some senators had left the capital to return to their states for the customary five-month break that lasted until the first week in December. Senate leaders, however, had other plans for members before an adjournment would be possible. At the top of their list of unfinished business was one of the notorious Alien and Sedition Acts.

An excerpt from the Sedition Act of 1798.

The Senate's new rule provided that less than a quorum could authorize expenses for the sergeant at arms to bring absent members back to the chamber. The office of sergeant at arms had recently been created specifically for chasing down absent senators and reluctant witnesses needed to conduct Senate business. Those senators who had prematurely left town without a sufficient excuse would be required to pay whatever expenses the sergeant at arms incurred in returning them.

On Independence Day 1798, the Senate used this new rule to call back enough senators to enact one of the most repressive statutes in American history. The Sedition Act of 1798 reflected growing national hysteria over the possibility of war with France. In an effort to silence journalists supporting anti-administration views, the act's framers provided punishments that included fines and imprisonment for those who publicly criticized Congress or the president.

More than a dozen journalists were ultimately prosecuted under this statute before it expired in 1801. The resulting widespread public anger at the administration of John Adams helped elect Thomas Jefferson president in 1801 and shifted control of the Senate to Jefferson's Democratic-Republican Party.

Further Reading

Miller, John C. *Crisis in Freedom: The Alien and Sedition Acts.* Boston: Little Brown, 1951.

Smith, James Morton. *Freedom's Fetters: The Alien and Sedition Laws and American Civil Liberties.* Ithaca, N.Y.: Cornell University Press, 1967.

March 27, 1800

The Senate Holds an Editor in Contempt

Should it be possible to send someone to jail for publishing the text of a bill while it is still before the Senate? On March 27, 1800, a majority of senators believed the answer to that question to be a resounding 'yes.'

Two years earlier, at a time of national paranoia over possible war with France, a Federalist-dominated Congress, supporting the administration of President John Adams, had passed the infamous Alien and Sedition Acts. The 1798 Sedition Act targeted journalists loyal to the opposition Democratic-Republican Party, formed around the leadership of Adams' vice president, Thomas Jefferson. That statute provided for the imprisonment of any person who wrote, published, or uttered any false or malicious statement about the president or Congress.

By early 1800, with Congress still meeting in Philadelphia, Senate Federalists launched a campaign against William Duane, the hard-hitting editor of that city's influential Republican newspaper, the *Aurora*. In February, Duane published a Federalist-sponsored Senate bill, leaked to him by three Republican senators. The purpose of the leaked bill was to establish a special committee for the coming election. Composed of six senators, six representatives, and the chief justice, the committee would review electoral college ballots and decide which ones should be counted. In his outraged reporting on this blatantly unconstitutional device to swing the election to Adams, Duane mistakenly indicated that the bill had already passed the Senate.

Duane's error gave Senate Federalists an excuse to create a "committee on privileges."

This panel quickly concluded that he had illegally breached Senate privileges by publishing the bill and that he was guilty through his false statements of exciting against senators "the hatred of the good people of the United States."

On March 24, Duane complied with a Senate order to appear in its chamber to hear the charges on which a party-line majority had found him guilty—without trial—and to comment before the Senate passed sentence. Allowed a two-day continuance to confer with counsel, he decided not to return. When the Senate cited him for contempt and ordered his arrest, Duane went into hiding until Congress adjourned several weeks later.

By the time the new session convened in November 1800, the government had moved from Philadelphia to Washington. The disruption of the move, together with the subsequent election victories that would place Jefferson in the White House and his fellow Democratic-Republicans in control of Congress, concluded this bizarre chapter of Senate history.

William Duane, editor of the Aurora *newspaper in Philadelphia.*

Further Reading

Rosenfeld, Richard N. *American Aurora: A Democratic-Republican Returns.* New York: St. Martin's Press, 1997.

November 17, 1800

The Senate Moves to Washington

A late fall storm snarled travel along the east coast. Senators trying to reach Washington from their homes in time for the new session experienced frustrating delays. A heavy blanket of snow forced cancellation of a welcoming parade.

On November 17, 1800, following a 10-year stay in Philadelphia, the Senate of the Sixth Congress met for the first time in the Capitol Building. Work on the Capitol had begun in 1793, but materials and labor proved to be more expensive than anticipated. Facing major funding shortfalls, the building's commissioners in 1796 decided to construct only the Senate wing. Although some third-floor rooms remained incomplete by moving day, the wing was substantially ready to receive along with the Senate, the House, the Supreme Court, the Library of Congress, and district courts.

When Congress arrived in Washington in 1800, only the north wing of the Capitol had been completed.

When the Senate convened in the ground-floor room now restored as the old Supreme Court chamber, only 15 of the necessary 17 members answered the quorum call. Four days later, the Senate finally achieved its first Washington quorum and, with the House, notified President John Adams that Congress awaited any communication he might wish to make. The following day, the president arrived in the crowded, leaky, and unheated—but elegantly appointed—Senate Chamber. He began his annual address to the joint session by congratulating members on their new seat of government and—pointedly—"on the prospect of a residence not to be changed." He added, optimistically, "Although there is some cause to apprehend that accommodations are not now so complete as might be wished, yet there is great reason to believe that this inconvenience will cease with the present session."

As President Adams continued with a lackluster address—the last annual message any president would personally deliver to Congress for the next 113 years—the chilled members sadly contemplated the unfinished Capitol and its rustic surroundings. While some fondly recalled Philadelphia's "convenient and elegant accommodations," as the Senate had put it in a resolution of thanks when departing that city six months earlier, a New York senator privately offered what is perhaps the first known instance of "Washington bashing." He volunteered sarcastically that the city was not so bad. To make it perfect, it needed only "houses, cellars, kitchens, well informed men, amiable women, and other little trifles of this kind."

Further Reading

Ferling, John. *John Adams: A Life*. Knoxville, Tenn.: University of Tennessee Press, 1992.

Thompson, C. Bradley. *John Adams & The Spirit of Liberty*. Lawrence: University Press of Kansas, 1998.

Young, James Sterling. *The Washington Community, 1800-1828*. New York: Harcourt Brace Jovanovich, 1966.

CHAPTER II

THE "GOLDEN AGE" OF THE SENATE

1801-1850

No Hissing

Thomas Jefferson published A Manual of Parliamentary Practice for the Use of the Senate of the United States *in 1801.*

O n a quiet December morning in 1800, a well-dressed gentleman knocked on the door at the Capitol Hill residence of publisher Samuel Smith. When the publisher's wife, Margaret Bayard Smith, greeted him, she had no idea who he was. But, she liked him at once, "So kind and conciliating were his looks and manners." Then her husband arrived and introduced her to the vice president of the United States, Thomas Jefferson.

Jefferson had come to deliver a manuscript for publication. Mrs. Smith admiringly noted the vice president's "neat, plain, but elegant handwriting." Weeks later, on February 27, 1801, Jefferson returned to receive a copy of his newly printed book. It bore the title, *A Manual of Parliamentary Practice for the Use of the Senate of the United States.*

Three years earlier, in 1797, Jefferson had approached his single vice-presidential duty of presiding over the Senate with feelings of inadequacy. John Adams, who had held the job since the Senate's founding in 1789, knew a great deal about Senate procedure and—of equal importance—about British parliamentary operations. Yet, despite Adams' knowledge, senators routinely criticized him for his arbitrary and inconsistent parliamentary rulings.

In his first days as vice president, Jefferson decided to compile a manual of legislative procedure as a guide for himself and future presiding officers. He believed that such an authority, distilled largely from ancient books of parliamentary procedure used in the British House of Commons, would minimize senators' criticism of presiding officers' rulings, which in those days were not subject to reversal by the full Senate.

Jefferson arranged his manual in 53 topical sections, running alphabetically from "Absence" to "Treaties." He began the section entitled "Order in Debate" with a warning to members based on his own observation of legislative behavior. Even today, his admonition might suitably appear on the wall of any elementary school classroom. "No one is to disturb another [person who is speaking] by hissing, coughing, spitting, speaking or whispering to another."

Although Jefferson's original manuscript has long since disappeared, a personal printed copy, with notes in his own handwriting, survives at the Library of Congress.

Jefferson's Manual, with its emphasis on order and decorum, changed the way the Senate of his day operated. Years later, acknowledging Jefferson's brilliance as a parliamentary scholar, the U.S. House of Representatives adopted his Senate *Manual* as a partial guide to its own proceedings.

Further Reading

U.S. Congress. Senate. *A Manual of Parliamentary Practice for the Use of the Senate of the United States,* by Thomas Jefferson. 103rd Cong., 1st sess., 1993. S. Doc. 103-8.

"Dear Diary"

In recent years, courts have taken an active interest in diaries kept by public officials. This has created a "chilling effect" among those who might otherwise be inclined to record their experiences for a future generation and has led some to predict that no senator in her or his right mind would ever again keep a diary. That would be most unfortunate. And it would run counter to a well-established tradition in Senate history.

The first person elected to the U.S. Senate, Pennsylvania's William Maclay, is remembered for only one thing during his service from 1789 to 1791—that he kept a diary. Without it, we would know next to nothing about what went on behind the Senate's closed doors during the precedent-setting First Congress. Maclay's experience gives added force to the truism that one sure way to shape the historical record is to keep a diary. Historians will sooner turn to a richly detailed diary than plow thorough seemingly endless boxes of archived paper or computer disks.

Another of the Senate's notable diary keepers began his task early in the 19th century. New Hampshire's Federalist Senator William Plumer first put quill to paper on October 17, 1803, when the Senate met in special session to consider ratification of the Louisiana Purchase treaty. Decades before the Senate made any regular effort to report its proceedings beyond the sketchy outline of its official journal, Senator Plumer kept a full record of Senate sessions until his term expired three-and-a-half years later. His diary provides unique information on the Louisiana treaty debate, including his outburst at President Thomas Jefferson for taking the Senate's approval for granted. The president, by publicly supporting the treaty before the Senate had a chance to take it up, was, in Plumer's words, destroying the Senate's "freedom of opinion."

In the 1970s, Vermont Senator George Aiken compiled and published an excellent modern-era Senate diary. Although he first came to the Senate in 1941, he did not began his diary until 1972, when he was the Senate's second most senior incumbent. He proceeded by dictating his thoughts every Saturday for 150 weeks until his retirement in 1975. He hoped, above all, that his diary would show "how events can change their appearance from week to week and how the attitude of a Senator can change with them."

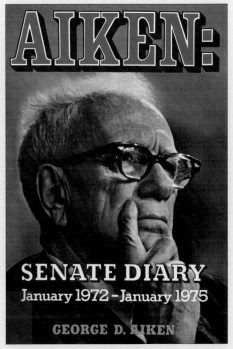

George Aiken of Vermont (1941-1975) published his diary in 1976.

Further Reading

Aiken, George D. *Aiken: Senate Diary, January 1972-January 1975.* Brattleboro, VT: Stephen Greene Press, 1976.

Bowling, Kenneth R. and Helen E. Veit, eds. *The Diary of William Maclay and other Notes on Senate Debates.* Baltimore: Johns Hopkins Press, 1988.

Brown, Everett Somerville, ed. *William Plumer's Memorandum of Proceedings in the United States Senate,* 1803-1807. New York: MacMillan, 1923.

The Senate Tries a Supreme Court Justice

On November 30, 1804, for the third time in its brief history, the Senate began an impeachment trial. The first trial in 1798 and 1799 had involved a senator previously expelled on grounds of treason. Because that senator no longer served, the Senate dismissed the case citing lack of jurisdiction. The second trial, in 1804, removed a federal judge for reasons of drunkenness and probable insanity. More than the first two proceedings, however, this third trial challenged the Senate to explore the meaning of impeachable crimes.

Samuel Chase had served on the Supreme Court since 1796. A staunch Federalist and a volcanic personality, Chase showed no willingness to tone down his bitter partisan rhetoric after Jeffersonian Republicans gained control of Congress in 1801. Representative John Randolph of Virginia orchestrated impeachment proceedings against Chase, declaring he would wipe the floor with the obnoxious justice. The House accused Chase of refusing to dismiss biased jurors and of excluding or limiting defense witnesses in two politically sensitive cases. Its trial managers hoped to prove that Chase had "behaved in an arbitrary, oppressive, and unjust way by announcing his legal interpretation on the law of treason before defense counsel had been heard." Highlighting the political nature of this case, the final article of impeachment accused the justice of continually promoting his political agenda on the bench, thereby "tending to prostitute the high judicial character with which he was invested, to the low purpose of an electioneering partizan."

At the time the Senate took up the case against the Federalist justice, its members included 25 Jeffersonian Republicans and 9 Federalists. Chase appeared before the Senate on January 4, 1805, to declare that he was being tried for his political convictions rather than for any real crime or misdemeanor. His defense team, which included several of the nation's most eminent attorneys, convinced several wavering senators that Chase's conduct did not warrant his removal from office. With at least six Jeffersonian Republicans joining the nine Federalists who voted not guilty on each article, the Senate on March 1, 1805, acquitted Samuel Chase on all counts. A majority voted guilty on three of the eight articles, but on each article the vote fell far short of the two-thirds required for conviction. The Senate thereby effectively insulated the judiciary from further congressional attacks based on disapproval of judges' opinions. Chase resumed his duties at the bench, where he remained until his death in 1811.

Impeached by the House, Supreme Court Justice Samuel Chase was acquitted by the Senate.

Further Reading

Rehnquist, William. *Grand Inquests: The Historic Impeachments of Justice Samuel Chase and President Andrew Johnson.* New York: William Morrow, 1992.

March 2, 1805

Indicted Vice President Bids Senate Farewell

Aaron Burr continues to fire the imagination. Charming, shrewd, and brilliant, Burr won a Senate seat in 1791 by defeating Treasury Secretary Alexander Hamilton's father-in-law, Philip Schuyler. In the Senate, this brash New Yorker made many enemies among establishment Federalists by vigorously opposing Hamilton's financial system and President George Washington's foreign policy. Although he left the Senate after one term, he returned in 1801 as vice president.

Widely respected as a skilled parliamentarian and an impartial presiding officer, Burr took positions that alienated his fellow Jeffersonian Republicans. In 1804, with no chance of reelection as vice president, he sought the New York governorship. He credited his resulting defeat, in part, to Alexander Hamilton's private comment that he was a dangerous and devious man. This led to the infamous July 1804 duel at which he killed Hamilton. Although indicted for murder in New York and New Jersey, Burr never stood trial. Instead, he returned to Washington in November 1804 for the new congressional session.

Burr's previously chilly relations with President Thomas Jefferson and other key Republicans suddenly warmed and Jefferson even invited him to dine at the White House. This renewed show of respect related to the fact that Burr would be soon be presiding at the Senate impeachment trial of Federalist Supreme Court Justice Samuel Chase. Ignoring Republican efforts to sway him, Burr conducted that trial "with the dignity and impartiality of an angel, but with the rigor of a devil." On March 1, 1805, the Senate acquitted Chase.

Burr chose the following day to bid the Senate farewell. He ended his brief remarks with a singularly brilliant expression of the Senate's uniqueness under the Constitution. The Senate, he said, "is a sanctuary; a citadel of law, of order, and of liberty; and it is here—it is here, in this exalted refuge; here, if anywhere, will resistance be made to the storms of political phrenzy and the silent arts of corruption; and if the Constitution be destined ever to perish by the sacrilegious hands of the demagogue or the usurper, which God avert, its expiring agonies will be witnessed on this floor." As Burr walked from the chamber, his promising career in ruins, members spontaneously began to weep. Few of those present would ever forget this moment of high drama.

Aaron Burr, senator from New York (1791-1797), vice president of the United States (1801-1805).

Further Reading

Fleming, Thomas. *Duel: Alexander Hamilton, Aaron Burr, and the Future of America*. New York: Basic Books, 1999.

Kennedy, Roger G. *Burr, Hamilton, and Jefferson: A Study in Character*. New York: Oxford University Press, 2000.

Rogow, Arnold A. *A Fatal Friendship: Alexander Hamilton and Aaron Burr*. New York: Hill and Wang, 1998.

First Senator Buried in Congressional Cemetery

In life, Connecticut Senator Uriah Tracy was known as a witty and compelling speaker and a forceful leader of the Federalist Party. In death, he acquired the dubious distinction of becoming the first senator to be buried in Congressional Cemetery.

These sandstone cenotaphs in Congressional Cemetery, designed by Capitol architect Benjamin Latrobe, memorialize members who died in office.

The 30-acre graveyard, overlooking the banks of the Anacostia River, dates from the early 1800s when Washington's Christ Church set aside plots within its cemetery for members of Congress who died in office. Some members were permanently interred there, starting with the 55-year-old Tracy following his death on July 19, 1807. For others, it served only as a temporary resting place until the seasons changed and the dirt roads home became passable. The distinguished Capitol architect Benjamin Latrobe designed massive square memorials—or cenotaphs (literally: empty tomb)—in memory of each deceased incumbent member. By 1877, more than 150 of these stout monuments dotted the burial ground, although only 80 bodies actually rested beneath them. Latrobe had wanted them built of marble, but Congress chose to save money by using sandstone. As the sandstone monuments discolored and deteriorated, Senator George Hoar of Massachusetts exclaimed that the mere sight of them added a "new terror to death." About that time, Congress chose to stop erecting cenotaphs.

Perhaps the most notable among the cemetery's 60,000 residents is Elbridge Gerry, signer of the Declaration of Independence, delegate to the Constitutional Convention, House member, and vice president under James Madison. Gerry became seriously ill late in 1814 as a result of the burdens of the War of 1812 and, according to a biographer, his "relentless socializing." On November 23, determined to preside over the Senate, he set out for the Capitol, but suffered a fatal stroke on the way.

Near Vice President Gerry's monument is the grave of Samuel Otis, the first secretary of the Senate, who died in office after 25 years of never missing a day on the job. Not far from Otis is the tomb of Isaac Bassett, one of the Senate's first pages, who came to the Senate as a boy in 1831 and remained until 1895, an elderly white-bearded doorkeeper. Several members of the press have joined this congressional gathering, including the first photojournalist, Mathew Brady, and one of the first women journalists in Washington, Anne Royall.

With the establishment of Arlington Cemetery after the Civil War, Congressional Cemetery yielded its active role as the chief national burying ground.

Further Reading

Johnson, Abby Arthur. "'The Memory of the Community': A Photographic Album of Congressional Cemetery." *Washington History* 4 (Spring/Summer 1992): 26-45.

April 25, 1808

Senator John Smith Resigns Under Fire

He was the first senator to be indicted and he came close to becoming the second senator—after William Blount in 1797—to be expelled. With his political and business careers in shambles, John Smith reluctantly resigned from the Senate on April 25, 1808.

One of Ohio's first two senators, Smith took his oath of office on October 25, 1803. Almost nothing is known of his earliest years, including his parents' names or his place of birth. A large and gregarious man with a talent for impassioned oratory, he established himself as a preacher in the 1790s and then moved on to the greater financial rewards of life as a trader, supplying military posts near Cincinnati. He entered political life and won election to the Ohio territorial legislature where he led a successful campaign for statehood.

While in the Senate, Smith continued his profitable trading ventures in Louisiana and West Florida and pursued numerous land investment schemes. In 1805, former Vice President Aaron Burr sought his support in organizing a military expedition against Spanish Florida. Although Smith claimed he had no interest in Burr's plot to force secession of Spanish territories, he agreed to provide supplies for the proposed expedition. When President Thomas Jefferson later issued an alert, charging that Burr's actual purpose was an invasion of Mexico, Smith responded patriotically by financing weapons to defend against the Burr expedition and delivering those weapons to New Orleans. These travels caused him to miss weeks of Senate sessions and led the Ohio legislature to charge him with dereliction of duty and to demand his resignation.

Although Smith ignored that demand, he found his troubles increasing as a court in Richmond, Virginia, indicted him in mid-1807 for participating in Burr's conspiracy. As he traveled to Richmond, he learned that the court had acquitted Burr on a technicality and had dropped his own case.

Soon after the Senate convened in late 1807, members opened an investigation into Smith's conduct. A defense team that included prominent Baltimore lawyer Francis Scott Key argued that Smith might have been naive but that he was no traitor. By a vote of 19 to 10—one short of the two-thirds required for expulsion—Smith retained his seat. Concluding that his political career was over, he then resigned. Forced into bankruptcy, he moved to the Louisiana Territory where he lived his remaining years in poverty.

John Smith of Ohio (1803-1808), the first senator to be indicted, came one vote short of the two-thirds needed to expel him from the Senate.

Further Reading

Wilhelmy, Robert W. "Senator John Smith and the Aaron Burr Conspiracy." *Cincinnati Historical Society Bulletin* 28 (Spring 1970): 39-60.

The Senate Convenes in Emergency Quarters

On September 19, 1814, the Senate began a new session in a state of profound crisis. Four weeks earlier, invading British troops had reduced all but one of Washington's major public buildings to smoking rubble. That August 24 blaze had particularly devastated the Capitol's Senate wing, honeycombed with rotting wooden floors and containing the Library of Congress' tinder-dry collection of books and manuscripts. The conflagration reduced the Senate Chamber's marble columns to lime, leaving the room, in one description, "a most magnificent ruin."

President James Madison arranged for Congress to meet temporarily at the city's only available building, Blodgett's Hotel, on Eighth and E Streets, Northwest. The hotel also housed the U.S. Patent Office. At the time of the invasion, a quick-thinking superintendent had saved the building by explaining that it housed a large collection of patent models, which belonged to individual inventors and therefore should be protected as private property.

British troops set fire to the Capitol on the evening of August 24, 1814, causing extensive damage.

The 19 senators who gathered in Blodgett's hastily fitted Senate Chamber on that mid-September day had many questions. Should the government remain in Washington? Might it not resettle in the more comfortable city of Philadelphia, its home in the 1790s? If it continued in Washington, should the blistered Capitol and blackened White House be rebuilt? Or should members follow a Louisiana senator's suggestion to construct an "unadorned" capitol, located conveniently near Georgetown? He reasoned, "Our laws to be wholesome need not be enacted in a palace." Should members give priority to funding construction of legislative chambers while leaving the unpopular president's mansion until later? And should they move the cabinet offices closer to Congress? The House of Representatives agreed to this, only to change its mind after hearing stories, dating from Congress' Philadelphia days, of how frequent interruptions by senators and representatives had complicated the work of the all-too-accessible cabinet officers.

Members studied and debated these issues almost until the March 1815 adjournment, when they authorized President Madison to borrow from local banks to rebuild, on their existing sites, the Capitol, White House, and cabinet quarters. When members returned in December, they moved to a new temporary structure on the site of today's Supreme Court Building. They hoped it would be a brief stay, but construction delays and cost overruns kept them there for another four years.

Further Reading
Pitch, Anthony S. *The Burning of Washington: The British Invasion of 1814.* Annapolis: Naval Institute Press, 1998.

October 10, 1814

The Senate Buys Jefferson's Library

When British forces burned the Capitol in August 1814, they fueled the fire with 3,000 books from the small room that then served as the congressional library. Among the Senate's first orders of business, as it convened in temporary quarters 10 blocks from the gutted Capitol, was to obtain a new library. In September, former President Thomas Jefferson had written to offer his own library—the largest personal collection of books in the nation. "I have been fifty years in making it, and have spared no pains, opportunity or expense, to make it what it now is. While residing in Paris I devoted every afternoon . . . in examining all the principal bookstores, turning over every book with my own hands, and putting by everything which related to America . . ." Recognizing that the nation lacked spare funds during the war emergency, Jefferson explained that he would accept whatever price Congress wished to pay and would take his payments in installments. Appraisers valued the nearly 6,500 volumes at $23,950.

On October 10, 1814, the Senate quickly and unanimously agreed to pay this amount. When the measure reached the House of Representatives, however, it encountered spirited opposition. Reading the collection's inventory, sharp-eyed representatives contended there were too many works in foreign languages. Some titles, including those by Voltaire, Locke, and Rousseau, seemed too philosophical—too literary—for the presumed needs of Congress. In the midst of a war, they contended, Congress had greater priorities than buying expensive libraries for which it lacked secure housing. With the failure of a first round of crippling amendments, the determined opponents, including New Hampshire Representative Daniel Webster, proposed buying the entire collection and then returning to Jefferson "all books of an atheistical, irreligious, and immoral tendency."

House members who supported the purchase held a slim majority. They conceded that every major library contained some books "to which gentlemen might take exception," but argued there was simply no other collection available for purchase to equal this one. One witness to this debate observed that the measure's supporters responded to the zealous and vehement opposition "with fact, wit, and [well-placed] argument." Ultimately, they prevailed, but by a slim margin of 10 votes. As the supporters predicted, this collection went on to serve as a "most admirable" base upon which to establish a national library.

From 1824 until 1897 the Library of Congress was located in the Capitol's west central portion.

Further Reading

Conway, James. *America's Library: The Story of the Library of Congress, 1800-2000*. New Haven: Yale University Press, 2000.

October 11, 1814

The Senate Elects a New Secretary

Imagine the chaos. Seven weeks earlier, the army of a foreign power had set fire to all but one of Washington's public buildings. The Capitol lay in a smoldering ruin. August 24, 1814, had been one of the darkest days in the war with Great Britain. By September, however, the marauding British had withdrawn and President James Madison had called Congress into emergency session at the Patent Office.

On October 11, the Senate prepared to elect a new secretary—its principal administrative, legislative, and financial officer—to help manage the chaos. Samuel Otis, secretary of the Senate for the past 25 years had recently died. As the first person to hold that office, Otis had firmly stamped the position with his own style and personality. But the 73-year-old Otis had also made a few enemies in recent years among senators who questioned the aging man's competence.

The election of his successor proved to be a contentious affair. After considering 9 candidates through 10 separate ballots, the Senate selected former Senator Charles Cutts of New Hampshire.

Cutts inherited the thankless job of directing two relocations, as the Senate moved through the mud and chaos of a shattered city to larger temporary quarters the following year and then, in 1819, to the restored Capitol.

Secretary of the Senate Charles Cutts (1814-1825) directed the relocation of the Senate to temporary quarters after British forces burned the Capitol on August 24, 1814.

The Senate took this occasion to strengthen the secretary's accountability for its administrative and financial operations. Early in 1823, members approved legislation requiring the secretary to submit, at the end of each congressional session, a statement of the names and compensation of all persons employed and all expenditures from the contingent fund. (Today, this volume is known to Senate staffers seeking to learn their colleagues' salaries as the "Green Book.")

Secretary Cutts presented his first annual report in 1823. Soon the Senate adopted a rule that suggested unhappiness with Cutts. At the start of the next congressional session, the secretary would be required to stand for reelection at the start of each Congress, rather than continuing to serve "during good behavior." (The indefinite term reflected the need to have officers carry over from one Congress to the next at a time of rapid turnover among members.)

Predictably, at the first opportunity, the Senate retired Cutts in favor of another unemployed former senator, Walter Lowrie of Pennsylvania. (Lowrie had the misfortune of representing a state whose legislature believed service in the Senate to be a temporary honor that should not extend beyond a single six-year term.) Soothing the senatorial distrust that had plagued Cutts, Lowrie easily won reelection through the next five Congresses and served until he chose to retire in 1836.

Further Reading
National Intelligencer, October 13, 1814, front page.

March 19, 1816

Salary Storm

Consider having your salary level tied to the market price of wheat. That was one of the proposals the Constitution's framers considered as they wrestled with the politically explosive issue of how to set pay rates for members of Congress. In the Congress under the Articles of Confederation, which served as the national legislature at the time the framers were meeting, members were paid at various rates by their individual states.

Deciding only that members should be paid from the U.S. Treasury, the framers left it up to Congress to set the actual amounts.

Soon after Congress convened in 1789, both houses agreed to a constitutional amendment that would delay implementation of any congressional salary changes until after the next election for all House members. This would allow the voters an indirect voice in this inherently contentious matter. Unfortunately for members seeking political cover, more than two centuries passed before the necessary number of states ratified this plan as the Constitution's 27th Amendment.

The First Congress decided to play it safe and compensate senators and representatives at the rate paid to the Constitution's framers—six dollars for every day they attended a session. Before long, however, senators began to argue that they deserved a higher rate than House members. They cited the inconvenience of setting aside their customary livelihoods for the six long years of a Senate term and the presumed extra burdens of advising and consenting to treaties and nominations. The House initially refused to take the Senate proposal seriously, but eventually consented to a seven-dollar Senate rate to take effect five years later and to last only one session.

As the years passed, members became increasingly dissatisfied with their rates of pay.

On March 19, 1816, they voted to abandon the six-dollar daily rate, which had amounted to about $900 a year for those who attended regularly, in favor of a $1,500 annual salary. Supporters reasoned that this would make Congress more efficient because members would be less likely to prolong sessions to pile up more daily salary.

Members failed to anticipate the firestorm of public outrage. Georgians hanged their senators in effigy. An unusually large percentage of incumbent House members lost their elections or chose not to run that fall. At the next session, Congress repealed the raise and quietly returned to a daily rate.

Forty years would pass before Congress again dared to adopt a fixed annual salary.

This financial ledger records nearly a century of salary and mileage payments to senators, from 1790 to 1881.

Further Reading
U.S. Congress. Senate. *The Senate, 1789-1989*, Vol. 2, by Robert C. Byrd. 100th Congress, 1st sess., 1991. S. Doc.100-20. Chapter 15.

The Senate Creates Permanent Committees

For its first quarter-century, the Senate tried to operate without permanent legislative committees. From 1789 until December 1816, the Senate relied on three-to-five-member temporary—or "select"—committees to sift and refine legislative proposals. A late 18th-century guidebook to "how a bill becomes a law" would have explained the process in three steps. First, the full Senate met to discuss the broad objectives of a proposed bill. Next, members elected a temporary committee to convert the general ideas expressed during that floor discussion into specific bill text. The senator who received the most votes automatically became chairman. This system ensured that committees would consist only of those who basically supported the proposed legislation and that activist members would have more committee assignments than those who were less engaged in the legislative process. In the third step, after the committee sent its recommendations to the full Senate, it went out of existence.

PLAN of the ATTIC STORY of the NORTH WING of the CAPITOL U.S. as authorized to be built. 1817

The rooms along the western side of the north wing's top floor were designed for Senate committees.

In 1806, concerned over the increasing amounts of time consumed in electing dozens of temporary committees each session, the Senate began to send new legislation to previously appointed select committees that had dealt with similar topics. Soon, the Senate also began dividing the president's annual State of the Union message into sections by subject matter and referring each section to a different select committee.

The emergency conditions of the War of 1812 accelerated the transition from temporary to permanent committees by highlighting the importance of legislative continuity and expertise. In December 1815, at the start of a new Congress and with the war ended, the Senate appointed the usual select committees to consider the president's annual message, but, when those panels completed that task, the presiding officer assigned them bills on related subjects, thereby keeping them in operation. During that session, however, the Senate also appointed nearly 100 additional temporary committees. Once again the upper house was spending excessive amounts of time voting on committee members.

On December 10, 1816, the Senate took the final step and formally converted 11 major select panels into permanent "standing" committees. This action ensured that those committees, each with five members, would be available not only to handle immediate legislative proposals, but also to deal with ongoing problems and to provide oversight of executive branch operations.

Further Reading

U.S. Congress. Senate. *The Senate, 1789-1989*, Vol. 2, by Robert C. Byrd. 100th Congress, 1st sess., 1991. S. Doc.100-20. Chapter 9.

November 16, 1818

Youngest Senator

When the Senate convened on November 16, 1818, it set a record never likely to be broken. Members on that occasion, however, probably did not realize they were making history—and violating the Constitution—in administering the oath of office to Tennessee's 28-year-old John Henry Eaton.

The framers of the Constitution set the minimum age of Senate service at 30 years. They arrived at that number by adding five years to the 25-year minimum they had established for House members, reasoning that the deliberative nature of the "senatorial trust" called for a "greater extent of information and stability of character" than would be needed in the House.

Apparently no one asked John Eaton how old he was. In those days of large families and poorly kept birth records, he may not have been able to answer that question. Perhaps it was only later that he determined the birth date that now appears on his tombstone, confirming his less-than-constitutional age. Had someone in 1818 chosen to challenge his seating, Eaton could have pointed to the Senate's 1816 decision to seat Virginia's 28-year-old Armistead Mason, or the 1806 precedent to admit 29-year-old Henry Clay.

Within a few years of Eaton's swearing-in, the Senate began to pay closer attention to such matters. This issue then lay dormant for more than a century until the 1934 election of Rush Holt, a 29-year-old West Virginia Democrat. During his campaign, Holt had pledged to wait six months into the 1935 session until his 30th birthday to be sworn in. While he was waiting, his defeated Republican opponent, former incumbent Senator Henry Hatfield, filed a petition with the Senate charging that Holt's failure to meet the constitutional age requirement invalidated his election. Hatfield therefore asked that he be declared the winner, having received the highest number of votes among eligible candidates.

The Senate dismissed Hatfield's arguments, observing that the age requirement applies at the time of oath taking rather than the time of election, or the time the term began. It also reiterated that the ineligibility of the winning candidate gives no title to the candidate receiving the next highest number of votes. On June 21, 1935, Holt followed in the line of Eaton, Mason, and Clay as the Senate's fourth youngest member. In January 1973, the distinction of becoming the youngest since Holt—at the age of 30 years, 1 month, and 14 days—went to Delaware's Joseph Biden.

John Henry Eaton, senator from Tennessee (1818-1829).

Further Reading
McKellar, Kenneth. *Tennessee Senators as Seen by One of their Successors.* Kingsport, Tenn.: Southern Publishers, Inc., 1942.

March 4, 1825

Presiding Officer Stripped of Powers

The 1820s brought a decided shift away from the previously unhurried pace of Senate Chamber floor activity. Debates over the Missouri Compromise suddenly thrust issues of slavery and territorial expansion onto the Senate's agenda. The resulting turmoil caused the body's leaders to look for ways to streamline floor procedures.

They decided that the time had come to change the way that the Senate selected its committee chairmen and members. From its earliest years, the Senate had laboriously voted separately for each chairman and each member. With the emergence of stronger political parties in the early 1820s, this slow process offered unlimited opportunities for endless partisan wrangles.

In 1823, the Senate abandoned this system in favor of allowing the presiding officer to appoint committees. At a time when the vice presidency was vacant for several years, or otherwise occupied by infirm individuals who seldom appeared in the Senate Chamber, members thought of the "presiding officer" as the Senate president pro tempore—one of their own number. No one doubted that the president pro tempore would make selections satisfying to the majority.

All of this abruptly changed in March 1825 with the arrival of a vigorous new vice president—South Carolina's John C. Calhoun, a former House member and war secretary, and active presidential aspirant. Senators immediately recognized his brilliance and its attendant dangers.

By the time he took office, Calhoun had split with President John Quincy Adams and the president's powerful ally, Secretary of State Henry Clay. He believed Adams and Clay had corruptly influenced the outcome of the 1824 presidential election, which had been decided in the House of Representatives. Allies of Adams and Clay watched carefully as Calhoun became the first vice president to make Senate committee assignments under the 1823 rules change. To no one's surprise in that bitterly partisan era, Calhoun appointed prominent administration opponents to the chairmanships of the Senate's major standing committees.

Within weeks, Adams and Clay partisans arranged for a Senate rules change. Once again, the full Senate would elect all committee chairmen and members. And, for the first time, the Senate allowed its members to appeal and reverse decisions made by the presiding officer. Never again would a vice president enjoy the power that, ever so briefly, had fallen into the hands of John C. Calhoun.

John C. Calhoun, senator from South Carolina (1832-1843, 1845-1850), vice president of the United States (1825-1832).

Further Reading
Niven, John. *John C. Calhoun and the Price of Union*. Baton Rouge: Louisiana State University Press, 1988.

January 26, 1830

The Most Famous Senate Speech

When the debate started, it focused on the seemingly prosaic subjects of tariff and public land policy. By the time it ended nine days later, the focus had shifted to the vastly more cosmic concerns of slavery and the nature of the federal Union. Observers then and since have considered Massachusetts Senator Daniel Webster's closing oration, beginning on January 26, 1830, as the most famous speech in Senate history.

The debate began with a proposal by a Connecticut senator to limit federal land sales in the West. Responding for the West, Missouri Senator Thomas Hart Benton condemned this as a trick to safeguard the supply of cheap labor for manufacturers in the Northeast.

South Carolina Senator Robert Hayne entered the debate at that point as a surrogate for Vice President John C. Calhoun. Hayne agreed that land sales should be ended. In his opinion, they enriched the federal treasury for the benefit of the North, while draining wealth from the West. At the heart of his argument, Hayne asserted that states should have the power to control their own lands and—ominously—to disobey, or "nullify" federal laws that they believed were not in their best interests. Hayne continued that the North was intentionally trying to destroy the South through a policy of high tariffs and its increasingly vocal opposition to slavery.

Daniel Webster rose to Hayne's challenge. In a packed Senate Chamber, Webster used his organ-like voice to great effect as he began a two-day speech known as his "Second Reply to Hayne." In response to Hayne's argument that the nation was simply an association of sovereign states, from which individual states could withdraw at will, Webster thundered that it was instead a "popular government, erected by the people; those who administer it are responsible to the people; and itself capable of being amended and modified, just as the people may choose it should be."

Webster's Reply to Hayne, *by George P. A. Healy, portrays Webster's famous floor speech.*

The impact of Webster's oration extended far beyond the Senate Chamber to establish him as a national statesman who would lead the debate over the nature of the Union for the next tumultuous 20 years.

Following his speech, Webster encountered Hayne at a White House reception. When Webster asked the South Carolina senator how he was doing, Hayne relied, "None the better for you, sir."

Further Reading
Remini, Robert. *Daniel Webster: The Man and His Time*. New York: W.W. Norton, 1997.

43

Henry Clay Celebrates a First

Question: Who was the first U.S. senator to win the presidential nomination of his political party?

In December 1831, that senator's party—known as the National Republicans—met in Baltimore to conduct the first major national political convention. In previous presidential elections, parties had produced candidates through state conventions, and caucuses held in state legislatures and in the U.S. Congress. The last congressional caucus had taken place in 1824 and included only 66 of Congress' 261 members.

As the nation grew and means of communication improved, parties realized the importance of orchestrating a national event to energize supporters. The National Republicans chose Baltimore because it was conveniently near Washington, where many of their delegates also served in Congress.

As a former House Speaker and secretary of state, Henry Clay in 1831 could easily have won the necessary number of electoral votes without the added formality of a national convention. But his party wanted to take no chances in its campaign to dislodge Democrat Andrew Jackson from the White House.

In addition to supporting the innovation of a national party convention, Clay had decided that his standing would be enhanced if he could return to public office as a member of the United States Senate. This move reflected the growing stature of the Senate in that era as it moved out of the shadow of the House of Representatives. Eight years earlier, Andrew Jackson had made the same tactical decision. In doing this, both men risked humiliation at the hands of political opponents in their state legislatures. A defeat for a Senate seat would certainly tarnish a subsequent presidential bid. Indeed, the Kentucky legislature elected Henry Clay to the Senate in November 1831 by a margin of only nine votes.

Clay remained in Washington during the December Baltimore convention, at which 155 delegates from 18 of the nation's 24 states met in a large saloon and chose him unanimously on December 13, 1831.

The following spring, as the campaign got underway, 300 young National Republicans visited Washington to support their candidate. Known as "Clay's Infant-School," they experienced an unexpected treat on May 7, 1832, when the candidate himself rode down from the Senate to accept their ceremonial nomination.

Since 1832, 14 other incumbent senators, including three Republicans and four Democrats, have received their parties' nomination. In 1920, Warren Harding became the first among them to win the presidency; in 1960 John F. Kennedy became the second.

Henry Clay ran for president of the United States in 1824, 1832, and 1844. This 1844 Whig election banner features Clay and his running mate, Theodore M. Frelinghuysen.

Further Reading

Remini, Robert. *Henry Clay: Statesman for the Union.* New York: W.W. Norton, 1991.

June 24, 1834

First Cabinet Rejection

Relations between the Senate and the president had become so embittered that the president delayed submitting the names of his recent cabinet appointees for confirmation until the final week of the congressional session. By June of 1834, the Senate stood evenly divided between supporters of President Andrew Jackson and anti-Jackson men. The president's assault on the Second Bank of the United States, launched two years earlier, had precipitated this split and led to the formation of the opposition Whig Party. In March, the Senate had censured Jackson for his efforts to remove government funds from that federally chartered quasi-private institution. When Jackson formally protested this extra-constitutional act, the Senate refused to print his message in its journal.

Nine months earlier, Jackson had selected Roger Taney, the architect of his anti-bank policies, as secretary of the treasury. Senators complained that the unconfirmed Taney held his office illegally. As Jackson biographer Robert Remini has written, "Whether this was true did not disturb Jackson one whit." Yet Jackson knew that sooner or later he would have to send Taney's name to the Senate and, in Remini's words, "he knew that senators would tear into the nomination like ravenous wolves to get revenge for the removal of the deposits and poor Taney would be made to bear much of the pain and humiliation."

Finally, on June 23, 1834, Jackson sent forth Taney's nomination. On the next day a pro-bank majority in the Senate, including both senators from Taney's Maryland, denied him the post by a vote of 18 to 28, making him the first cabinet nominee in history to suffer the Senate's formal rejection.

The following year the deeply insulted Jackson returned Taney's name to the Senate as associate justice of the Supreme Court. Opponents blocked a vote on the last day of that session and tried unsuccessfully to eliminate one seat from the Court. When the Senate reconvened in December 1835, under a slim margin of Democratic control, Jackson sent it a new Taney nomination, this time to fill a vacancy for chief justice of the United States. Following extended maneuvering and bitter debate, the Senate confirmed Taney.

In preparing to leave office a year later, Jackson wrote to a friend that he was greatly looking forward to seeing his loyal supporter, president-elect Martin Van Buren, whom the Senate had rejected for a diplomatic post in his first administration, sworn into office by Chief Justice Taney.

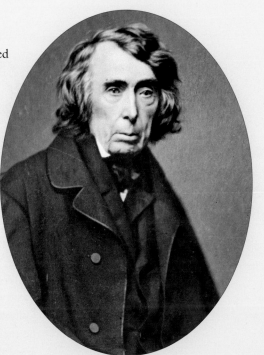

The Senate rejected Roger B. Taney's nomination as secretary of the treasury.

Further Reading

Remini, Robert. *Andrew Jackson and the Course of American Democracy*, 1833-1845. New York: W.W. Norton, 1984.

March 16, 1836

Senate Rejects Calhoun's "Gag Rule"

On March 16, 1836, South Carolina's John C. Calhoun stormed out of the Senate Chamber. The Senate had just rejected a proposal that he believed would save the nation unnecessary bloodshed.

In a speech delivered several days earlier, Calhoun had warned Congress against interfering with the South's system of slave labor. "The relation which now exists between the two races," he said, "has existed for two centuries. It has grown with our growth and strengthened with our strength. It has entered into and modified all our institutions, civil and political. We will not, cannot permit it to be destroyed."

Gag rule motion from the House of Representatives, 1837.

A growing number of petitions to Congress demanding the abolition of slavery in the District of Columbia had caused Calhoun to speak out. While many believed that slavery could not be abolished in the states where it existed without a constitutional amendment, the senders of those petitions reasoned that since Congress had exclusive jurisdiction over the District, it had the power to outlaw slavery there.

Few members in the Senate of 1836 cared about abolishing slavery in the District of Columbia. Yet, they faced two options. One was to accept the petitions and then bury them in a committee. This procedure preserved the basic right of citizens to petition their government, while protecting the interests of members from the slave states.

John C. Calhoun believed it was time to end this hypocrisy. Under his plan, the Senate would accept no anti-slavery petitions. In his opinion, Congress had no business considering emancipation. If that issue ever reached the floor of the Senate or House, there would be no end to it; it would shake the Union at its foundations.

Most senators wanted this irritating issue to disappear. They feared that Calhoun's proposal to bar the Senate door to these petitions would inadvertently benefit the small and regionally isolated anti-slavery movement. Overnight, the troublesome enemies of slavery could be transformed into noble champions of civil liberties.

After rejecting Calhoun's plan on March 16, the Senate devised a curious, complex, and obscure delaying procedure. It would vote not on whether to receive the petition itself—this would dignify the petition—but on whether to accept the question of receiving the petition.

This indirect method produced enough confusion to provide political cover for all members regardless of position. It was a classic example—a quarter century before the Civil War—of postponing the inevitable.

Further Reading

Miller, William Lee. *Arguing About Slavery: The Great Battle in the United States Congress.* New York: Alfred A. Knopf, 1996.

January 16, 1837

The Senate Reverses a Presidential Censure

A unique sheet of time-weathered paper rests in a green steel vault at the National Archives Building. Careful inspection reveals that it was originally created as page 552 of the Senate's 1834 handwritten legislative journal. Because of the document's great significance, someone later sliced it out of the bound journal to make it easier to display.

The yellowed document symbolizes a titanic struggle in the Senate of the 1830s between allies of Democratic President Andrew Jackson and the forces of Whig Senator Henry Clay. Its most striking visual feature is a rectangular box, formed of thin black lines, which encloses 34 words. Inscribed by the secretary of the Senate on March 28, 1834, they read as follows: "Resolved that the President in the late Executive proceedings in relation to the public revenue, has assumed upon himself authority and power not conferred by the Constitution and laws, but in deroga-tion of both."

This message was placed in the journal following the Senate's vote to censure Jackson for refusing to provide documents related to his plan to remove government funds from the privately run Bank of the United States. This censure, totally without constitu-tional authorization, united the Senate's "Great Triumvirate" of Clay, Daniel Webster, and John C. Calhoun against Jackson and his Senate ally, Missouri's Thomas Hart Benton.

For the next three years, Benton worked tirelessly to remove this blot from Jackson's record and from the Senate's official journal. Early in 1837, with less than two months remaining in the president's final term, and with majority control back in Democratic hands, Benton called for a vote. By a five-vote margin, the Senate agreed to reverse its earlier censure. On January 16, 1837, the secretary of the Senate carried the 1834 Senate Journal into the chamber, drew careful lines around its text, and wrote, "Expunged by order of the Senate."

Pandemonium swept the galleries. When a disgruntled Whig sympathizer ignored the presiding officer's repeated calls for order, that officer directed the sergeant at arms to arrest the man and haul him onto the Senate floor. After the Senate voted to free the demonstrator, he approached the presiding officer and demanded, "Am I not permitted to speak in my own defense?" The outraged presiding officer ordered him removed from the chamber and the Senate adjourned amidst the tumult.

The Great Tumble Bug of Missouri, Bent-on Rolling his Ball, *depicts Missouri Senator Thomas Hart Benton as an insect rolling a large ball labeled "Expunging Resolution" uphill toward the Capitol.*

Further Reading

Holt, Michael F. *The Rise and Fall of the American Whig Party: Jacksonian Politics and the Onset of the Civil War.* New York: Oxford University Press, 1999.

Wilentz, Sean. *The Rise of American Democracy: Jefferson to Lincoln.* New York: W. W. Norton, 2005.

The Senate Elects a Vice President

Richard M. Johnson, senator from Kentucky (1819-1829), vice president of the United States (1837-1841).

The presidential election of 1800 revealed a need to amend the U.S. Constitution. The original system for electing presidents provided that the candidate receiving a majority of Electoral College votes would become president, while the runner up would become vice president. The 1800 election resulted in a tie between Thomas Jefferson and Aaron Burr. Under the Constitution, this stalemate sent the election to the House of Representatives, which chose Jefferson. The states soon ratified a 12th amendment to the Constitution, requiring separate contests for the offices of president and vice president.

To balance the role of the House in electing a president when the Electoral College fails to do so, the 12th Amendment requires the Senate to handle that responsibility for vice-presidential contests. The Senate must choose between the two top electoral vote getters, with at least two-thirds of its members present.

The Senate has exercised this power only once. In the election of 1836, which made Martin Van Buren president, Kentucky's former Democratic Senator Richard M. Johnson fell one electoral vote short of a majority among four vice-presidential candidates.

A controversial figure, who openly acknowledged his slave mistress and their daughters, Johnson had served in Congress for 30 years and was a close friend of the outgoing president, Andrew Jackson. His many detractors alleged that he owed his vice-presidential nomination to his dubious claim that during the War of 1812 he killed the Indian chieftain Tecumseh. This claim produced his vice-presidential campaign slogan, "Rumpsey, Dumpsey, Colonel Johnson killed Tecumseh."

On February 8, 1837, by a vote of 33 to 16, the Senate elected Johnson vice president. Johnson apologized to the Senate for not having paid more attention to its procedures while a senator and hoped that "the intelligence of the Senate will guard the country from any injury that might result from the imperfections of its presiding officer."

During his four years in office, Johnson broke 17 tie votes, a record exceeded by only one of his vice-presidential successors (Schuyler Colfax, 1869-1873). When not presiding over the Senate, Johnson could regularly be found in Kentucky, operating his tavern.

Johnson's erratic behavior—believing his slave mistress had been unfaithful, he sold her and married her sister—combined with his chronic financial problems added to President Martin Van Buren's political difficulties and contributed to the defeat of their ticket in the election of 1840.

Further Reading

U.S. Congress. Senate. *Vice Presidents of the United States, 1789-1993*, by Mark O. Hatfield, with the Senate Historical Office. 104th Congress, 2d sess., 1997. S. Doc. 104-6.

A Senate Leader Apologizes

Three major portraits of Henry Clay occupy prime space in the Capitol. In each of them, the Kentucky statesman wears the genial look of a man confident about his place in history. In March of 1841, however, Clay looked worried. He was in deep trouble.

The trouble began when Senator William King of Alabama rose on the Senate floor to defend a fellow Democrat against a verbal attack by Clay, a leader of the Whig Party. For years, the two men had clashed over the era's great polarizing issues.

The issue that divided King and Clay at the start of the new Congress in March 1841 related to selection of a private contractor to handle the Senate's printing needs. With the Whigs now in control of the Senate's majority, Clay as their leader had sought to dismiss Democrat Francis Blair, editor of the *Washington Globe*, as official Senate printer and to hire a Whig printer. Clay said he "believed the *Globe* to be an infamous paper, and its chief editor an infamous man." When King responded that Blair's character would "compare gloriously" to that of Clay, the Kentucky senator jumped to his feet and shouted, "That is false, it is a slanderous base and cowardly declaration and the senator knows it to be so."

King answered ominously, "Mr. President, I have no reply to make—none whatever. But Mr. Clay deserves a response." King then wrote out a challenge to a duel and delivered it to Clay. Only then did Clay realize what trouble his hasty words had unleashed.

As Clay and King selected seconds and prepared for the imminent encounter, the Senate sergeant at arms arrested both men and turned them over to a local court. Clay posted a $5,000 bond as assurance that he would keep the peace, "and particularly towards William R. King." King insisted on "an unequivocal apology."

On March 14, 1841, Clay formally apologized to King and noted that he should have kept his intense feelings to himself. King then delivered his own apology. After King finished, Clay walked to the Alabama senator's desk and said sweetly, "King, give us a pinch of your snuff." As both men shook hands, senators burst into applause. Clay brightened and once again looked as if he were ready for the portrait painter.

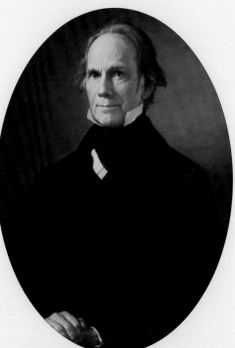

Henry Clay, senator from Kentucky (1806-1807, 1810-1811, 1831-1842, 1849-1852).

Further Reading

Remini, Robert. *Henry Clay: Statesman for the Union*. New York: W.W. Norton, 1991.

Vagabond Statue

Statue of George Washington, by Horatio Greenough, 1841.

On July 31, 1841, a sailing vessel from Leghorn, Italy, docked at the Washington Navy Yard. It carried a massive 10-foot-high, 12-ton marble statue of a seated man wearing only a Roman toga. The artist was the noted American sculptor Horatio Greenough; the marble man, modeled after the Greek god Zeus, was President George Washington. Several years earlier, Congress had commissioned Greenough to prepare this work for permanent display in the recently completed Capitol Rotunda.

Controversy erupted almost immediately. Capitol officials directed that the piece be placed at the center of the Rotunda. Sculptor Greenough protested. He wanted it moved off to the side so that light coming through an opening at the top of the wooden dome, which at that time covered the Rotunda, would strike Washington's face at a flattering angle. By placing the statue in the center, the nearly vertical light would, he feared, shade the lower portions of the face "and give a false and constrained effect to the whole monument." He lost that argument.

The second point of controversy related to the work's design. Despite the era's neo-classical revival, few on Capitol Hill seemed ready for a half-naked father-of-the-country with well-developed and fully exposed shoulder muscles. His upraised right arm, draped with what appeared to be a towel across his biceps, gave the impression that he was preparing for a bath. Within weeks, incensed members of Congress demanded the work's removal. Sculptor Greenough seized the opportunity for a better location and suggested a perch on the Capitol's west front. He also lost that argument.

Two years after workmen had hauled the 12-ton statue up the east-front stairs, they hauled the work back down and placed it in the center of the Capitol's eastern plaza. During the winter of 1844, carpenters built a small shed to protect the underdressed patriarch from snow and ice. Come spring, the unsightly shed was removed; it was seldom replaced in the winters that followed.

As decades passed, the elements pitted and discolored the marble. Finally, a charitable Congress took pity on the snow-covered president in the parking lot. In 1908, the sculpture made another journey—to the indoor warmth of the Smithsonian Institution. Today, this historical curiosity resides on the second floor of the National Museum of American History. While the setting is less grand than that of the Capitol Rotunda, at least the lighting is perfect.

Further Reading

U.S. Congress. Senate. *History of the United States Capitol: A Chronicle of Design, Construction, and Politics,* by William C. Allen. 106th Congress, 2d sess., 2001. S. Doc. 106-29.

March 26, 1848

The Senate Arrests a Reporter

On March 26, 1848, the Senate arrested a journalist and imprisoned him in a Capitol committee room. This unusual event occurred during one of the most turbulent decades in American history. Throughout the 1840s, territorial disputes with Mexico over the Republic of Texas, and with Great Britain over Oregon, inflamed the Senate's proceedings. Out of this agitation emerged a question that the framers of the Constitution, 60 years earlier, thought they had answered affirmatively: Could the Senate keep a secret?

By the 1840s, many political observers believed the framers had been overly optimistic. In 1844, the Senate censured a member for releasing confidential treaty documents to a newspaper. Two years later, senators investigated the *Washington Daily Times* for unauthorized publication of the Oregon boundary settlement. When the reporter willingly identified his sources, including a Senate doorkeeper, the accused individuals heatedly swore to their innocence. Tired of this finger pointing, the Senate punished the *Times* by banning its reporters from the press gallery. The last straw fell in March 1848, when the *New York Herald* published the secret treaty ending the war with Mexico.

Denying that Secretary of State James Buchanan leaked the document, President James Polk guessed that the culprit must be a senator. John Nugent, the reporter who prepared the treaty story for the *Herald*, added weight to the president's theory by observing that the best leakers were those same senators who most strongly defended the Senate's practice of considering treaties behind closed doors.

Under questioning, Nugent refused to disclose his sources to Senate investigators, saying only that in this instance they were neither senators nor Senate officers. The frustrated investigating committee thereupon ordered him to be arrested and confined to one of the Senate's committee rooms. As the *Herald* retaliated by publishing the names of the Senate's most cooperative leakers, Nugent spent his captivity in comfort, receiving a doubled salary while issuing his regular columns under the dateline "Custody of the Sergeant at Arms." Each evening he accompanied the sergeant at arms to that officer's home for a good meal and a comfortable night's sleep. From time to time, the full Senate summoned Nugent to answer questions, but always without success. After a month, the Senate realized the futility of further incarceration and released its prisoner on the face-saving grounds of protecting his health. Who actually leaked the treaty? The historical evidence points to Secretary of State Buchanan.

James Buchanan, senator from Pennsylvania (1834-1845), secretary of state (1845-1849), president of the United States (1857-1861).

Further Reading
Ritchie, Donald A. *Press Gallery: Congress and the Washington Correspondents.* Cambridge: Harvard University Press, 1991.

March 4, 1849

President for a Day?

On a statue in Kansas City, Missouri, an inscription reads, "David Rice Atchison, 1807–1886, President of the U.S. [for] one day." The day of President Atchison's presumed presidency occurred on March 4, 1849.

A proslavery Democrat, David Atchison served in the U.S. Senate from 1843 to 1855. His colleagues elected him president pro tempore on 13 occasions. In those days, the vice president regularly attended Senate sessions. Consequently, the Senate chose a president pro tempore to serve only during brief vice-presidential absences.

Until the 1930s, presidential and congressional terms began at noon on March 4. In 1849, that date fell on a Sunday, causing President Zachary Taylor to delay his inauguration until the next day. For some, this raised the question of who was president from noon of March 4 to noon of March 5. Today, we understand that Taylor automatically became president on the fourth and could have begun to execute the duties of his office after taking the oath privately.

In 1849, the Senate president pro tempore immediately followed the vice president in line of presidential succession. That era's ever-present threat of sudden death made it essential to keep an unbroken order of succession. To ensure that there was a president pro tempore in office during adjournment periods, the vice president customarily left the Senate Chamber in an annual session's final days so that the Senate could elect this constitutional officer. Accordingly, the Senate duly elected Atchison on March 2, 1849. His supporters, to the present day, claim that the expiration of the outgoing president's and vice president's terms at noon on March 4 left Atchison with clear title to the job.

Unfortunately for Atchison's shaky claim, his Senate term also expired at noon on March 4. When the Senate of the new Congress convened the following day to swear in the new senators and vice president, with no president pro tempore, the secretary of the Senate called members to order.

No one planning to attend Taylor's March 5 inauguration seems to have realized that there had been a President Atchison in charge. Nonetheless, for the rest of his life, Atchison enjoyed polishing this story, describing his presidency as "the honestest administration this country ever had."

David Rice Atchison, senator from Missouri (1843-1855).

Further Reading

Parrish, William E. *David Rice Atchison of Missouri: Border Politician*. Columbia: University of Missouri Press, 1961.

March 7, 1850

Speech Costs Senator his Seat

Ask anyone familiar with the Senate's history to name a famous floor speech that is commonly identified by the date on which it was given and you will almost certainly receive one answer, "The Seventh of March Speech."

On March 7, 1850, Massachusetts Senator Daniel Webster rose in the Senate Chamber to stake his career, his reputation, and perhaps the nation's future on the success of a speech that he hoped would unite moderates of all sections in support of Kentucky Senator Henry Clay's proposed "Compromise of 1850."

He began his "Seventh of March" address with the immortal lines, "Mr. President, I wish to speak today, not as a Massachusetts man, nor as a Northern man, but as an American, and a member of the Senate of the United States. . . . I speak for the preservation of the Union. Hear me for my cause." The Massachusetts statesman then spoke for three and a half hours—a relatively brief performance for one known to have given an after dinner speech lasting five hours.

Webster contended that it was pointless to argue about the continuation of slavery where it already existed—it was not going away—or to worry about extending slavery into the arid lands of the southwest, where plantation agriculture stood no chance of flourishing. Asserting that slaveholders were entitled to the protection of their property, he urged strengthening of fugitive slave statutes.

Thanks to the recently introduced telegraph, Webster's address quickly appeared in newspapers throughout the nation. Nearly everywhere but in his native New England, Webster won high praise for moral courage. It was said that his speech slammed into New England with the force of a hurricane. Many there believed that he must have cut a deal with southern leaders to win their promised support for the presidency. Horace Mann called it a "vile catastrophe," that Webster, who had walked with the gods, had now descended to consort with "harlots and leeches." Ralph Waldo Emerson cried, "'Liberty! Liberty!' Pho! Let Mr. Webster, for decency's sake shut his lips for once and forever on this word. The word 'Liberty' in the mouth of Mr. Webster sounds like the word 'love' in the mouth of a courtesan."

His political base in ruins, Webster soon resigned from the Senate and finished his public career as secretary of state.

The United States Senate, A.D. 1850, *by Robert Whitechurch, depicts Henry Clay presenting his program of compromise to the Senate. Daniel Webster is seated with head in hand,* left foreground.

Further Reading

Remini, Robert V. *Daniel Webster: The Man and His Time.* New York: W.W. Norton, 1997.

Wiltse, Charles M., ed. *The Papers of Daniel Webster.* Hanover, NH: University Press of New England, 1974–1989.

Bitter Feelings in the Senate Chamber

John C. Calhoun died on March 31, 1850. Two days later, Vice President Millard Fillmore conducted his funeral in the Senate Chamber. On April 3, 1850, responding to the deeply unsettled atmosphere spawned by the South Carolina statesman's death and the festering slavery issue, the vice president addressed the Senate. His voice tinged with disappointment, he noted that when he first became the Senate's presiding officer a year earlier, he had assumed he would not be burdened with maintaining order in a body famous for its courtesy and collegiality. Times had changed.

In the earliest years, the Senate had given its presiding officer the sole power to call senators to order for inappropriate

SCENE IN UNCLE SAM'S SENATE.

Cartoonist Edward Clay lampooned the dramatic scene on the Senate floor between Henry Foote and Thomas Hart Benton.

language or behavior. The decision was not subject to appeal to the full Senate. This practice changed in 1828, thanks to John C. Calhoun, who at that time was proving to be an unusually active vice president—too active to suit the taste of many senators. The Senate revised its rule to allow members, as well as the vice president, to call other members to order for offensive behavior. If the Senate objected to the vice president's subsequent ruling on that call, it could overrule him by majority vote.

In his April 1850 address, Vice President Fillmore lamented that, since many senators appeared reluctant to call their colleagues to order, he would do his duty to contain the first spark of disorder before it ignited a conflagration that would be more difficult to control. "A slight attack, or even insinuation, of a personal character, often provokes a more severe retort, which brings out a more disorderly reply, each Senator feeling a justification in the previous aggression."

Two weeks later, Fillmore's worst fears were realized. When he ruled Missouri Senator Thomas Hart Benton out of order, Kentucky's Henry Clay, no friend of Benton, angrily charged that the vice president's action was an attack on the power and dignity of the Senate. The ensuing debate sparked a bitter exchange between Benton and Mississippi Senator Henry Foote. As the burly Benton pushed aside his chair and moved menacingly up the center aisle toward the diminutive Foote, Foote pulled a pistol. Pandemonium swept the chamber. Benton bellowed, "I have no pistols! Let him fire! Stand out of the way and let the assassin fire!" Fillmore quickly entertained a motion to adjourn, a bit wiser about the near impossibility of maintaining order in a deeply fractured Senate.

Further Reading

Chambers, William. *Old Bullion Benton: Senator from the New West, Thomas Hart Benton, 1782-1858*. New York: William N. Chambers, 1956. Reissued, New York: Russell & Russell, 1970.

CHAPTER III

WAR AND RECONSTRUCTION

1851-1880

July 4, 1851

Capitol Cornerstone Dedicated

On the Fourth of July, 1851, sunny and unseasonably mild weather attracted large crowds to the Capitol's east front plaza. The festive multitudes looked forward to a day of parades, speeches, and fireworks. These events were to celebrate the laying of a cornerstone as the beginning of a major Capitol construction project.

Five new states had entered the Union over the previous six years. This expansion added to the membership of Congress and strained the capacities of the Capitol's already overcrowded legislative chambers.

The recently enacted Compromise of 1850 had eased fears that the nation would soon break apart over the issue of permitting slavery in states created from the nation's western territories. The resulting burst of confidence in the future of the Union led Congress to authorize an expansion of the Capitol. These extensions would provide new Senate and House chambers and much-needed committee rooms.

Shortly before noon on July 4, 1851, a colorful parade reached the Capitol. It included President Millard Fillmore, several veterans of the Revolutionary War, and three individuals who had witnessed the placing of the building's original cornerstone 58 years earlier.

Into a specially fashioned granite block—believed to have been placed in the northeast corner of the new House wing—Capitol Architect Thomas U. Walter set current newspapers, documents, and $40.44 in new coins from the Philadelphia mint. Using the same trowel that President George Washington had employed in setting the 1793 cornerstone, a Masonic official performed a sealing ceremony.

Then all eyes turned to the east front steps for a view of the nation's foremost orator, former Senator Daniel Webster. In his two-hour address, Webster compared the United States of that day with the nation at the time of the first cornerstone laying. He also noted that he had placed a brief handwritten statement under the cornerstone. That statement included his message to future generations. "If it shall be the will of God that this structure shall fall from its base, that its foundation be upturned, . . . Be it known that on this day the Union of the United States of America stands firm, that their Constitution still exists unimpaired, and with all its original usefulness and glory; growing every day stronger and stronger in the affections of the great body of the American people, and attracting more and more the admiration of the world."

An artillery salute and fireworks on the mall concluded this most jubilant Independence Day.

The Capitol is shown under construction in Present State of the Capitol at Washington, *dated 1853.*

Further Reading

U.S. Congress. Senate. *History of the United States Capitol: A Chronicle of Design, Construction, and Politics,* by William C. Allen. 106th Congress, 2d sess., 2001. S. Doc. 106-29.

June 5, 1852

First Senator Nominated as Vice President

What an imposing name: Senator King. Throughout the history of the Senate, four Kings have been senators. In June 1852, one of them—William Rufus Devane King of Alabama—became the first senator to gain a major party's nomination for the vice presidency. Several months later, he won that office, but then gained the dark distinction of becoming the only vice president to die before getting to exercise that position's responsibilities.

When William King received his party's vice-presidential nomination on June 5, 1852, he had served in the Senate for more than 28 years, making him at that time the second longest-serving senator in history. In those days, the Senate elected a president pro tempore to serve only during the absence of the vice president. King had been a frequent choice as president pro tempore. His Senate colleagues considered the warm-hearted and even-tempered King to be an excellent presiding officer. They saw him as a man of sound judgment and rich experience who could be stern "when public interests or his personal honor required it." At a time when the vice president's only significant duty was to preside over the Senate, King seemed to be the ideal man for the job.

Although King and his presidential running mate Franklin Pierce won the 1852 election, deteriorating health kept him from returning to the Senate Chamber in his new role. Describing himself as looking like a skeleton, the vice president-elect traveled to Cuba to seek a cure for his tuberculosis. There, by special act of Congress, he took his oath as the nation's unlucky 13th vice president. After several weeks, King returned to his home in Alabama, where he died just five weeks into his term and without ever reaching the nation's capital.

From William King to John Edwards in 2004, 25 incumbent Democratic and Republican senators have received their party's vice-presidential nomination. On four occasions, the candidates on both sides of the ticket were senators, such as the 1928 race that pitted Majority Leader Charles Curtis against Minority Leader Joseph Robinson. In the years since World War II, as the vice presidency has taken on wider responsibilities, senators have been increasingly willing to accept their party's nomination. Of the 25 senatorial candidates for vice president since 1852, 13 won the office. But only two—Harry Truman and Lyndon Johnson—continued directly to the White House, in each case because of the death of the incumbent president.

William R. King, senator from North Carolina (1819-1844, 1848-1852), served as vice president of the United States from March 24, 1853 until his death on April 18, 1853.

Further Reading

U.S. Congress. Senate. *Vice Presidents of the United States, 1789-1993*, by Mark O. Hatfield with the Senate Historical Office. 104th Congress, 2d sess., 1997. S. Doc. 104-16.

June 29, 1852

Henry Clay Dies

Henry Clay died of tuberculosis in Washington on June 29, 1852. The 75-year-old Kentucky statesman had spent his lengthy public career setting records. He was the first of three senators who began their service under the constitutionally required age of 30. He won election as Speaker of the House on his first day in that body. He engineered the only Senate censure of a president. He built the Whig Party. He ran three times (1824, 1832, and 1844) as a candidate for the presidency. For successfully forging compromise solutions to issues that threatened to shatter the Union, at his death he became the first person to lie in state in the Capitol Rotunda.

By today's tenure standards, Clay's service in the Senate was relatively brief—a total of only 16 years between his first term in 1806 and his death in 1852. Yet he dominated American political life for much of that period and set a standard for what it means to be a successful United States senator. With Daniel Webster and John C. Calhoun, the other two members of the Senate's so-called Great Triumvirate, Clay excelled as an orator. Each of the three senators developed a unique speaking style. Webster's strength lay in his use of richly cultivated language. Calhoun succeeded on the power of his intellect, where substance took precedence over style. Clay's success grew not from language or substance, but from the personal style of his voice and mannerisms. One biographer reported that he "was more a debater than orator. Invariably dramatic, if not flamboyant, he regularly mesmerized his audience with his histrionics." Another wrote that Clay changed his "rhetorical costumes" depending on the occasion and location of his speaking engagements.

Alternatively haughty and captivating, Clay charmed even those who differed with his policies and principles. When he resigned from the Senate in 1842 to prepare for the 1844 presidential election, he apologized for the "ardor of temperament" that had led him, on occasion, "to use language offensive and susceptible of ungracious interpretation towards my brother senators." Perhaps John C. Calhoun had some of that language in mind when, setting a memorable definition for the nature of friendship among senators, he observed, "I don't like Clay. He is a bad man, an imposter, a creator of wicked schemes. I wouldn't speak to him, but, by God, I love him!"

This symbolic group portrait eulogizing recent legislative efforts to preserve the Union—notably the Compromise of 1850—features Henry Clay of Kentucky, Daniel Webster of Massachusetts, and John C. Calhoun of South Carolina.

Further Reading

Holt, Michael F. *The Rise and Fall of the American Whig Party: Jacksonian Politics and the Onset of the Civil War.* New York: Oxford University Press, 1999.

Remini, Robert V. *Henry Clay: Statesman for the Union.* New York: W.W. Norton, 1991.

May 22, 1856

The Caning of Senator Charles Sumner

On May 22, 1856, the "world's greatest deliberative body" became a combat zone. In one of the most dramatic and deeply ominous moments in the Senate's entire history, a member of the House of Representatives entered the Senate Chamber and savagely beat a senator into unconsciousness.

The inspiration for this clash came three days earlier when Senator Charles Sumner, a Massachusetts antislavery Republican, addressed the Senate on the explosive issue of whether Kansas should be admitted to the Union as a slave state or a free state. In his "Crime Against Kansas" speech, Sumner identified two Democratic senators as the principal culprits in this crime—Stephen Douglas of Illinois and Andrew Butler of South Carolina. He characterized Douglas to his face as a "noise-some, squat, and nameless animal . . . not a proper model for an American senator." Andrew Butler, who was not present, received more elaborate treatment. Mocking the South Carolina senator's stance as a man of chivalry, the Massachusetts senator charged him with taking "a mistress . . . who, though ugly to others, is always lovely to him; though polluted in the sight of the world, is chaste in his sight—I mean," added Sumner, "the harlot, Slavery."

Representative Preston Brooks was Butler's South Carolina kinsman. If he had believed Sumner to be a gentleman, he might have challenged him to a duel. Instead, he chose a light cane of the type used to discipline unruly dogs. Shortly after the Senate had adjourned for the day, Brooks entered the Senate Chamber, where he found Sumner busily attaching his postal frank to copies of his "Crime Against Kansas" speech.

Moving quickly, Brooks slammed his metal-topped cane onto the unsuspecting Sumner's head. As Brooks struck again and again, Sumner rose and lurched blindly about the chamber, futilely attempting to protect himself. After a very long minute, it ended.

Bleeding profusely, Sumner was carried away. Brooks walked calmly out of the chamber without being detained by the stunned onlookers. Overnight, both men became heroes in their respective regions.

Surviving a House censure resolution, Brooks resigned, was immediately reelected, and soon thereafter died at age 37. Sumner recovered slowly and returned to the Senate, where he remained for another 18 years. The nation, suffering from the breakdown of reasoned discourse that this event symbolized, tumbled onward toward the catastrophe of civil war.

Frank Leslie's Illustrated Newspaper *depicted the dramatic assault on Senator Charles Sumner in the Senate Chamber.*

Further Reading

Donald, David. *Charles Sumner and the Coming of the Civil War.* New York, Knopf, 1976.

January 4, 1859

The Senate's New Chamber

By 1820, long lines of interested observers began to form at the entrance to the Senate Chamber. That year's Missouri Compromise guaranteed an equal balance in the Senate between states that permitted slavery within their borders and those that did not. By contrast, representation in the House of Representatives, whose membership was apportioned according to population, was shifting to favor northern and western states against proslavery interests of the South.

Consequently, the Senate's theater-like chamber became the principal forum for debate over the issue of whether to permit the expansion of slavery into the nation's newly acquired territories and the states that would form in these areas.

In an effort to accommodate its rapidly increasing number of visitors, the Senate authorized construction of a second gallery. Soon that gallery became packed and impatient visitors pressed for overflow space on the Senate floor. In the years ahead, the Senate alternately liberalized and tightened its regulations governing special access to the floor. Between 1845 and 1850, congestion on the floor grew worse as five newly admitted states contributed 10 additional senators. Long before the availability of separate office buildings, the Senate's 62 members spent much time at their chamber desks and resented the crowding.

In September 1850, as the space situation turned critical, Congress appropriated $100,000 to add new Senate and House wings. This massive project doubled the Capitol's original space. Lasting 17 years and employing 700 workers, this became one of the largest and most expensive construction projects in 19th-century America. No other building could compare in cost, scale, complexity, and richness.

On January 4, 1859, members of the Senate solemnly proceeded to their new chamber. The next day's *New York Herald* described the room as light, graceful, and "finely proportioned." The iron ceiling contained 21 brilliantly adorned glass panels that emitted light through a skylight in the roof or from gas jets placed just beneath it. A special heating and ventilating system was designed to offer year-round comfort. The spacious new galleries accommodated up to 600 visitors and for several years made that chamber a popular site for off-hours theatrical events and lecture programs.

Within months of their arrival, however, members began to complain about poor acoustics, inadequate lighting, chilling drafts, and the deafening sound of rain echoing on the glass-paneled ceiling. Only the looming crisis of secession and civil war stopped plans for an immediate reconstruction of that space—but the complaining continued for at least another century.

The Senate Chamber under construction in 1857.

Further Reading

U.S. Congress. Senate. *History of the United States Capitol: A Chronicle of Design, Construction, and Politics*, by William C. Allen. 106th Congress, 2d sess., 2001. S. Doc. 106-29.

Senator Killed in a Duel

Throughout the Senate's history, members have taken satisfaction from setting records. One exception was California Senator David Broderick. In September 1859, Broderick established a record that remains unbroken. He became the first sitting senator to die in a duel.

Broderick was born in Washington, D.C., in 1820, the son of a stonemason who worked on the Capitol. His family later moved to New York City, where Broderick worked as a stonemason and a saloonkeeper. He read constantly and became a shrewd student of human nature as he observed the superheated political culture of New York City's ward politics. An antislavery Democrat in search of a political future, he joined the 1849 gold rush to California. He settled in San Francisco, where he quickly made a fortune in real estate.

Elected to the California state senate, Broderick rapidly became a power broker within the Democratic Party's antislavery wing and set his eyes on a seat in the U.S. Senate. He used his power in the legislature to stall, for nearly two years, a vote on the reelection of Senator William Gwin, a member of his party's proslavery faction. Finally, in 1857, California's other Senate seat opened and Broderick negotiated a deal with Gwin under which Broderick would take that seat's full six-year term, leaving Gwin the four-year balance of the blocked seat. Broderick's price for supporting Gwinn was full control of California's federal patronage appointments.

California's 1859 state election contest deepened the antagonism between Gwin's proslavery and Broderick's anti-slavery factions. During the campaign, California Chief Justice David Terry, an ally of Senator Gwin, denounced Broderick as no longer a true Democrat. In Terry's opinion, Broderick was following the "wrong Douglas." He had abandoned Democratic Party leader Stephen Douglas in favor of "black Republican" leader Frederick Douglass. Broderick angrily responded that Terry was a dishonest judge and a "miserable wretch." For these words, Terry challenged Broderick to a duel.

The men met early on the morning of September 13 at a field south of San Francisco. After Broderick's pistol discharged prematurely, Terry coolly aimed and fired into Broderick's chest. The senator's death endowed a rough-and-tumble political operator with a martyr's crown and accelerated the downward spiral to civil war. Terry was acquitted of the crime and went on to serve the Confederacy. Years later, in 1889, he too was gunned down, by a bodyguard after threatening the life of a U.S. Supreme Court justice.

David Broderick, senator from California (1857-1859).

Further Reading
Williams, David. *David C. Broderick: A Political Portrait.* San Marino: Huntington Library, 1969.

January 21, 1861

Jefferson Davis Delivers Farewell Speech

By any standard, this scene has to rank as one of the most dramatic events ever enacted in the chamber of the United States Senate. Would-be spectators arrived at the Capitol before sunrise on a frigid January morning. Those who came after 9 a.m., finding all gallery seats taken, frantically attempted to enter the already crowded cloakrooms and lobby adjacent to the chamber. Just days earlier, the states of Mississippi, Florida, and Alabama had joined South Carolina in deciding to secede from the Union. Rumors flew that Georgia, Louisiana, and Texas would soon follow.

On January 21, 1861, a fearful capital city awaited the farewell addresses of five senators. One observer sensed "blood in the air" as the chaplain delivered his prayer at high noon. With every senator at his place, Vice President John Breckinridge postponed a vote on admitting Kansas as a free state to recognize senators from Florida and Alabama.

When the four senators completed their farewell addresses, all eyes turned to Mississippi's Jefferson Davis—the acknowledged leader of the South in Congress. Tall, slender, and gaunt at the age of 52, Davis had been confined to his bed for more than a week. Suffering the nearly incapacitating pain of facial neuralgia, he began his valedictory in a low voice. As he proceeded, his voice gained volume and force.

"I rise, Mr. President, for the purpose of announcing to the Senate that . . . the state of Mississippi . . . has declared her separation from the United States." He explained that his state acted because "we are about to be deprived in the Union of the rights which our fathers bequeathed to us." Davis implored his Senate colleagues to work for a continuation of peaceful relations between the United States and the departing states. Otherwise, he predicted, interference with his state's decision would "bring disaster on every portion of the country."

Absolute silence met the conclusion of his six-minute address. Then a burst of applause and the sounds of open weeping swept the chamber. The vice president immediately rose to his feet, followed by the 58 senators and the mass of spectators as Davis and his four colleagues solemnly walked up the center aisle and out the swinging doors.

Later, describing the "unutterable grief" of that occasion, Davis said that his words had been "not my utterances but rather leaves torn from the book of fate."

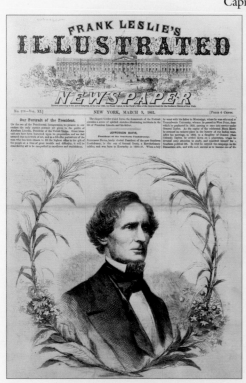

Jefferson Davis, senator from Mississippi (1847-1851, 1857-1861).

Further Reading

Davis, William C. *Jefferson Davis: The Man and His Hour, A Biography.* New York: HarperCollins, 1991.

March 4, 1861

Hannibal Hamlin Takes the Vice-Presidential Oath

March 4, 1861, was a sad day for Hannibal Hamlin. On that day, he gave up the Senate seat he had held for 12 years to become vice president of the United States.

At high noon, Hamlin called the Senate to order and swore in newly elected senators. Shortly after 1 p.m., he welcomed into the chamber outgoing President James Buchanan and President-elect Abraham Lincoln. Then the entire assemblage rose and proceeded to the Capitol's east front for Lincoln's inaugural.

Hannibal Hamlin owed his classical name to the influence of his grandfather, who loved the great military figures of ancient history. Tall, with piercing black eyes and olive-colored skin, the courteous and affable Hamlin proved to be a natural politician.

In 1860, as Republican Party leaders worked to arrange a successful presidential ticket, they decided that Hamlin, a former Democrat from Maine, would politically and geographically balance Lincoln, a former Whig from Illinois. When an excited supporter interrupted Hamlin at a card game in Washington to give him news of his nomination in Chicago, the irritated senator complained the distraction ruined the only good hand he had had all evening. With great reluctance, he accepted the offer.

After his election, Lincoln tapped Hamlin's experience as an influential senator for leads about suitable cabinet choices. Based on this early collaboration, some speculated that Lincoln might actually make effective use of his vice president. They were wrong. Hamlin's value to Lincoln was as a senior senator. Once Hamlin took up his vice-presidential duties, his usefulness ended. Although he hated being vice president, he again sought the nomination in 1864. Party leaders, however, dumped him—Maine was by then safely Republican—in favor of Andrew Johnson, from the politically crucial border state of Tennessee.

With little to do as vice president, Hamlin had enlisted as a private in the Maine state coast guard at the start of the Civil War. In 1864, his unit was called to active duty. Promoted to corporal, the vice president drilled troops, guarded buildings, and peeled potatoes. When his three-month tour ended in September, he rejoined the political ranks to campaign for the ticket of Lincoln and Johnson.

Abraham Lincoln once said, "Hamlin has the Senate on the brain and nothing more or less will cure him." On March 4, 1869, Hamlin happily resumed his old seat in the Senate and pronounced himself cured.

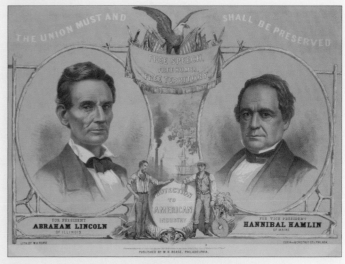

1860 campaign banner featuring presidential candidate Abraham Lincoln and vice-presidential candidate Hannibal Hamlin.

Further Reading

U.S. Congress. Senate. *Vice Presidents of the United States, 1789-1993*, by Mark O. Hatfield with the Senate Historical Office. 104th Congress, 2d sess., 1997. S. Doc. 104-16.

Soldiers Occupy the Senate Chamber

On April 15, 1861, the day after Fort Sumter fell, President Abraham Lincoln issued a call for 75,000 troops. Within three days, Washington swarmed with arriving volunteers to await a feared Confederate onslaught.

On April 19, 1861, the Sixth Massachusetts Regiment took up residence in the Senate Chamber following a bloody encounter in Baltimore with secessionist sympathizers. With the Senate in adjournment, a doorkeeper described the soldiers' arrival. "They were a tired, dusty, and bedraggled lot of men, showing every evidence of the struggle which they had so recently passed through. . . . Immediately upon entering the Capitol, they rushed into the Senate Chamber, the galleries, committee rooms, marble room, and wherever they could find accommodations." The doorkeeper continued, "Everything that was possible was done to make them comfortable as the circumstances permitted. But it almost broke my heart to see the soldiers bring armfuls of bacon and hams and throw them down upon the floor of the marble room. Almost with tears in my eyes, I begged them not to grease up the walls and the furniture."

Upwards of 4,000 troops eventually occupied the building. This overwhelming human influx proved costly. The Senate Chamber—in use for just two years—was described as filthy and "alive with lice." There a marauding soldier took his bayonet to the desk that Confederate president Jefferson Davis had occupied as a senator just three months earlier. Other soldiers wrote letters home on Senate stationery and conducted raucous mock sessions.

In the basement, bread ovens belched sooty smoke that damaged books in the Library of Congress' adjacent quarters. Without adequate sanitation facilities, the Capitol had quickly become "like one grand water closet [with a] stench so terrible" that only the most strongly motivated would enter the building. Ten weeks later, as members returned for an emergency session in hastily cleansed chambers, the sounds and smells of nearby troops reminded all of the extraordinary challenges that lay ahead.

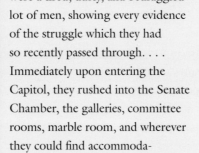

Union troops at the Capitol.

Further Reading
U.S. Architect of the Capitol, Office of the Curator. "Quartering Troops in the Capitol During the Civil War." November 1995.

July 11, 1861

Ten Senators Expelled

For what reasons should the Senate expel a member? The Constitution simply states that each house of Congress may "punish its Members for disorderly Behavior, and, with the Concurrence of two thirds, expel a Member." When the Senate expelled William Blount in 1797 by a nearly unanimous vote, it had reason to believe he was involved in a conspiracy against the United States.

Sixty-four years later, at the start of the Civil War, senators again turned to this constitutional safeguard. Between December 1860 and June 1861, 11 of the nation's 34 states had voted to withdraw from the Union. What was the status of their 22 senators at the beginning of the 37th Congress? Some were no longer senators because their terms had expired. Others sent letters of resignation. Still others, believing their seats no longer existed, simply left without formal notice. Several remained, despite their states' departure.

During a brief special session in March 1861, weeks before the start of hostilities, the Senate decided to consider these seats as vacant to avoid officially recognizing that it was possible for a state to leave the Union.

On the Fourth of July 1861, with open warfare in progress, President Abraham Lincoln convened Congress to deal with the emergency. With all hope of reconciliation gone, the Senate took up a resolution of expulsion against its 10 missing members. The resolution's supporters argued that the 10 were guilty, like Blount years before, of conspiracy against the government. In futile opposition, several senators contended that the departed southerners were merely following the dictates of their states and were not guilty of personal misconduct.

On July 11, 1861, the Senate quickly expelled all 10 southern senators by a vote of 32 to 10. By the following February, the Senate also expelled four border-state senators for their open support of the Confederacy. Since 1862, despite considering expulsion in an additional 16 instances, the Senate has removed no member under this provision.

Map showing secession of the Southern states.

Further Reading

U.S. Congress. Senate. *United States Senate Election, Expulsion and Censure Cases, 1793-1990*, by Anne M. Butler and Wendy Wolff. 103rd Congress, 1st sess., 1995. S. Doc. 103-33.

Senator Killed in Battle

He was a skilled lawyer, a renowned orator, and a member of the president's inner circle. He was also the only United States senator ever to die in a military engagement.

By the 1830s, Edward Dickinson Baker had become one of Illinois' most prominent lawyers and a close friend of Abraham Lincoln. In 1844, he won a seat in the U.S. House of Representatives, defeating Lincoln for the Whig Party nomination. At the start of the Mexican War in 1846, Representative Baker raised a regiment of troops and led them to the front. To boost congressional support for the unpopular war, he returned to the House Chamber in full uniform, lobbied his colleagues, resigned his seat, and rejoined his troops. After the war, he returned to another Illinois congressional district and, although a resident of that district for only three weeks, easily won a House seat. By 1852, he had left Congress to take up a lucrative law practice in San Francisco. A highly regarded orator, he earned national fame with his eulogy in 1859 at the funeral of California's U.S. Senator David Broderick, who had been killed in a duel with a former chief justice of that state.

Senator Edward D. Baker of Oregon was killed by Confederate forces at the Battle of Ball's Bluff while serving as a colonel in the Union army.

By 1860, Baker had moved to Oregon and won a seat in the U.S. Senate. When the Civil War began, he again raised a militia unit and appeared before his legislative colleagues in full uniform. On October 21, 1861, with Congress out of session and Confederate forces closing in on Washington, Senator-Colonel Baker went off to war.

Lightly schooled in military tactics, Baker gamely led his 1,700-member brigade across the Potomac River 40 miles north of the capital, up the steep ridge known as Ball's Bluff, and into the range of waiting enemy guns. He died quickly—too soon to witness the stampede of his troops back over the 70-foot cliffs to the rock-studded river below. Nearly 1,000 were killed, wounded, or captured. This disaster led directly to the creation of the toughest congressional investigating committee in history—the Joint Committee on the Conduct of the War.

Eighty years later, during the early months of World War II, members of Congress began turning up in combat zones with their reserve units. Despite the appeal of having senators saluting generals, the War Department banned the active duty service of all members, preserving the dubious distinction of Senator Edward Dickinson Baker.

Further Reading

Blair, Harry, and Rebecca Tarshis. *Colonel Edward D. Baker: Lincoln's Constant Ally*. Portland: Oregon Historical Society, 1960.

Holien, Kim Bernard. *The Battle of Ball's Bluff*. Orange, Va.: Moss Publications, 1985.

Tap, Bruce. *Over Lincoln's Shoulder: The Committee on the Conduct of the War*. Lawrence: University Press of Kansas, 1998.

February 5, 1862

Friendship or Treason?

He was a large man who walked with a swagger. Despite his limited formal education, he built a flourishing law practice and rose rapidly in the world of Indiana Democratic politics. Abrupt and hot-tempered, he was among the shrewdest of his state's political figures.

By 1845, Jesse Bright had become president of the Indiana state senate. Capitalizing on an opportunity to break a tied vote on the selection of a United States senator, he engineered his own election to that office.

In the Senate, Bright's knowledge of the chamber's rules and precedents won him the post of president pro tempore on several occasions. In the 1850s, however, he lost many of his natural political allies who were uncomfortable with his increasing support of legislation to protect slavery in the nation's territories. By 1860, his ownership of a Kentucky farm and 20 slaves led antislavery Indiana legislators to consider asking the Senate to declare Bright's seat vacant. As southern states began to leave the Union, Bright opposed the use of force against them, believing they would soon return.

The July 1861 Battle of Bull Run proved a disaster for Union troops—and for Jesse Bright. During the battle, Union forces captured an arms merchant as he attempted to cross into Confederate territory. They discovered that he carried a letter of introduction to Confederate president Jefferson Davis. The letter, highly deferential in tone, was signed by United States Senator Jesse Bright.

When the Senate took up the matter in January 1862, Bright explained that the captured arms supplier was a former client of his law practice. Although he claimed not to remember writing the letter, he asserted that it was only natural to introduce a friend to Davis, until recently a Senate colleague. Finally, Bright noted that the letter was dated March 1—before any fighting began. Aware that the Senate's Republican majority caucus had already determined his fate, Bright took the Senate floor on February 5, 1862, to state his case, if only "for posterity." He then gathered his belongings and walked solemnly from the chamber. Moments later, by a vote of 32 to 14, Bright became the 14th and final senator expelled by the Senate during the Civil War. No senator has been expelled since his time.

After a doomed Senate reelection bid, Bright served in the Kentucky legislature and went on to earn a fortune from his investments in West Virginia coal mines.

The United States Senate expelled Senator Jesse Bright of Indiana for disloyalty to the Union during the Civil War, despite his efforts to defend himself against the charges.

Further Reading

U.S. Congress. Senate. *United States Senate Election, Expulsion and Censure Cases, 1793-1990*, by Anne M. Butler and Wendy Wolff. 103rd Congress, 1st sess., 1995. S. Doc. 103-33.

Creating Another Senate

Anyone interested in the United States Senate might also be curious about another significant senate from our past—the Senate of the Confederate States of America. Early in 1861, as the southern states began to withdraw from the Union, their representatives established a Provisional Congress. That temporary single-house legislature drafted a constitution for the Confederacy that closely resembled the U.S. Constitution. It provided for a legislature consisting of a house and senate. Under this plan, the Confederate Senate was to operate like the U.S. Senate, with similar methods of election, terms of office, standing committees, rules of procedure, and legislative powers.

The Confederate Congress convened for the first time on February 18, 1862, at the Virginia state capitol in Richmond. Its House of Representatives claimed the ornate chamber formerly used by the Provisional Congress, leaving to the smaller Senate a dingy room on an upper floor. Unhappy with these inelegant quarters, Confederate senators appropriated the chamber of the state senate whenever that body was not in session.

Front view of the capitol building in Richmond, Virginia, 1865.

On its first day of operation, the Confederate Senate counted 20 of its 26 members present and elected Virginia's Robert M. T. Hunter president pro tempore. Hunter had served in the U.S. Congress as Speaker of the House and as a three-term senator. He was one of 10 former U.S. senators elected to the Confederate Senate.

Unlike the U.S. Senate, the Confederate Senate conducted many sessions behind closed doors and operated without formal political parties.

In its earliest months, under the pressure of wartime emergency, the Confederate Congress granted President Jefferson Davis most of what he requested. By the time the Second Confederate Congress convened in 1864, however, serious military reverses reawakened long-simmering political divisions. Factors such as former party affiliations, earlier levels of commitment to secession, and whether Union forces were occupying their respective states became increasingly evident in members' voting behavior. Deepening divisions among Confederate senators and representatives made it almost impossible for them to legislate constructively.

On March 18, 1865, as encircling Union forces tightened their grip on Richmond, the Confederate Senate held its last session, and hastily left town.

Because the Confederate Senate held many of its sessions in secret, did not use official reporters of debates to record public proceedings, and lost extensive records to the chaos of war, today we know very little about its operations.

Further Reading
Yearns, Wilfred Buck. *The Confederate Congress*. Athens, Ga.: University of Georgia Press, 1960.

February 22, 1862

Washington's "Farewell Address"

No Senate tradition has been more steadfastly maintained than the annual reading of President George Washington's 1796 Farewell Address. In this letter to "Friends and Citizens," Washington warned that the forces of geographical sectionalism, political factionalism, and interference by foreign powers in the nation's domestic affairs threatened the stability of the Republic. He urged Americans to subordinate sectional jealousies to common national interests.

The Senate tradition began on February 22, 1862, as a morale-boosting gesture during the darkest days of the Civil War. Citizens of Philadelphia had petitioned Congress to commemorate the forthcoming 130th anniversary of Washington's birth by reading the Address at a joint meeting of both houses.

Tennessee Senator Andrew Johnson introduced the petition in the Senate. "In view of the perilous condition of the country," he said, "I think the time has arrived when we should recur back to the days, the times, and the doings of Washington and the patriots of the Revolution, who founded the government under which we live."

Two by two, members of the Senate proceeded to the House Chamber for a joint session. As they moved through Statuary Hall, they passed a display of recently captured Confederate battle flags. President Abraham Lincoln, whose son Willie had died two days earlier, did not attend. But members of his cabinet, the Supreme Court, and high-ranking military officers in full uniform packed the chamber to hear Secretary of the Senate John W. Forney read the Address.

Early in 1888—the centennial year of the Constitution's ratification—the Senate recalled the ceremony of 1862 and had its presiding officer read the Address on February 22. Within a few years, the Senate made the practice an annual event.

Every year since 1896, the Senate has observed Washington's birthday by selecting one of its members, alternating parties, to read the 7,641-word statement in legislative session. Delivery generally takes about 45 minutes. In 1985, Florida Senator Paula Hawkins tore through the text in a record-setting 39 minutes, while in 1962, West Virginia Senator Jennings Randolph, savoring each word, consumed 68 minutes.

At the conclusion of each reading, the appointed senator inscribes his or her name and brief remarks in a black, leather-bound book. In 1956, Minnesota Senator Hubert Humphrey wrote that every American should study this memorable message. "It gives one a renewed sense of pride in our republic. It arouses the wholesome and creative emotions of patriotism and love of country."

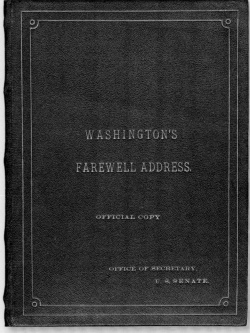

After the annual reading of Washington's "Farewell Address," senators inscribe their names and brief remarks in this leather-bound book.

Further Reading
U.S. Congress. Senate. *Washington's Farewell Address.* 105th Congress, 2d sess., 1998. S. Doc.105-22.

Senator Resigns to Protest Loyalty Oath

James A. Bayard, senator from Delaware (1851-1864, 1867-1869).

Oath-taking by newly elected members of Congress continues a constitutional rite that is nearly as old as the Republic. While this practice dates from a simple 14-word statement enacted by the First Congress in 1789, the current oath is a product of the 1860s—drafted by Civil War-era members of Congress intent on ensnaring traitors.

The original oath served nicely for nearly three-quarters of a century. By 1861, however, the outbreak of the Civil War gave particular urgency to the previously routine act of oath-taking. At a time of uncertain and shifting loyalties, President Abraham Lincoln ordered all federal civilian personnel to retake the 1789 oath. By 1862, members of Congress who believed the Union had more to fear from northern traitors than southern soldiers enacted the so-called Ironclad Test Oath. Added to the first oath, this text required civil servants and military officers to swear not only to future loyalty but also to affirm that they had never previously engaged in disloyal conduct.

Although Congress did not initially extend the 1862 Test Oath to its own members, many took it voluntarily. Angered by those senators who refused this symbolic act, such as Delaware Democrat James A. Bayard, Massachusetts Republican Charles Sumner engineered a January 25, 1864, rules change making the Test Oath mandatory for all senators.

Senator Bayard contended that the Test Oath ignored the president's pardoning power. Looking ahead to the postwar era, he warned that the Test Oath would block any southern senator-elect who arrived in the Senate with a presidential pardon and a certificate of election. If he took the oath, swearing no past disloyalty to the Union, he would perjure himself; if he refused the oath, he would not be seated. The Delaware senator also feared that this oath set a dangerous precedent, as future congresses could add other requirements related to past behavior that could limit membership eligibility. He believed Congress could require, for instance, that senators swear to their temperance, chastity, and monogamy. Bayard took the oath on January 29, 1864, and then immediately resigned in protest.

In 1868, Congress exempted southerners from the Test Oath by creating an alternate vow, the language of which was nearly identical to today's pledge. Northerners angrily pointed to the new law's unfair double standard of requiring loyal Unionists to take the harsh Test Oath while ex-Confederates were offered the less-demanding 1868 version. Finally, in 1884, a new generation of lawmakers quietly repealed the deeply inflaming wartime oath.

Further Reading
Hyman, Harold M. *Era of the Oath: Northern Loyalty Tests during the Civil War and Reconstruction.* Philadelphia: University of Pennsylvania, 1954.

March 6, 1867

Appropriations Committee Created

On March 6, 1867, the Senate established its Committee on Appropriations—51 years after creating its other major standing committees. Why did the body wait so long and why did the members choose to act in 1867?

In the Senate's earliest years, the Finance Committee handled most appropriations, but it did so in an increasingly haphazard manner. Agency heads, wishing to appear frugal, typically understated their funding needs to the House of Representatives and then, in a congressional session's hectic final days, quietly turned to the less-disciplined Senate for increases that generally survived conference committee review. When agencies ran out of money, the threat of suspended operations usually convinced Congress to replenish their coffers. When agencies ran a surplus, they spent it as they pleased. But the Civil War had vastly expanded and complicated federal spending. The lack of centralized control in the Senate, tolerable in an earlier era, now strongly played to the president's advantage. No less than the power of the purse was at stake.

By March of 1867, a newly strengthened Radical Republican majority in the Senate, determined to block President Andrew Johnson's lenient policies for readmission of former Confederate states, saw reform of the appropriations process as a potent weapon in that struggle. Following the House of Representatives' recent successful example, they created a separate Committee on Appropriations.

The seven-member panel rapidly became a Senate powerhouse. And just as rapidly, the large majority of senators who did not serve on it came to resent the appropriators' use of their funding power to shape policy. After tolerating the committee for 32 years—institutional change comes slowly to the Senate—members in January 1899 adopted a rule stripping Appropriations of seven major funding bills and awarding them to the respective legislative committees. Not until 1922 did the Appropriations Committee recapture the full jurisdiction that it exercises today.

Senate Appropriations Committee room, as it appeared early in the 20th century. The room was originally designed for the Senate Committee on Naval Affairs.

Further Reading

U.S. Senate. Committee on Appropriations. *Committee on Appropriations, 138th Anniversary, 1867-2005*, United States Senate. 109th Congress, 1st sess., 2005. S. Doc. 109-5.

The Senate Votes on a Presidential Impeachment

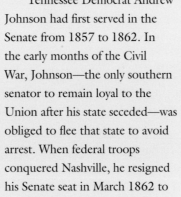

Spectators packed the Senate galleries to watch as the Senate voted on whether to remove President Andrew Johnson from office.

It is an old favorite among trivia-question writers. "Who was the only former American president to serve in the United States Senate?" The answer is identical to that for another popular civics question: "Who was the first president to be impeached in the House and tried by the Senate?"

Tennessee Democrat Andrew Johnson had first served in the Senate from 1857 to 1862. In the early months of the Civil War, Johnson—the only southern senator to remain loyal to the Union after his state seceded—was obliged to flee that state to avoid arrest. When federal troops conquered Nashville, he resigned his Senate seat in March 1862 to accept President Lincoln's appointment as military governor of Tennessee. In 1864, he won election as vice president and took up his duties the following March. Following Abraham Lincoln's assassination in April 1865, he moved to the White House to serve as president for the balance of the term.

Johnson's impeachment is a complex story, but one important issue related to a vital Senate prerogative—the confirmation of presidential nominations. In the eight decades since the 1787 framing of the Constitution, the question had repeatedly arisen, "If the Senate is responsible for confirming appointees, does it also have a role in removing them?"

In 1867, as President Johnson's relations with Congress rapidly deteriorated, the Senate and House passed, over his veto, the Tenure of Office Act. That act required officeholders confirmed by the Senate to remain in place until the Senate approved their successors. When Johnson subsequently defied Congress by firing Secretary of War Edwin Stanton, the House of Representatives impeached the president for violating the Tenure of Office Act.

On May 16, 1868, the Senate voted 35 to 19 to remove President Andrew Johnson from office—one vote short of the necessary two-thirds. For many of these 54 senators, this was unquestionably the single most difficult vote of their congressional careers. Seven Republican senators courageously defied their party's leadership and voted with the 12 Democratic senators to acquit the president—thereby saving him and, possibly, the institution of the presidency.

In January 1875, Johnson won back his former Senate seat after a hotly contested struggle that forced the Tennessee legislature through 56 separate ballots. On March 5, 1875, Johnson took his Senate oath before the same body that only seven years earlier had failed by a single vote to remove him from the White House. During the 19-day Senate special session, he delivered one major address—on political turmoil in Louisiana—and then returned to Tennessee, where he died four months later.

Further Reading

Trefousse, Hans L. *Andrew Johnson: A Biography*. New York: W.W. Norton, 1989.

U.S. Congress. Senate. *Vice Presidents of the United States, 1789-1993*, by Mark O. Hatfield with the Senate Historical Office. 104th Congress, 2d sess., 1997. S. Doc. 104-16.

September 8, 1869

William Fessenden Dies

Today, the name "Fessenden" brings to mind no immediate political association. On September 8, 1869, however, it identified perhaps the most significant senator of the entire Civil War era—William Pitt Fessenden, Republican of Maine. When the 62-year-old Fessenden died on that day, his Senate colleagues genuinely grieved at the loss of a legislative giant.

Fessenden came to the Senate in February 1854, at the start of a bitter three-month debate over the Kansas-Nebraska Act. After only nine days in office, he delivered a powerful floor speech accurately predicting that if the measure were enacted, opening the nation's western territories to slavery, it would set the North and South on a course toward inevitable disunion.

During the Civil War, Fessenden chaired the Senate Finance Committee, which also served as the Senate's principal appropriating committee. Long hours under enormous pressure regularly brought him to the point of physical exhaustion as he worked to shape vital wartime funding legislation. He once said he was "content to work like a dog" while "leaving all the jabber to others." Fessenden's quick temper intimidated colleagues and lobbyists who appeared before his committee. To those whose expensive requests seemed at odds with his priorities for waging the war, he barked, "It is time for us to begin to think a little more about the money!"

When Fessenden reluctantly left the Senate in 1864 to serve as treasury secretary, he found the treasury nearly empty. After negotiating a bond issue that produced the revenue necessary to conclude the war, he returned to the Senate in 1865. As chairman of the Joint Committee on Reconstruction, he worked for a temperate plan to reunite the nation under congressional—not presidential—leadership. Although he disliked President Andrew Johnson, he opposed his 1868 impeachment and used his influence with six other Senate Republicans to gain the essential votes for Johnson's acquittal. In 1869, Fessenden became chairman of the recently established Committee on Appropriations, but died before he could place his mark on that panel.

As a practical and cautious behind-the-scenes senator who concentrated on fiscal and monetary policy, Fessenden failed to attract the attention that journalists and historians have given to the Radical Republicans, like Charles Sumner, who concentrated on slavery issues. Today, Sumner is remembered in the Capitol with an oil portrait and marble bust. Fessenden lies largely forgotten in an unmarked family grave in Portland, Maine.

*William Pitt Fessenden,
senator from Maine
(1854-1864, 1865-1869).*

Further Reading
Jellison, Charles A. *Fessenden of Maine, Civil War Senator.* Syracuse: Syracuse University Press, 1962.

First African-American Senator

O n February 25, 1870, visitors in the Senate galleries burst into applause as Mississippi senator-elect Hiram Revels entered the chamber to take his oath of office. Those present knew that they were witnessing an event of great historical significance. Revels was about to become the first African American to serve in Congress.

Born 42 years earlier to free black parents in Fayetteville, North Carolina, Revels become an educator and minister of the African Methodist Episcopal Church. During the Civil War, he helped form regiments of African-American soldiers and established schools for freed slaves. After the war, Revels moved to Mississippi, where he won election to the state senate. In recognition of his hard work and leadership skills, his legislative colleagues elected him to one of Mississippi's vacant U.S. Senate seats as that state prepared to rejoin the Union.

Revels' credentials arrived in the Senate on February 23, 1870, and were immediately blocked by a few members who had no desire to see a black man serve in Congress. Masking their racist views, they argued that Revels had not been a U.S. citizen for the nine years required of all senators. In their distorted interpretation, black Americans had only become citizens with the passage of the 1866 Civil Rights Act, just four years earlier. His supporters dismissed that statement, pointing out that he had been a voter many years earlier in Ohio and was therefore certainly a citizen.

Massachusetts Senator Charles Sumner brought the debate to an end with a stirring speech. "The time has passed for argument. Nothing more need be said. For a long time it has been clear that colored persons must be senators." Then, by an overwhelming margin, the Senate voted 48 to 8 to seat Revels.

Three weeks later, the Senate galleries again filled to capacity as Hiram Revels rose to make his first formal speech. Seeing himself as a representative of African-American interests throughout the nation, he spoke—unsuccessfully as it turned out—against a provision included in legislation readmitting Georgia to the Union. He correctly predicted that the provision would be used to prohibit blacks from holding office in that state.

When Hiram Revels' brief term ended on March 3, 1871, he returned to Mississippi, where he later became president of Alcorn College.

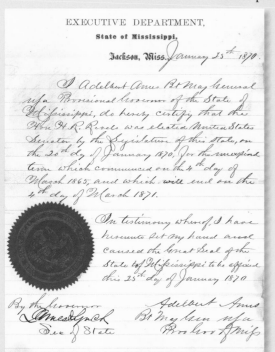

Hiram Revels' credentials presented to the U.S. Senate on February 23, 1870.

Further Reading

U.S. Congress. Senate. *The Senate, 1789-1989*, Vol. 2, by Robert C. Byrd. 100th Congress, 1st sess., 1991. S. Doc.100-20. Chapter 24.

January 17, 1871

The Battle of Three Brothers

There has never been a Senate election race quite like it. In January 1871, Delaware's Democratic Senator Willard Saulsbury notified his state's legislature that he wished that body to reelect him to the office he had held for two terms. He expected no serious opposition from that small and solidly Democratic body in gaining the 16 votes necessary for election. Yet, to his frustration, two other candidates emerged. Not only were these contenders from his own party, they were also from his own family—his two elder brothers.

Saulsbury's political difficulties stemmed from his abuse of alcohol. That problem had been evident in a dramatic scene played out in the Senate Chamber years earlier.

During an 1863 filibuster, Saulsbury angrily referred to President Abraham Lincoln as a "weak and imbecile man." When Vice President Hannibal Hamlin, as presiding officer, ordered him to take his seat, Saulsbury refused. Hamlin then directed the sergeant at arms to "take the senator in charge." Responding, "Let him do so at his expense," Saulsbury drew a pistol and threatened to shoot the officer. Days later, a more sober Saulsbury—facing a resolution of expulsion—apologized and the Senate dropped the matter.

By 1871, Delaware Democrats had had enough of Saulsbury's embarrassing outbursts. Party leaders quietly approached his brother, Gove Saulsbury, a physician who had just completed a term as governor. The ambitious Gove Saulsbury controlled 14 of the needed 16 votes. The other brother, Eli Saulsbury, a quiet and temperate man, counted three supporters, while 13 others remained loyal to Willard. If Gove could attract just two of either brother's allies, he would have the election.

After three deadlocked ballots, Willard —angry at Gove's betrayal—released his supporters to vote for brother Eli. With this switch, Eli Saulsbury won the election. He would remain in the Senate for the next 18 years.

From the 1850s to the 1880s, Delaware's two Senate seats were occupied under an informal political arrangement known as the "Saulsbury-Bayard Compact." With no significant Republican party to offer a serious challenge, the Saulsbury family controlled one seat as its personal right, while the Bayard family took the other. This kind of blatant political manipulation in the state legislature added force to a growing campaign for a constitutional amendment requiring direct popular election of senators.

As the historically unique 1871 election demonstrated, however, for the time being Delaware politics remained just family politics.

Willard Saulsbury, senator from Delaware (1859-1871).

Eli Saulsbury, senator from Delaware (1871-1889).

Further Reading

Franseth, Gregory S., L. Rebecca Johnson Melvin, and Shiela Pardee. "The End of an Era in Delaware: The Practical Politics of Willard Saulsbury, Jr." *Collections* 11 (2003): 1-27.

U.S. Congress. Senate. *The Senate, 1789-1989*, Vol. 2, by Robert C. Byrd. 100th Cong., 1st sess., 1991. S. Doc. 100-20. Chapter 5.

The Senate Ends Franked Mail Privilege

Franking privileges—the ability to send mail by one's signature rather than by postage—date back to the 17th-century English House of Commons. The American Continental Congress adopted the practice in 1775 and the First Congress wrote it into law in 1789. In addition to senators and representatives, the president, cabinet secretaries, and certain executive branch officials also were granted the frank. In those days, every newspaper publisher could send one paper postage-free to every other newspaper in the country.

Until the 1860s, members of Congress spent a great deal of time carefully inscribing their names on the upper right-hand corner of official letters and packages. One member boasted that if the envelopes were properly arranged, he could sign as many as 300 per hour. After the Civil War, senators and representatives reduced the tedium of this chore by having their signatures reproduced on rubber stamps.

Intended to improve the flow of information across a vast nation, the franking privilege lent itself to abuse and controversy. Stories circulated of members who routinely franked their laundry home and who gave their signatures to family and friends for personal use. Legend had it that one early 19th-century senator even attached a frank to his horse's bridle and sent the animal back to Pittsburgh. Critics accused incumbents of flooding the mails with government documents, speeches, and packages of seeds to improve their chances of reelection.

In 1869, the postmaster-general, whose department was running a large deficit, recommended that Congress and federal agencies switch to postage stamps. Responding to charges of governmental extravagance, the 1872 Republican Party platform carried a plank that demanded the frank's elimination. When Congress returned to session following the 1872 election, many senators decided to deliver on that campaign promise.

On January 31, 1873, the Senate voted to abolish the congressional franking privilege after rejecting a House-passed provision that would have provided special stamps for the free mailing of printed Senate and House documents.

Within two years, however, Congress began to make exceptions to this ban, including free mailing of the *Congressional Record*, seeds, and agricultural reports. Finally, in 1891, noting that its members were the only government officials required to pay postage, Congress restored full franking privileges. Since then, the franking of congressional mail has been subject to ongoing review and regulation.

A cartoon from Harper's Weekly, *1860, depicting a senator preparing to ship his laundry home using the franking privilege.*

Further Reading

Pontius, John S. "Franking." In *The Encyclopedia of the United States Congress*, edited by Donald C. Bacon, et al. New York: Simon & Schuster, 1995.

U.S. Congress. Senate. "Franking." In *Precedents Relating to the Privileges of the Senate of the United States*, compiled by George P. Furber. Washington, D.C.: GPO, 1893.

March 11, 1874

Charles Sumner Dies

Early in the morning of March 11, 1874, 63-year-old Massachusetts Senator Charles Sumner suffered a massive heart attack. The mortally ill senator said that his only regrets about dying were that he had not finished preparing his collected writings for publication and that the Senate had not yet passed his civil rights bill. He expired that afternoon. Not since the death of Abraham Lincoln in 1865 had the nation grieved so deeply at the loss of one of its statesmen.

From the time he first took his oath as a senator 23 years earlier, Sumner had eloquently campaigned against racial inequality. His first speech in the Senate attacked the 1850 law that allowed the use of federal resources to capture runaway slaves. Only three other senators joined him in that politically risky campaign—one that was as unpopular in his home state as it was in the South. In the mid-1850s, he helped found the Republican Party as a coalition of antislavery political factions.

Tall and handsome, Sumner was also pompous and arrogant. Those latter traits got him into deep trouble in May 1856. At one point in a three-hour speech attacking slavery in Kansas, he described South Carolina Senator Andrew Butler as "an ignorant and mad zealot." Several days later, a House member who was related to Butler entered the Senate Chamber and savagely beat Sumner for those remarks.

The attack transformed Sumner into a northern hero, solving his political problems at home, and effectively guaranteeing him a lifetime seat in the Senate. When he died in 1874, his funeral was conducted in the Senate Chamber and he lay in state in the Capitol Rotunda. Individual states competed for the honor of having his body displayed in their capitols.

Sumner would surely have been pleased to know that he has been memorialized on all three floors of the U.S. Capitol's Senate wing. Constantino Brumidi's portrait in Room 118 depicts Sumner as a senator of ancient Rome. That classical motif appears also in a third-floor marble portrait bust by noted 19th-century sculptor Martin Milmore. The grandest work, however, is located just outside the Senate Chamber. In the last year of his life, a tired and ill Sumner sat for a formal oil portrait by artist Walter Ingalls. In the finished work, Ingalls tactfully borrowed from a much earlier Mathew Brady photograph, leaving for posterity an image of a benevolent Sumner in his youthful prime.

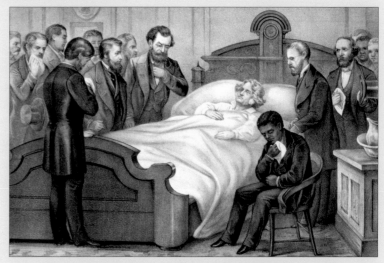

Currier & Ives lithograph depicting the death of Senator Charles Sumner of Massachusetts (1851-1874).

Further Reading

Donald, David. *Charles Sumner and the Rights of Man*. New York, Knopf, 1970.

U.S. Congress. Senate. *United States Senate Catalogue of Fine Art*, by William Kloss and Diane Skvarla. 107th Congress, 2d sess., 2002. S. Doc. 107-11.

War Secretary's Impeachment

An impeachment trial for a secretary of war occupied much of the Senate's time during May 1876.

At issue was the behavior of William Belknap, war secretary in the administration of President Ulysses Grant. A former Iowa state legislator and Civil War general, Belknap had held his cabinet post for nearly eight years. In the rollicking era that Mark Twain dubbed the Gilded Age, Belknap was famous for his extravagant Washington parties and his elegantly attired first and second wives. Many questioned how he managed such a grand life style on his $8,000 government salary.

By early 1876, answers began to surface. A House of Representatives' committee uncovered evidence supporting a pattern of corruption blatant even by the standards of the scandal-tarnished Grant administration.

Secretary of War William Belknap, standing left, appeared before a congressional committee to face corruption charges.

The trail of evidence extended back to 1870. In that year, Belknap's luxury-loving first wife assisted a wheeler-dealer named Caleb Marsh by getting her husband to select one of Marsh's associates to operate the lucrative military trading post at Fort Sill in Indian territory. Marsh's promise of generous kickbacks prompted Secretary Belknap to make the appointment. Over the next five years, the associate funneled thousands of dollars to Marsh, who provided Belknap regular quarterly payments totaling over $20,000.

On March 2, 1876, just minutes before the House of Representatives was scheduled to vote on articles of impeachment, Belknap raced to the White House, handed Grant his resignation, and burst into tears.

This failed to stop the House. Later that day, members voted unanimously to send the Senate five articles of impeachment, charging Belknap with "criminally disregarding his duty as secretary of war and basely prostituting his high office to his lust for private gain."

The Senate convened its trial in early April, with Belknap present, after agreeing that it retained impeachment jurisdiction over former government officials. During May, the Senate heard more than 40 witnesses, as House managers argued that Belknap should not be allowed to escape from justice simply by resigning his office.

On August 1, 1876, the Senate rendered a majority vote against Belknap on all five articles. As each vote fell short of the necessary two thirds, however, he won acquittal. Belknap was not prosecuted further; he committed suicide in 1890.

Years later, the Senate finally decided that it made little sense to devote its time and energies to removing from office officials who had already removed themselves.

Further Reading

Bushnell, Eleanore. *Crimes, Follies and Misfortunes: The Federal Impeachment Trials.* Urbana: University of Illinois Press, 1992. Chapter 8.

February 5, 1877

The Florida Case

On the third floor of the United States Capitol, to the left of the Senators' Family Gallery entrance, hangs a large historical picture. This dramatic oil painting, in a richly gilded Victorian frame, bears the title: *The Florida Case before the Electoral Commission, February 5, 1877.*

On the night of the presidential election in November 1876, the headline of the *New-York Tribune* proclaimed "Tilden Elected." That verdict, of course, was premature. Although Democrat Samuel Tilden had won 250,000 more votes than Republican Rutherford B. Hayes, neither man gained an undisputed electoral-vote majority. To reach the 185 electoral votes necessary for election, Tilden needed one more vote; Hayes needed 20. Together, Oregon, Florida, South Carolina, and Louisiana controlled 20 disputed electoral votes.

Without statute or precedents to help it determine which sets of electors to count in these states, Congress set up an advisory commission of five senators, five representatives, and five Supreme Court justices. The commission's eight Republicans and seven Democrats met in the Capitol's Supreme Court chamber—currently restored as the Old Senate Chamber—for nine days at the beginning of February 1877. Commission members sat at the justices' bench; counsel for both sides occupied desks nearby; and members of the press jammed the gallery directly behind the seated commissioners. Each day, members of Congress, cabinet officers, and others forming a "who's who" of social and political Washington, packed every available inch of chamber floor space.

The painting on the Capitol's third floor brilliantly captures that epic scene. It is the work of Cornelia Fassett, a talented artist, Washington hostess, and mother of eight who specialized in portraits of notable government figures. During the summer of 1877, several months after the electoral commission rendered its party-line verdict in favor of Hayes, Fassett set up a temporary studio in the Supreme Court chamber. There she worked to capture the commission's architectural setting. She then filled her canvas with carefully detailed likenesses of 260 prominent Washington figures—some taken from private sittings, others from Mathew Brady photographs. Among these figures are 30 senators, Senate clerks, Senate wives and children, and Fassett herself, with sketch pad in the lower center of the picture.

The Florida Case before the Electoral Commission, *by Cornelia A. Fassett, 1879.*

Early in 1879, after heated debate, the Senate defeated a bill to purchase the picture on the grounds that the event was "so recent" and one "about which party passions are still excited." Several years later, however, with those passions cooled, Congress quietly acquired the painting.

Further Reading

U.S. Congress. Senate. *The Senate, 1789-1989*, by Robert C. Byrd, Vol. 1. 100th Congress, 1st sess., 1988. S. Doc.100-20. Chapter 17.

U.S. Congress. Senate. "The Florida Case before the Electoral Commission." In *United States Senate Catalogue of Fine Art*, by William Kloss and Diane K. Skvarla. 107th Congress, 2d sess., 2002. S. Doc. 107-11.

Senator for Three States

James Shields, senator from Illinois (1849-1855), senator from Minnesota (1858-1859), senator from Missouri (1879).

James Shields holds a Senate service record that no other senator is ever likely to surpass. He began his Senate career in 1849 representing Illinois. Shields had successfully turned a wound suffered several years earlier in the Mexican War to political advantage, defeating incumbent Senator Sidney Breese, a fellow Democrat. One political wag joked about Shields' lucky "Mexican bullet." "What a wonderful shot that was! The bullet went clean through Shields without hurting him, or even leaving a scar, and killed Breese a thousand miles away."

Supporters of the defeated Breese petitioned the Senate to refuse to seat Shields on grounds that he had not been a U.S. citizen for the required nine years. An Irish immigrant, he had filed naturalization papers eight and a half years earlier. This raised the question of whether the citizenship requirement had to be satisfied at the time of election or by the beginning of Senate service.

A coalition of Whigs and disaffected Democrats voted to invalidate Shields' election. The Whigs expected this would deprive the Democrats of a seat for more than a year. Under Illinois law, only the state legislature could fill a vacancy created by a voided election, and the legislature was not scheduled to convene for another 18 months. The Democratic governor foiled

this plan, however, by calling a special session of the legislature. That body again elected Shields, who by then had satisfied the citizenship requirement.

Six years later, failing to win reelection, Shields moved to the Minnesota Territory, where he helped establish colonies for poor Irish immigrants. In 1858, he became one of Minnesota's first two U.S. senators. When Shields and his colleague drew lots to determine when their respective Senate terms would expire, Shields got the term with less than a year remaining. Failing to win reelection, he moved to California. During the Civil War, he served as a general in the Union army and later moved to Missouri.

On January 22, 1879, in failing health, 73-year-old James Shields won election to represent Missouri—his record-setting third state in the U.S. Senate. By then, he had become a beloved figure among Americans of Irish heritage and his election to an uncompleted term with only six weeks remaining served as an expression of that affection. He died soon after completing his final Senate service: the uniquely distinguished senator from Illinois, Minnesota, and Missouri.

Source
Castle, Henry A. "General James A. Shields, Soldier, Orator, Statesman." *Collections of the Minnesota Historical Society* 15 (May 1915): 711-30.

February 14, 1879

A Former Slave Presides over the Senate

On February 14, 1879, a Republican senator from Mississippi presided over the Senate. In this instance, the Senate's customary practice of rotating presiding officers during routine floor proceedings set a historical milestone. The senator who temporarily assumed these duties had a personal background that no other senator, before or since, could claim: he had been born into slavery.

Blanche K. Bruce was born 38 years earlier near Farmville, Virginia. The youngest of 11 children, he worked in fields and factories from Virginia to Mississippi. Highly intelligent and fiercely ambitious, Bruce gained his earliest formal education from the tutor hired to teach his master's son.

At the start of the Civil War, Bruce escaped slavery by fleeing to Kansas. He attended Oberlin College for two years and then moved to Mississippi, where he purchased an abandoned cotton plantation and amassed a real estate fortune. In 1874, while Mississippi remained under postwar military control, the state legislature elected Bruce to the U.S. Senate. Several years earlier, that legislature had sent the Senate its first African-American member when it elected Hiram Revels to fill out the remaining months of an unexpired term.

Blanche Bruce's Senate service got off to a sour start when Mississippi's other senator, James Alcorn, refused to escort him to the front of the chamber to take his oath of office. As Bruce started down the aisle alone, New York Republican Roscoe Conkling moved to his side and completed the journey to the rostrum. The grateful senator later named his only son Roscoe Conkling Bruce.

Withdrawal of the military government in Mississippi ended Republican control of that state's political institutions and any chance that Bruce might serve more than a single term. That term, however, proved to be an active one as he advocated civil rights for blacks, Native Americans, Chinese immigrants, and even former Confederates. It was during a heated debate on a bill to exclude Chinese immigrants that Bruce made history at the presiding officer's desk.

After leaving the Senate, Bruce held a variety of key government and educational posts until his death in 1898.

Blanche Kelso Bruce, senator from Mississippi (1875-1881).

Source

Mann, Kenneth Eugene. "Blanche Kelso Bruce: United States Senator Without a Constituency." *Journal of Mississippi History* 38 (May 1976): 183-98.

CHAPTER IV

ORIGINS OF THE MODERN SENATE

1881-1920

A Dramatic Tiebreaker

Chester Arthur served as vice president of the United States, from March 4 to September 20, 1881, when he assumed the presidency upon the death of President Garfield.

On March 18, 1881, early in a special session called to consider nominations received from newly inaugurated Republican President James Garfield, the vice president's hands trembled as he reached for the roll-call-vote tally sheet. In a Senate Chamber packed with senators, House members, and even the chief justice of the United States, Republican Vice President Chester Arthur announced the result of a vote to select a Republican slate of committee chairmen and members. Those in favor: 37; those opposed: 37. When the vice president cast his tie-breaking vote in favor of the Republican slate, the chamber exploded in volleys of cheers and boos.

The triumphant Republicans then moved to elect a secretary of the Senate and sergeant at arms. At this point, a newspaper correspondent observed that the Democratic senators "were not in a hilarious mood. Their countenances were those of mourners at a funeral. Behind their desks was a grim row of clerks witnessing with solemn interest the proceedings that would deprive them of snug positions." With the Senate equally divided on organizational questions, the Democrats had hoped to strike a bargain. While grudgingly accepting a one-vote Republican margin on each committee, they insisted on retaining the officers they had selected when they controlled the Senate of the previous Congress. The Republicans refused to negotiate.

The resulting stalemate disrupted Senate business for the next two months. With several Republicans absent due to illness, the Democrats were able to stall a vote on the staffing issue by leaving the chamber each time Republicans tried to muster the majority quorum necessary to conduct business.

Soon a split developed within Republican ranks over Garfield's nominee to fill a key New York City federal post. Both of New York's Republican senators opposed that choice and were angry with Garfield for ignoring their views. In a tactical move, they dramatically resigned from the Senate, expecting that their state legislature would soon reelect them and thereby send the White House a message about their political standing within New York.

The Republican resignations gave the Democrats a two-vote Senate majority. But in the interest of wrapping up the deadlocked special session, Democrats agreed not to reopen the issue of committee control. In return the Republicans conceded the staffing issue—at least until the next session. Within months, however, the assassination of President Garfield dampened any desire for further battles over the management of this closely divided Senate.

Further Reading

U.S. Congress. Senate. *The Senate, 1789-1989*, Vol. 1, by Robert C. Byrd. 100th Congress, 1st sess., 1988. S. Doc.100-20.

May 16, 1881

Both New York Senators Resign

Brilliant and handsome, ambitious and arrogant, New York Republican Roscoe Conkling was one of the most compelling and colorful members of the late-19th-century Senate. Described as "a veritable bird of paradise amidst a barnyard of drabber fowl," Conkling sported green trousers, scarlet coats, gold lace, striped shirts, and yellow shoes.

Soon after his arrival in 1867, this flamboyant orator became one of the Senate's principal Republican leaders. Conkling built a strong state political machine through his control over New York City's patronage-rich customs house. When an investigation uncovered a record of graft and corruption under customs collector and Conkling protégé Chester Arthur, a bitter struggle split the Republican Party. This partisan disarray helped the Democrats, in the 1878 elections, gain control of both houses of Congress for the first time in 18 years.

When James Garfield won the 1880 Republican presidential nomination, he tried to placate Conkling and his faction of the party by selecting Chester Arthur as his running mate. Once Garfield took office, however, he shifted direction and nominated as the New York City customs collector a candidate who lacked Conkling's endorsement. When the appointment reached the Senate Chamber, a colleague reported that Conkling "raged and roared like a bull for three mortal hours," claiming a violation of "senatorial courtesy." Garfield further baited the furious senator by boldly responding that he was the head of the government and not "the registering clerk of the United States Senate." When it became clear that the president had the votes needed to confirm his nominee, Conkling took a gamble and persuaded his Senate colleague Thomas Platt to join him.

On May 16, 1881, both New York senators resigned their seats, confident that the state legislature would vindicate them with speedy reelection. In returning with this refreshed mandate, Conkling believed he would be able to humiliate his party's president and control the Republican legislative agenda.

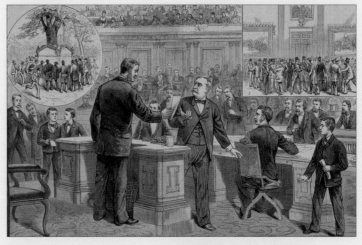

In an 1881 showdown with President Garfield over patronage, Roscoe Conkling and Thomas Platt of New York resigned from the Senate.

Unfortunately for Conkling and Platt, the state legislature took a dim view of this unorthodox scheme. As members deliberated throughout the summer, a deranged patronage seeker shot and mortally wounded President Garfield. When the legislature, in a wave of revulsion against Conkling's tactic, selected two others to fill the Senate seats, Garfield murmured from his deathbed, "Thank God." Thus ended Roscoe Conkling's remarkable political career.

Further Reading

Jordan, David M. *Roscoe Conkling of New York: Voice in the Senate*. Ithaca: Cornell University Press, 1971.

Platt, Thomas Collier. *The Autobiography of Thomas Collier Platt*. Edited by Louis J. Lang. New York: Arno Press, 1974.

Henry B. Anthony, "Father of the Senate," Dies

Henry B. Anthony, senator from Rhode Island (1859-1884).

At the height of his career, Rhode Island Republican Senator Henry B. Anthony was known to his colleagues as the "Father of the Senate"—the longest-serving member among them—a source of wisdom and stability in unsettled times.

In 1868, when the chief justice of the United States directed the Senate clerk to call the roll at the climactic moment of President Andrew Johnson's impeachment trial, Anthony's name stood at the head of the alphabet. "Mr. Senator Anthony," the chief justice intoned, "How say you? Is the respondent, Andrew Johnson, president of the United States, guilty or not guilty . . . ?" Anthony's response—meaningful because it was the first to be given and because he was known to be a supporter of Johnson—echoed like a thunder clap across the tense chamber: "Guilty!"

A rough-and-tumble old-time politician, Anthony did not hesitate—in the words of one modern writer—to employ "political legerdemain and bribery" to gain his objectives. His break with Andrew Johnson came after the president began directing Rhode Island patronage appointments to Anthony's political adversaries.

On September 2, 1884, Anthony died at age 69. This politically adroit former newspaper editor and state governor had served continuously in the Senate for the 25 years since 1859. Only two others in Senate history to that time had held longer terms.

In an era when the Senate selected its president pro tempore more for popularity than seniority, and made that choice each time the vice president was away from the Senate Chamber, members picked "Father" Anthony a record-setting 17 times.

Americans of his day knew Anthony as a powerful orator, who delivered famous funeral orations for notable senators including Stephen Douglas and Charles Sumner. Today, Anthony's name is known only to a few for its association with a Senate rule designed to keep measures that have been cleared for floor action from being bottled up on the Senate calendar.

Long before the Senate developed the position of majority leader to decide which items on its calendar would be given priority consideration, the "Anthony Rule" attempted to limit floor debate by allowing senators to speak no more than five minutes on certain measures before voting. It has since fallen into disuse, perhaps underscoring a biographer's assessment that Anthony was "one of the type of senators whose services lie rather in the exercise of judgment and practical wisdom than in any [lasting] contribution to law or practice."

Further Reading
Dove, Robert B. "Anthony Rule." In *The Encyclopedia of the United States Congress*, edited by Donald E. Bacon, et al. New York: Simon & Schuster, 1995.

May 13, 1886

The Senate's Oldest Art Collection

Day and night, throughout the year, 20 grim-faced men keep watch over the Senate Chamber. Stationed in the gallery, they never speak. A visitor might ask who they are and how they got there.

These silent sentinels memorialize those who held the office of vice president of the United States between 1789 and 1885. They got to their gallery niches because the Senate agreed on May 13, 1886, to commission marble portrait busts to honor their service, under the Constitution, as presidents of the Senate.

An unveiling earlier in 1886 of a portrait bust in memory of Henry Wilson inspired this plan. Wilson, a popular vice president, had died 11 years earlier in the Vice President's Room, near the Senate Chamber. The notable American sculptor Daniel Chester French produced the Wilson bust, placed on permanent display in the Vice President's Room.

Sculptor French assisted the Senate in establishing guidelines for the larger collection and agreed to prepare the first entry—a likeness of the body's first president, John Adams. French accepted the Adams commission despite his misgivings about the paltry $800 fee the Senate had set for each of these marble portraits. He said, "I consider it an honor and worth a great deal to have a bust of mine in so important a position. I do not know how many sculptors you will find who will look at it in the same way."

The Senate unveiled the portrait busts of John Adams and Thomas Jefferson on its 100th anniversary in 1889. By 1898, all 20 of the gallery's niches were occupied, and the Senate provided that additional busts be placed throughout its Capitol wing. Today, each of nation's first 44 vice presidents, from Adams to Dan Quayle, occupies a place in this special Senate Pantheon. Tennessee's Andrew Johnson will forever share a corner with Kentucky's John Breckinridge, whom he supported in 1860 for the presidency, denounced in 1863 for his military attacks on Tennessee, and pardoned in 1868 for his service as Confederate secretary of war.

Outside the chamber, the growing collection is arranged in chronological order throughout the second-floor hallways. Two of the Senate's best story-tellers—John Nance Garner and Alben Barkley—flank the chamber's south entrance. Several paces to the right, Lyndon Johnson looks directly at Richard Nixon, the political adversary who followed him to the White House. Nixon casts his eyes slightly to the left, however, eternally avoiding Johnson's steady gaze.

A bust of Henry Wilson, senator from Massachusetts (1855-1873), vice president of the United States (1873-1875), became the inspiration for the vice-presidential bust collection.

Further Reading

U.S. Congress. Senate. *United States Senate Catalogue of Fine Art*, by William Kloss and Diane K. Skvarla. 107th Congress, 2d sess., 2002. S. Doc. 107-11.

Confederate General Elected
Secretary of the Senate

In the several decades that followed the Civil War, the Democratic Party—long associated with the states of the former Confederacy—struggled to restore its standing as a national political organization. After the 1892 elections, many Democrats believed they had finally succeeded. In those contests, for the first time since the war, they captured the presidency and gained control of both houses of Congress. Symbolizing their return to national power, Senate Democrats replaced the incumbent secretary of the Senate—a former Union army general—with a former Confederate general.

In the late 1850s, North Carolina native William Ruffin Cox actively encouraged the states of the Old South to secede from the Union. A prosperous lawyer, he studied military tactics and, at his own expense, equipped a light artillery battery. When war came, he organized and led a Confederate infantry company. During the May 1863 Chancellorsville Campaign, Cox lost three-quarters of his regiment in just 15 minutes of fighting. In June 1864, he accompanied General Jubal Early on a raid designed to capture Washington. They reached Silver Spring, Maryland—the closest threat to the capital of any rebel unit—before withdrawing in the face of superior forces.

After the war, William Cox returned home to Raleigh, resumed his law practice, and joined former secessionists in organizing a political faction that eventually restored Democratic rule to North Carolina. He represented a North Carolina district in the U.S. House of Representatives from 1881 to 1887.

When the Democrats elected Cox as secretary in August 1893, several Republican senators objected to the Senate's departure from its pre-Civil War practice "when a political change of the Senate did not cause a change of its executive officers." While noting that only four individuals had served as secretary during the Senate's first 72 years, a Republican leader acknowledged that "a new order of things has come and we on this side of the chamber recognize it fully and bow to the inevitable."

A man of "striking physical appearance, cultured and courtly," Cox carried out his Senate responsibilities "with acceptance and distinction." When the Republicans regained the Senate majority two years later, party leaders agreed to keep him in office. This decision owed much to his genial nature, but even more to the political realities of a Republican caucus sharply divided on larger policy issues. Finally, in 1900, a strengthened Republican caucus decided to make a change and the 69-year-old Cox retired.

William Ruffin Cox, secretary of the Senate (1893-1900).

Further Reading

Raleigh [N.C.] *News and Observer,* December 27, 1919. Obituary.

U.S. Congress. *Congressional Record.* 53rd Cong., spec. sess., April 6, 1893, 97-99.

June 17, 1894

Senate Service Record Set

Perhaps the moral of this story is that those who run for president need to take special care in choosing who will place their name in nomination at their party's national convention. In 1880 John Sherman was a major contender for the Republican nomination. A former chairman of the House Ways and Means Committee and the Senate Finance Committee, he won further distinction as secretary of the treasury in the Rutherford Hayes administration. Sherman asked his former Ohio colleague, Representative James A. Garfield, to nominate him at the convention. "You ask for his monuments," Garfield told the delegates, "I point you to 25 years of national statutes. Not one great beneficial law has been placed on our statute books without his intelligence and powerful aid." Unfortunately for Sherman, the convention deadlocked, passed over front-runners like himself, and instead nominated the eloquent James Garfield.

Although he never became president, Sherman was one of the Senate's most illustrious members. In addition to chairing the Finance Committee, he also chaired the committees on Agriculture and Foreign Relations, served as president pro tempore, and headed the Senate Republican Conference.

John Sherman grew up in Ohio with seven siblings, including the future Civil War General William Tecumseh Sherman. Trained as a lawyer, he won election to the U.S.

House of Representatives, where he served from 1855 until he entered the Senate in 1861. There, Sherman specialized in financial policy, sponsoring legislation to finance operations of the Union army and to establish a national banking system. As an anti-inflation, sound-money advocate, Sherman crafted laws to reduce the national debt and end the free coinage of silver.

After his service as secretary of the treasury, Sherman returned to the Senate in 1881, ironically to replace Garfield, whose election to the Senate had been superseded by his election to the presidency. In the Senate, Sherman sponsored the landmark Sherman Antitrust Act. He served until 1897, when another Ohioan, President William McKinley, nominated him for secretary of state.

Sherman captured one other Senate distinction. On June 17, 1894, he became the longest-serving senator in history, breaking the nearly 30-year service record that Thomas Hart Benton had set back in 1851. When Sherman left the Senate in 1897, his tenure approached 32 years. In the 110 years since his departure, 29 senators have exceeded Sherman's record length of service. There is no better measure of the increased attractiveness of Senate service in modern times.

John Sherman, senator from Ohio (1861-1877, 1881-1897).

Further Reading

Sherman, John. *John Sherman's Recollections of Forty Years in the House, Senate, and Cabinet, An Autobiography.* 2 vols. Chicago: Werner Company, 1895.

Capitol Gas Explosion

The stone floor in today's "small Senate rotunda" was blown away by the force of the gas explosion that rocked the Capitol on November 6, 1898.

As the shadows lengthened on a quiet Sunday afternoon in November 1898, two policemen pedaled their bicycles on a routine tour through a Capitol Hill neighborhood. Suddenly, a tremendous explosion shattered their conversation. They turned instinctively toward the Capitol, three blocks away, to witness a sheet of flame rising from the building's basement-level windows along the east front.

Moments earlier, another police officer inside the building had detected the odor of gas. Until recently, gas had been commonly used to light the Capitol's interior, so the officer was not unduly alarmed. At the moment he set out to investigate, a large volume of gas from a leaky meter in the basement was rising slowly to the level of an open flame in a lamp left burning for the gas company's meter reader. The resulting explosion, just north of the Rotunda on the Senate side, heaved the floor upward spewing brick, plaster, and dense black smoke in all directions. As the intense fire raced up an elevator shaft to the upper floors, it melted steel, cracked stone, and incinerated priceless records.

Gas pipes had honeycombed the Capitol since mid-century, when that fuel began to replace whale oil as the principal means of lighting the building. In 1865, 1,083 gas jets provided lighting for the Rotunda. On those rare occasions when evening sessions of Congress coincided with gala White House entertainments, the city lacked sufficient gas to fuel, at the same time, the East Room's chandeliers and the lighting apparatus above the Senate and House chambers. This spurred a search for a more reliable and safer means of lighting.

In the early 1880s, Capitol engineers experimented with electricity, but concluded that the flickering light of the primitive incandescent lamps was inadequate for the building's needs. Within a few years, however, advances in technology accelerated the installation of electric lights throughout the Capitol and by 1896 both chambers relied on this means of illumination.

For several more years, the Capitol employed chandeliers outfitted with both gas and electric lights. Then came the disastrous explosion of November 6, 1898. Although no one was injured, the blast reduced large portions of the interior to a 20-ton pile of debris. Thus ended the era of gas illumination in the United States Capitol.

Further Reading

U.S. Congress. Senate. *History of the United States Capitol: A Chronicle of Design, Construction, and Politics,* by William C. Allen. 106th Congress, 2d sess., 2001. S. Doc. 106-29.

December 28, 1898

Justin S. Morrill Dies

This significant late-19th-century senator lived in a Washington mansion that the architect of the Capitol designed specially for him. Renowned Capitol artist Constantino Brumidi decorated the ceiling of his drawing room. Every 14th of April, that ornate salon on Thomas Circle echoed to the merriment of the senator's birthday party, a highlight of Washington's spring social season. His portrait, which today hangs outside the Senate Chamber, captures the thoughtful image of a man to whom his colleagues in the 1890s accorded their ultimate term of respect: "Father of the Senate."

Justin Morrill was born in Stafford, Vermont in 1810. At age 15, he ended his formal schooling to become a storekeeper. Shrewd and hardworking, Morrill built a successful retail business, gaining the financial independence that allowed him to retire at age 38. He turned to politics and, in 1854, won a seat in the U.S. House of Representatives.

Morrill flourished in the House as a skilled behind-the-scenes negotiator and expert on the nation's financial affairs. During the Civil War, as chairman of the House Ways and Means Committee, he shaped legislation that created the nation's first income tax.

The Vermonter's greatest contribution during his 12 years in the House was the 1862 Land-Grant College Act. Sensitive about his own lack of educational opportunities, he pioneered a program that dedicated revenues from the sale of 17 million acres of federal lands to establish public institutions of higher education in every state.

In 1867, Morrill began the first of six terms in the Senate. By the time of his death on December 28, 1898, including his House tenure, he had served in Congress a record-setting 44 years and had chaired the Senate Finance Committee for 17 years—a record that still stands

As chairman of the Joint Committee on Public Buildings, Morrill guided legislation for construction of the Capitol Building's west front terrace, the Executive Office Building, and the unfinished portion of the Washington Monument. It was his idea to convert the old House chamber into a national statuary hall.

Justin Morrill's greatest construction legacy was the grand, Italian Renaissance-style Thomas Jefferson Building of the Library of Congress, which opened a year before he died. In his eulogy, a Senate colleague suggested honoring this singular representative and senator with a plaque in the new library's Great Hall. That proposal languished for decades, until 1997. On the occasion of the library building's centennial, Vermont's two senators at last implemented this most appropriate honor.

Justin S. Morrill, senator from Vermont (1867-1898).

Further Reading
Parker, William Belmont. *The Life and Public Services of Justin Smith Morrill.* 1924. Reprint. New York: Da Capo Press, 1971.

February 22, 1902

Senate Fistfight

From its earliest days, the Senate has followed a set of rules designed to promote courteous and respectful behavior among members while debating issues that frequently provoke strong feelings. Those rules include cautions not to interrupt another member while speaking and provisions for unruly members to be silenced until the presiding officer determines whether that member may proceed. Beyond these general guidelines, the Senate traditionally relied on common sense and "gentlemanly behavior" to keep tempers under control.

In 1856, the savage beating in the Senate Chamber of a senator by a House member sorely tested this arrangement. Members briefly considered, and then rejected, a rule providing that senators "shall avoid personality and shall not reflect improperly upon any state." The majority believed that "general parliamentary law grown out of the wisdom and experience of a thousand parliaments and senates" should be adequate to guide the Senate without adding to the rules whenever "anything exciting occurs."

This 1896 cartoon depicts Senator Benjamin Tillman as, "That South Carolina cyclone, or the terrible tantrums of the untamable Tillman."

Nearly 50 years later, when fists began to fly, this "hands-off" arrangement fell apart.

On February 22, 1902, John McLaurin, South Carolina's junior senator, raced into the Senate Chamber and pronounced that state's senior senator, Ben Tillman, guilty of "a willful, malicious, and deliberate lie." Standing nearby, Tillman spun around and punched McLaurin squarely in the jaw. The chamber exploded in pandemonium as members struggled to separate both members of the South Carolina delegation. In a long moment, it was over, but not without stinging bruises both to bystanders and to the Senate's sense of decorum.

Although Tillman and McLaurin had once been political allies, the relationship had recently cooled. Both were Democrats, but McLaurin had moved closer to the Republicans, who then controlled Congress, the White House, and a lot of South Carolina patronage. When McLaurin changed his position to support Republicans on a controversial treaty, Tillman's rage erupted. With McLaurin away from the chamber, he had charged that his colleague had succumbed to "improper influences."

On February 28, 1902, the Senate censured both men and reluctantly added to its rules the provision—echoing the proposals of a half-century earlier—that survives today as part of Rule XIX: "No senator in debate shall, directly or indirectly, by any form of words impute to another Senator or to other Senators any conduct or motive unworthy or unbecoming a Senator."

Further Reading
Simkins, Francis Butler. *Pitchfork Ben Tillman: South Carolinian.* Baton Rouge, 1944.

March 6, 1903

Senate Democratic Caucus Organizes

On March 6, 1903, the faction-ridden Senate Democratic caucus decided it was time to get organized. On that day, for the first time in the Senate's history, the caucus formally elected a chairman and a secretary, agreed to keep regular minutes of its proceedings, and took steps toward the adoption of a "binding rule."

When Republican President Theodore Roosevelt called the Senate into special session on March 5, 1903, to consider ratification of a Panama Canal treaty, the Democratic caucus unanimously selected Maryland's Arthur Gorman as chairman. The dominant figure in late 19th-century Maryland political life, Gorman was a masterful legislative strategist and party loyalist. Based on his informal service as Democratic leader in the 1890s, his Senate colleagues believed he was just the man to revitalize their heavily out-numbered party in the early 1900s.

Gorman convened the caucus on March 6, 1903, in a third-floor Capitol room that offered an expansive view of the building's East Front plaza. The newly elected secretary, Tennessee Senator Edward Carmack, presumably began to keep regular minutes. Although the formal record of that session has not survived, the following day's Washington Post provided a richly detailed account. The existing minutes begin with the meeting of March 16, 1903. Democratic senators who opposed the pending Panama Canal treaty sought to unite their party by proposing a rule that would bind all 33 members to any decision approved by two-thirds of the caucus. The action, agreed to later that year, marked the first time a party caucus sought to exercise such a binding rule.

Adoption of the binding rule promoted a distinction between the terms "caucus" and "conference." As these words came to be used, senators were in "caucus" when they discussed whether or not to bind the party's vote on a given issue; they were in "conference" when considering election of officers or general legislative business.

Arthur P. Gorman, senator from Maryland (1881-1899, 1903-1906).

Further Reading

Lambert, John R., Jr. *Arthur Pue Gorman*. Baton Rouge: Louisiana State University Press, 1953.

U.S. Congress. Senate. *Majority and Minority Leaders of the Senate*, by Floyd M. Riddick. 100th Congress, 2d sess., 1988. S.Doc. 100-29.

U.S. Congress. Senate. *Minutes of the Senate Democratic Conference: Fifty-eighth through Eighty-eighth Congress, 1903-1964,* Donald A. Ritchie, ed. 105th Congress, 1998. S. Doc. 105-20.

U.S. Congress. Senate. *Minutes of the Senate Republican Conference: Sixty-second Congress through Eighty-eighth Congress, 1911-1964*, Wendy Wolff and Donald A. Ritchie, eds. 105th Congress, 1999. S. Doc. 105-19.

April 28, 1904

Senate Office Building Authorized

On April 28, 1904, President Theodore Roosevelt signed legislation authorizing purchase of land for the Senate's first permanent office building—today called the Richard B. Russell Building.

With the original Capitol's completion in 1830, many believed Congress' space needs had been fully met. The next 20 years proved them wrong. The admission of seven new states led to growing demands for enlarged chambers and additional member and committee office space. In 1850, Congress authorized construction of new Senate and House wings that more than doubled the Capitol's length.

Twenty-five years after those wings opened in the late 1850s, unrelenting pressures for additional space caused Congress to authorize construction of terraces along the Capitol's west front. When completed in 1891, these terraces provided 50 small rooms for Senate use. This was not enough, however, to accommodate the Senate's nearly 60 committees and the 12 new members from the six states that had entered the Union in the previous two years. Consequently, as members moved into the new terrace rooms, they also voted to purchase a three-year-old, five-story apartment house.

Located on the corner of New Jersey and Constitution Avenues, the Maltby Building made it possible for every senator to have an office. This greatly irritated House members whose plan to acquire a similar structure on their side of Capitol Hill had fallen through. Why, they asked, should 76 senators have more space collectively than 332 House members? Several suggested, in vain, that the Senate share its Maltby space.

Soon, however, senators began to complain about their new Maltby quarters—stifling in summer, frigid in winter. The building had been constructed on the site of an old stable. Its heaviest component—the elevator shaft—settled seven inches into the underlying mire, carrying with it surrounding walls and floors. The city fire marshal considered the structure a firetrap. Although this deteriorating situation inspired the 1904 legislation for a permanent, fireproof office building, senators had little choice but to remain at Maltby until the new building's completion in 1909.

View of the Maltby Building, left center, *looking north from the Capitol.*

Further Reading

U.S. Congress. Senate. *History of the United States Capitol: A Chronicle of Design, Construction, and Politics*, by William C. Allen. 106th Congress, 2d sess., 2001. S. Doc. 106-29.

February 17, 1906

"Treason of the Senate"

In February 1906, readers of *Cosmopolitan* magazine opened its pages to this statement: "Treason is a strong word, but not too strong to characterize the situation in which the Senate is the eager, resourceful, and indefatigable agent of interests as hostile to the American people as any invading army could be." This indictment launched a nine-part series of articles entitled "Treason of the Senate."

The "Treason" series placed the Senate at the center of a major drive by Progressive Era reformers to weaken the influence of large corporations and other major financial interests on government policy making. Direct popular election of senators fit perfectly with their campaign to bring government closer to the people.

As originally adopted, the Constitution provided for the election of senators by individual state legislatures. In the years following the Civil War, that system became increasingly subject to bribery, fraud, and deadlock. As Congress took on a greater role in shaping an industrializing nation, those with a major business stake in that development believed they could best exert their influence on the U.S. Senate by offering financial incentives to the state legislators who selected its members.

The campaign for direct election of senators took on new force in 1906, following conviction of two senators on corruption charges. Each had taken fees for interceding with federal agencies on behalf of business clients. The resulting negative publicity inspired publisher William Randolph Hearst, then a U.S. House member and owner of *Cosmopolitan* magazine, to commission popular novelist David Graham Phillips to prepare a series of investigative articles.

Making the point that large corporations and corrupt state legislators played too large a role in selection of senators, these articles doubled *Cosmopolitan*'s circulation within two months. Yet, Phillips' obvious reliance on innuendo and exaggeration soon earned him the scorn of other reformers. President Theodore Roosevelt saw in these charges a politically motivated effort by Hearst to discredit his administration, and coined the term "muckraker" to describe the Phillips brand of overstated and sensationalist journalism.

For several decades before publication of Phillips' series, certain southern senators had blocked the direct election amendment out of fear that it would increase the influence of African-American voters. By 1906, however, many southern states had enacted "Jim Crow" laws to undermine that influence. The Phillips series finally broke Senate resistance and opened the way for the amendment's ratification in 1913.

Cast as a sinister-looking senator, New York's Chauncey Depew appeared on the cover of Cosmopolitan *when "The Treason of the Senate" series began in 1906.*

Further Reading

Phillips, David Graham. The Treason of the Senate. Edited with an introduction by George E. Mowry and Judson A. Grenier. Chicago: Quadrangle Books, 1964.

Ravitz, Abe C. David Graham Phillips. New York: Twayne Publishers, 1966.

April 19, 1906

Senator La Follette Delivers Maiden Speech

Robert La Follette, senator from Wisconsin (1906-1925).

Benjamin Disraeli never forgot his first attempt to deliver a speech as a brand new member of the British House of Commons. It was, perhaps, a legislator's worst nightmare. As he began to speak, other members started laughing. The more he spoke, the harder they laughed. Finally, humiliated, he gave up and sat down. As his parting shot, this future prime minister pledged, "The time will come when you shall hear me."

From the Senate's earliest days, new members have observed a ritual of remaining silent during floor debates for a period of time—depending on the era and the senator—that ranged from several months to several years. Some believed that by waiting a respectful amount of time before giving their so-called maiden speech, their more senior colleagues would respect them for their humility.

On April 19, 1906, Wisconsin Senator Robert La Follette was anything but humble. A 20-year veteran of public office, with service in the House and as his state's governor, he believed he had been elected to present a message that none of his more seasoned colleagues was inclined to deliver. La Follette waited just three months, an astoundingly brief period by the standards of that day, before launching his first major address. He spoke

for eight hours over three days; his remarks in the *Congressional Record* consumed 148 pages. As he began to speak, most of the senators present in the chamber pointedly rose from their desks and departed. La Follette's wife, observing from the gallery, wrote, "There was no mistaking that this was a polite form of hazing."

A year later, in 1907, Arkansas Senator Jeff Davis shocked Capitol Hill by waiting only nine days. The local press corps, keeping a count of such upstart behavior, noted that Davis was the fourth new senator in recent years who "refused to wait until his hair turned gray before taking up his work actively."

For most of the Senate's existence, the tradition of waiting several years before delivering a maiden speech has been more an ideal than reality. As one Senate insider explained, in this modern era of continuous and immediate news coverage, "the electorate wouldn't stand for it." The tradition, however, of paying attention to "maiden speeches," regardless of when they are delivered, remains important to senators, constituents, and home-state journalists.

Further Reading
"Few in Senate Hear La Follette," *Chicago Daily Tribune,* April 20, 1906, 10.
"Nettled at Empty Seats," *The Washington Post*, April 20, 1906, 4.

May 21, 1906

High Court Upholds Senator's Conviction

Daniel Webster had a great deal of trouble with his personal finances. While a senator, he maintained a busy law practice to supplement his congressional salary. On occasion, he took clients into the Senate Chamber to watch as he advocated their legislative interests. In the midst of a crucial 1833 battle to recharter the Bank of the United States, he reminded the bank's president that it was time for his retainer to be "refreshed."

In those days, before any formal prohibition on senatorial conflicts of interest, most of his Senate colleagues disdained Webster's blatant tactics, but a significant number saw nothing wrong with representing the interests of private clients before the federal agencies whose appropriations they controlled. By the time of the Civil War, however, the expansion of those appropriations and the federal government's growing regulatory role increased opportunities for corruption. Consequently, in 1864, Congress outlawed this practice and barred those found guilty from holding federal office.

In 1905, for the first and only time, two senators were convicted of violating the 1864 statute. Oregon's John Mitchell died as the Senate prepared expulsion proceedings. Kansas Senator Joseph Burton, found guilty of taking money to help a St. Louis company scuttle a U.S. Post Office mail fraud investigation, avoided Senate action pending his appeal.

On May 21, 1906, the U.S. Supreme Court upheld Burton's conviction, but ruled that the 1864 law's bar against federal office holding did not automatically vacate his Senate seat or require the Senate to expel him. Only the Senate could determine its members' eligibility for continued service. Within days Burton resigned to begin a six-month prison term.

Several weeks earlier, a colorful and forthright Texas senator named Joseph Bailey expressed a view he believed common among other members. Speaking 63 years before the Senate adopted its first ethics code, he said, "I despise those [senators] who think they must remain poor to be considered honest. I am not one of them. If my constituents want a man who is willing to go to the poorhouse in his old age in order to stay in the Senate during his middle age, they will have to find another senator. I intend to make every dollar that I can honestly make, without neglecting or interfering with my public duty."

Joseph Burton, senator from Kansas (1901-1906).

Further Reading

Baker, Richard Allan. "The History of Congressional Ethics." In *Representation and Responsibility: Exploring Legislative Ethics*, edited by Bruce Jennings and Daniel Callahan. New York: Plenum Press, 1985.

Russell Building Cornerstone Laid

I n April 1906, as workmen laid the cornerstone to what we know today as the Cannon House Office Building, President Theodore Roosevelt thrilled a large audience with a speech attacking muckraking journalists. That speech has since become a standard part of Roosevelt administration political folklore. Three months later, on the Senate side of Capitol Hill, a second cornerstone placement almost escaped public notice. On July 31, 1906, a handful of Senate employees, construction workers, and passers by watched as a crane operator lowered a large white block of Vermont marble into position. The highest-ranking official present, the Capitol superintendent, stood in the shade, fanning himself with a wide-brimmed Panama hat against the 90-degree heat.

Perhaps the Senate had good reason not to publicize its first office building. Three years later, on March 5, 1909, when the initial occupants moved into the grand Beaux Arts-style structure that is now designated the Richard Brevard Russell Senate Office Building, newspaper editors blasted the opening with headlines such as "New Building Fitted Up Regardless of Expense." Responding to a statement explaining that this was where senators' business activity would take place, *The New York Times* began, "When in the course of human events it became necessary for these ninety-two business gentlemen to have business offices, they erected a building that a thousand men would feel lonesome in." Noting its bronze ornamentation, mahogany furniture, gymnasium, telephone for each office, and running ice water, the same writer concluded, "It looks about as much like a prosaic business office building as a lady's boudoir does."

By today's standards, the space the building offered seems modest. Each senator received only two rooms. The senator's private office featured a fireplace, a large window, a double-kneehole "battleship" desk, six chairs, and a couch. The slightly smaller adjacent room housed the senator's personal staff, which at that time generally consisted of one secretary and one messenger. The building also contained eight committee rooms and a large, ornate conference room for party caucus meetings. Unlike its fraternal House twin, the Senate structure originally had only three sides, with an open courtyard facing First Street. By the early 1930s, expanding legislative activities and staff resources justified the addition of a fourth side along First Street, with 28 additional office suites. That occasion passed without much journalistic notice—muckraking or otherwise.

Laying the cornerstone of the Senate Office Building, July 31, 1906.

Further Reading

U.S. Congress. Senate. *History of the United States Capitol: A Chronicle of Design, Construction, and Politics,* by William C. Allen. 106th Congress, 2d sess., 2001. S. Doc. 106-29.

April 12, 1907

Woodrow Wilson's Changing Views of the Senate

In 1906, the president of Columbia University invited the president of Princeton University to deliver a series of lectures on American government. On April 12, 1907, Columbia students turned out to hear Princeton President Woodrow Wilson discuss the United States Senate.

In the 20 years since he had prepared his doctoral dissertation on Congress without ever visiting Congress, Wilson had gained considerable first-hand experience with the Senate. In 1907, he viewed the body with a spirit of cordiality and toleration. "There is no better cure for thinking disparagingly of the Senate than a conference with men who belong to it, to find out how various, how precise, how comprehensive their information about the affairs of the nation is; and to find, what is even more important, how fair, how discreet, how regardful of public interest they are."

Wilson noted sympathetically the "unmistakable condescension with which the older members of the Senate regard the President of the United States." Senior senators treat him "at most as an ephemeral phenomenon," because they have served longer than presidents and their "experience of affairs is much mellower than the President's can be; [they look] at policies with steadier vision than the President's; the continuity of the government lies in the keeping of the Senate more than in the keeping of the executive, even in respect to matters which are of the especial prerogative of the presidential office. A member of longstanding in the Senate feels that he is the professional, the President an amateur."

Over the following decade, conditioned by experience as governor of New Jersey and president of the United States, Wilson acquired a decidedly darker view of executive-legislative relations. In 1913, he denounced senators delaying a vote on a conference report as "a lot of old women." In 1917, those who filibustered armaments legislation were "a little group of willful men." In 1919, asked to accept reservations to the Treaty of Versailles offered by Senate Foreign Relations Committee chairman Henry Cabot Lodge, he said, "Never! I'll never consent to adopt any policy with which that impossible name is so prominently identified."

Never in American history was there a president better equipped by training and experience to work constructively with the Senate. Considering the tragic flaws of the Treaty of Versailles, never were there more serious consequences of his failure to do so.

Woodrow Wilson, circa 1902, as president of Princeton University.

Further Reading

Wilson, Woodrow. *Congressional Government: A Study in American Politics.* Boston: Houghton, Mifflin and Company, 1885.

Wilson, Woodrow. *The Papers of Woodrow Wilson*, edited by Arthur S. Link. 69 volumes. Princeton: Princeton University Press, 1966-1994.

August 4, 1908

William Allison Dies

He sits watchfully at the entrance to the Senate Chamber. His world-weary eyes cautiously examine those who pass busily before him. His white hair and neatly trimmed beard give a sense of solemn gravity to this statesman of an age long past. When he died on August 4, 1908, 79-year-old William Boyd Allison, Republican of Iowa, had served in the Senate for 35 years—longer than any other member in history to that time. He spent his entire Senate career on the Appropriations Committee and chaired that panel for a quarter-century—a record for leading a Senate committee that is not ever likely to be broken. He also sat on the Finance Committee for 30 years and chaired the Senate Republican Conference for the final 12 years of his life.

William Allison's extraordinary Senate career began with a stinging political defeat. After losing a race for the post of county attorney in his native Ohio, Allison decided to leave the state in search of a climate more favorable to his political ambitions. He settled in Iowa, joined a small law firm in Dubuque, and built a successful record of defending the interests of the major railroads vital to that region's economic development. That success assured him the financial backing necessary to pursue his public career. In 1873, after eight years in the U.S. House of Representatives, Allison moved to the Senate.

In the Senate, the dignified and unassuming Allison earned a reputation as a master conciliator and political moderate, successfully balancing the antagonistic interests of his state's farmers and railroads. He used his powerful committee assignments to forge and move to enactment legislation responsive to the leading issues of his day: tariff reform, currency stabilization, and railroad regulation.

A major national figure, the Iowa senator narrowly missed winning the Republican presidential nomination in 1888 and again in 1896. Happy to remain in the Senate, he turned aside offers to serve in the cabinets of that era's Republican presidents. Allison's death in 1908 brought an end to a decade in which he, with Republican senators Nelson Aldrich of Rhode Island, Orville Platt of Connecticut, and John Spooner of Wisconsin, directed the Senate and shaped the laws of the nation.

Soon after Allison's death, the Senate purchased the oil portrait that now hangs in a place of honor to the right of the Senate Chamber entrance, a few paces from the Republican side of the center aisle.

Known as the Senate Four, left to right, *Orville H. Platt of Connecticut (1879-1905), John C. Spooner of Wisconsin (1885-1891, 1897-1907), William B. Allison of Iowa (1873-1908), and Nelson W. Aldrich of Rhode Island (1881-1911) informally led the Senate at the turn of the 20th century.*

Further Reading
Sage, Leland L. *William Boyd Allison: A Study in Practical Politics.* Iowa City: State Historical Society of Iowa, 1956.

April 27, 1911

House Member Introduces Resolution to Abolish the Senate

"Whereas the Senate in particular has become an obstructive and useless body, a menace to the liberties of the people, and an obstacle to social growth; a body, many of the Members of which are representatives neither of a State nor of its people, but solely of certain predatory combinations, and a body which, by reason of the corruption often attending the election of its Members, has furnished the gravest public scandals in the history of the nation. . . ."

This text formed the preamble to a constitutional amendment introduced in the House of Representatives on April 27, 1911, by that chamber's first Socialist member, Victor Berger of Wisconsin. Continuing evidence of corrupted state legislative elections for U.S. senators and the Senate's apparent reluctance to follow the House in passing a constitutional amendment to require direct popular election of its members inspired Berger's resolution. It provided that all legislative powers be vested in the House of Representatives, whose "enactments . . . shall be the supreme law and the President shall have no power to veto them, nor shall any court have any power to invalidate them."

In his brief time as a member, the Milwaukee Socialist had made more enemies than friends among his House colleagues, which may explain why many in that body jumped so quickly to the Senate's defense with talk of enforcing the House ban against public criticism of the Senate.

As with nearly all of the more than 11,000 constitutional amendments proposed from 1789 to our own day, Berger's proposal died silently in committee. Yet, less than seven weeks later, perhaps nudged by Berger's gesture, the Senate approved its long-delayed direct-election resolution, which would soon be ratified as the Constitution's 17th Amendment.

Berger left the House in 1913, but remained a prominent social critic. For speaking against U.S. participation in World War I, he was convicted under the Espionage Act and sentenced to 20 years in prison—a sentence that the U.S. Supreme Court invalidated in 1921. In 1918 he lost a three-way race for the Senate, while polling more than a quarter of the votes cast. Later that year, he won back his old House seat, but that body refused to seat him. Following the dismissal of his conviction, he won the next three House elections and served there from 1923 to 1929.

Congressman Victor Berger of Wisconsin.

Further Reading
"Wants Senate Abolished," *New York Times*, April 28, 1911, 8.

Senate Deadlocked

Jacob Gallinger, senator from New Hampshire (1891-1918).

Augustus Bacon, senator from Georgia (1895-1914).

Soon after the Senate convened in April 1911, its members sensed they were witnessing the end of an era. Just a few years earlier, four senior Republicans had virtually ruled the Senate with the help of their party's two-to-one majority over the Democrats. Now, all four were gone. As a result of the recent 1910 mid-term elections, 10 new Democratic members bolstered the ranks of the minority. On the Republican side, a small but determined band of eight progressive insurgents worked to undermine their party's old-guard leadership much as their counterparts had done in the House of Representatives the year before in a successful revolt against the autocratic rule of Speaker Joseph Cannon.

Early in the session, illness forced the resignation of President pro tempore William Frye of Maine, another old-guard Republican. Frye had held that office for 15 of his 30 years in the Senate—a record that still stands. To replace him, the Senate Republican caucus nominated New Hampshire's Jacob Gallinger without dissenting votes. The insurgents, however, considered Gallinger one of the Senate's most reactionary members and were particularly angry because, as chairman of the party's committee on committees, he had denied them choice assignments. They concealed their opposition to his election until the full Senate took up the nomination on May 11, 1911.

When the clerk announced the results of the vote, the majority party candidate Gallinger shockingly trailed Democratic caucus nominee Augustus Bacon of Georgia. With several other senators receiving smaller numbers of votes, neither caucus candidate gained an absolute majority. After conducting six additional and equally fruitless ballots that day, the Senate—in an acrimonious mood—recessed without making a selection.

They tried again the following week, the following month, and the month after that. Each time the deadlock continued, as the Democrats held firm behind Bacon, and the eight insurgents voted for other candidates. Finally, on August 12, as pressure mounted for a decision on statehood for Arizona and New Mexico, and members agitated to escape Washington's wilting heat, party leaders brokered a compromise. Under that plan, Democrat Bacon would alternate as president pro tempore for brief periods during the remainder of the Congress with Gallinger and three other Republicans. Over the previous 15 years, one man had held the largely honorary post; over the next 15 months, five would. A new era seemed at hand.

Further Reading
U.S. Congress. Senate. *The Senate, 1789-1989*, Vol. 2, by Robert C. Byrd. 100th Congress, 1st sess., 1991. S. Doc.100-20. Chapter 6.

The Senate Guarantees Tenure to Union Vet Employees

The Civil War took more casualties than all other American wars combined. Well into the 20th century, tens of thousands of disabled veterans throughout the nation bore witness to that conflict's horrible cost. Many of those veterans and their relatives thronged the Capitol's corridors in the postwar era desperately seeking support through government pensions or congressional jobs.

Up to the time of World War I, the Senate staff included Civil War veterans working as clerks, elevator operators, and doorkeepers. Predominately soldiers of the Union Army, most of these men owed their appointments to Republican senators, who controlled the Senate—and thus the majority of its patronage— for all but four years between 1861 and 1913.

In 1911, the Democratic Party won control of the House of Representatives and narrowed the Republican majority in the Senate. The prospect of a Democratic-controlled Senate by 1913 inspired Idaho Republican Weldon Heyburn to sponsor a resolution guaranteeing permanent tenure to all Union veterans still on the Senate payroll. One of the last senators to "wave the bloody shirt" of hostility to the former Confederacy, Heyburn had won national notoriety for opposing federal funding of Confederate monuments.

On July 14, 1911, the Senate unanimously adopted Heyburn's resolution.

Two years later, after they did win control of the Senate, the Democrats met to decide whether to rescind the Heyburn resolution as part of a larger review of Senate staffing allocations. From the minutes of Democratic caucus deliberations, first published in 1998, we learn of their concern, shared by Republicans, to protect productive workers and weed out malingerers—regardless of party allegiance. We learn also of their desire to treat the Republican minority, in allocating patronage appointments, as the Republicans, over the years, had treated the Democratic minority.

Among the approximately 300 employees then on the Senate payroll, the majority caucus agreed to keep the 29 "old soldiers." They reasoned that a repeal of the Heyburn Resolution would "arouse a hostile excitement which would not be justified by the results." But the caucus also recommended that these aging veterans be reassigned to less challenging, lower-paid positions. By the standards of the times, this proved to be a politically suitable compromise— supporting veterans while reducing the Senate payroll.

Weldon Heyburn, senator from Idaho (1903-1912).

Further Reading

U.S. Congress. Senate. *Minutes of the Senate Republican Conference, 1911-1964*, edited by Wendy Wolff and Donald A. Ritchie. 105th Congress, 1999. S. Doc. 105-19.

U.S. Congress. Senate. *Minutes of the Senate Democratic Conference, 1903-1964*, edited by Donald A. Ritchie. 105th Congress, 1998. S. Doc. 105-20.

Senator Ousted

This cartoon reflects public sentiment against Senator William Lorimer of Illinois (1909-1912).

In 1873 Senator Samuel Pomeroy invited a state legislator for a midnight meeting in his hotel suite. There he handed him $7,000 to secure his vote in the upcoming state legislative balloting for reelection to the U.S. Senate. The legislator called a press conference, confessed to setting up Pomeroy for a bribery charge, displayed the cash, and ended a Senate career. Mark Twain and Charles Dudley Warner included a thinly disguised version of this widely publicized story in their 1873 novel *The Gilded Age*.

Over the next 40 years, charges of bribery were heard with increasing frequency as state legislatures struggled with their constitutional responsibility to elect U.S. senators. In 1890, Senate President pro tempore John Ingalls captured the rough-and-tumble spirit of those contests. "The purification of politics," he growled, "is an iridescent dream. Politics is the battle for supremacy. The Decalogue and the Golden Rule have no place in a political campaign. The object is success."

William Lorimer sympathized with Ingalls' famous remark as he won his Senate seat in 1909 following a lengthy and acrimonious deadlock in the Illinois legislature. Nearly a year into his term, Lorimer asked the Senate to investigate charges by the *Chicago Tribune* that he had obtained his seat through bribery and corruption. A Senate committee noted the Senate's practice of invalidating elections only if the accused senator had actively promoted the bribery and concluded that under such a standard Lorimer had done nothing wrong. After a rancorous six-week debate and despite considerable evidence against Lorimer, the Senate in March 1911 dropped the case. The resulting storm of public outrage, combined with an infusion of recently elected progressive-minded members, led the Senate on June 12, 1911, to approve a long-pending constitutional amendment providing for direct popular election of senators.

A week before the Senate vote on the constitutional amendment, additional public charges against Lorimer led the upper house to reopen his case. After hearing from 180 witnesses over the following year, a committee majority again found no clear trail of corruption. The full Senate, however, decided differently. On July 13, 1912, with the direct election amendment on its way to state ratification, the Senate declared Lorimer's 1909 election invalid. This action closed a major chapter in Senate history and accorded Lorimer the dubious distinction of being the last senator to be deprived of office for corrupting a state legislature.

Further Reading

Tarr, Joel A. *A Study in Boss Politics: William Lorimer of Chicago*. Urbana: University of Illinois Press, 1971.

U.S. Congress. Senate. *United States Senate Election, Expulsion and Censure Cases, 1793-1990*, by Anne M. Butler and Wendy Wolff. 103d Cong., 1st sess., 1995. S. Doc. 103-33.

January 28, 1913

Key Pittman Barely Elected

This Nevada Democrat barely made it to the Senate. On January 28, 1913, Key Pittman won a seat by a mere 89 votes. (In 1948, a Texas Democrat would become known as "Landslide Lyndon" for winning a Senate primary by 87 votes and in a 1964 Nevada general election Howard Cannon defeated Paul Laxalt by 84 votes.) Setting another record in that 1913 election, Pittman gained his seat by attracting a total of only 7,942 votes—the smallest number by which a U.S. Senate candidate has ever entered office. Key Pittman's election is noteworthy for a third reason. He won by a popular vote at a time when the Constitution still required state legislatures to elect senators. How was that possible?

By the second half of the 19th century, the state legislative election system had proven increasingly susceptible to deadlock and corruption. In the 1890s, the House of Representatives repeatedly passed constitutional amendments for direct popular election, only to see them die in the Senate. Early in the new century, more than half the states devised election systems that included a popular referendum for senators and a pledge by state legislative candidates to vote according to the referendum's results. Nevada operated under such a system. In 1910, that

state's voters had narrowly endorsed the Republican Senate incumbent. Although Democrats had regained control of the state legislature when it convened in 1911, they followed the will of the voters and awarded the seat to the Republican. He died soon thereafter, opening the way for Key Pittman to win the special election in 1912—the year the Senate finally agreed to a direct election amendment.

When the Nevada legislature met in January 1913, four months before the 17th Amendment's ratification, it formalized Pittman's slim popular-vote victory. Pittman went on to a colorful and productive 27-year Senate career. As one biographer notes, he "won advantages for his constituency by clever use of difficult domestic and foreign situations . . . [and by masterfully manipulating] amendments, riders, and especially conference committee compromises."

1918 photograph of Key Pittman, senator from Nevada (1913-1940).

Further Reading

Glad, Betty. *Key Pittman: The Tragedy of a Senate Insider.* New York: Columbia University Press, 1986.

March 15, 1913

Senate Banking Committee Established

Until 1913, the Senate operated without a banking committee. Unlike the House of Representatives, which had created its own banking panel in 1865, the Senate chose to refer banking and currency legislation to its Committee on Finance. When the Senate finally made its move on March 15, 1913, the two most responsible forces were Oklahoma Senator Robert Owen and that year's pending Federal Reserve Act.

Six years earlier, in 1907, Robert Owen had become one of Oklahoma's first two senators and, with Charles Curtis of Kansas, one of the Senate's first two members of Native American descent.

In his early 20s, Owen had moved with his mother from his native Virginia to live with her family in the Indian Territory's Cherokee Nation. He earned a law degree in the 1880s, became a federal Indian agent, and helped secure citizenship for residents of the Indian Territory, located adjacent to the Oklahoma Territory. He also successfully lobbied Congress to extend the provisions of the National Banking Act to the Indian Territory and organized a bank in Muskogee in 1890.

Members of the Senate Banking Committee, circa 1913.

Owen was a natural choice to become one of Oklahoma's first senators. A Progressive Democrat, he focused on national banking policy. Owen was particularly interested in creating an elastic system of currency to help the nation absorb the shock of financial panics such as the one that had occurred during his first year in the Senate.

Over the six years following the 1907 economic crisis, leaders in both houses of Congress became convinced of the need for a system to prevent a few large New York banks from controlling the vast majority of the nation's financial assets. A February 1913 House report on this dangerous concentration of wealth and influence finally led the Senate to conclude that it needed the full-time expertise of a separate committee on banking.

When Congress convened under Democratic control in March 1913, with a newly inaugurated Democratic president in the White House, pressures built for passage of legislation to create the Federal Reserve System. As a tireless sponsor of that legislation, Robert Owen became the new Senate Banking Committee's first chairman. With the aid of his House counterpart and President Woodrow Wilson, Owen overcame powerful opposing forces to secure passage of the Federal Reserve Act. His major substantive contribution to that act was its provision that the United States government rather than the banks would control the Federal Reserve Board.

Further Reading

Brown, Kenny L. "A Progressive from Oklahoma: Senator Robert Latham Owen, Jr." *Chronicles of Oklahoma* 62 (Fall 1984): 232-65.

May 28, 1913

Senators Require a Whip

Soon after Democrats took control of the Senate in 1913, they began to suffer from poor attendance at their party caucus meetings. Party leaders had decided to make key decisions on the Democratic administration's legislative priority—tariff reduction—in caucus rather than in the Finance Committee. This would allow Democrats to achieve a party position on politically sensitive tariff rates before confronting the Republican minority. Poor caucus attendance by those favoring tariff reduction, however, gave greater weight to Louisiana's two Democrats who vigorously supported high protective tariffs on imported sugar. Additional defections would have risked letting these senators significantly undermine the party's commitment to lower tariffs.

On May 28, 1913, the Democratic caucus convened with only 33 of its 50 members present. It unanimously adopted a resolution requesting regular attendance of all members. To enforce that agreement, the caucus then created the post of party whip. In doing so, they followed the example of both parties in the House of Representatives. Two years later, Senate Republicans also added the position of party whip to promote floor as well as caucus attendance.

As their first whip, Democrats chose a member with less than two months' service—Illinois Senator James Hamilton Lewis. Those who encountered "Ham" Lewis never forgot his elegant, courteous, and somewhat eccentric manner. Noted for his flowing red hair and carefully parted pink whiskers, he dressed in perfectly tailored clothes, wore beribboned eye glasses, carried a walking stick, and sprinkled his conversation with literary references.

Lewis lost his reelection bid in 1918 to publisher Medill McCormick, but he returned 14 years later, after defeating McCormick's widow, Ruth. When the Democratic whip's position fell vacant in 1933, as Senate Democrats again returned to the majority after an extended season in the minority, they elected Lewis to that post. Following his death in 1939, the Senate accepted a portrait of its first whip and later placed it near the chamber's entrance—perhaps to inspire senators of succeeding generations to timely attendance.

James Hamilton Lewis, senator from Illinois (1913-1919, 1931-1939).

Further Reading

U.S. Congress. Senate. *The Senate, 1789-1989*, Vol. 2, by Robert C. Byrd. 100th Congress, 1st sess., 1991. S. Doc.100-20. Chapter 8.

Senators Disclose Finances

On May 26, 1913, newly inaugurated President Woodrow Wilson warned the nation of the "extraordinary exertions" that lobbyists were making to kill his tariff reform legislation. Washington, he observed, "has seldom seen so numerous, so industrious, or so insidious a lobby. It is of serious interest to the country that the people at large should have no lobby and be voiceless in these matters, while great bodies of astute men seek to create an artificial opinion and to overcome the interests of the public for their private profit."

For the first time in 18 years, Democrats controlled both houses of Congress and the White House. President Wilson had made tariff reduction his top legislative priority. When the House easily approved the administration's bill, opponents believed they could stop it in the Senate, where Democrats held only a three-vote majority. This triggered the fierce lobbying campaign that so alarmed the president.

Within a week of the president's warning, on June 2, 1913, the Senate launched a formal investigation of the president's charges, instructing the Judiciary Committee "to report within ten days the names of all lobbyists attempting to influence such pending legislation and the methods which they have employed to accomplish their ends."

In its first 20th-century step toward public financial disclosure, the Senate required all of its members to explain under oath whether they had assets that might benefit from passage of any currently pending legislation. For six days, from morning to late evening, senators in groups of four paraded before a special Judiciary subcommittee to answer 11 prearranged questions. Humor and irony enriched their responses as members denied any dealings with "insidious" lobbyists. While the subcommittee struggled to define a "lobbyist," insidious or otherwise, Republicans joked that they had found one in President Wilson. Why not subpoena him to explain rumors that he planned to deny presidential patronage to Democrats who voted against the administration?

Proving that there is nothing so easy to start, or so difficult to end, as a congressional investigation, the "lobby committee" moved quickly from media frenzy to quiet obscurity, as it shifted its attention from 96 senators to scores of lobbyists in the weeks ahead. Although no "improper influences" were discovered, by temporarily weakening lobbying pressures on senators, this unique investigation gave Woodrow Wilson his first important legislative victory when Congress enacted the lower tariff rates he had championed.

This cartoon depicts Woodrow Wilson cutting into the Capitol dome with a knife labeled "lobby investigation," releasing birds labeled "lobbyists."

Further Reading

U.S. Congress. Senate. Committee on the Judiciary. *Maintenance of a Lobby to Influence Legislation.* Hearings before a Subcommittee, 63rd Cong., 1st sess. (1913).

March 9, 1914

Smoking Ban

On March 9, 1914, the Senate unanimously agreed to ban smoking in its chamber. Although senators never smoked in the chamber during public sessions, they happily brought out their cigars whenever the Senate went into executive session to consider nominations and treaties. During most executive sessions, until 1929, doorkeepers cleared the galleries and locked the doors. No longer on public display, members removed their ties and jackets, and lit their cigars. In this relaxed setting, senators more readily resolved their differences over controversial nominees and complex treaties.

In 1914, South Carolina Democrat Benjamin Tillman was one of the Senate's most senior members. Always a controversial figure, Tillman was best remembered for a speech at the 1896 Democratic National Convention in which he prodded President Grover Cleveland to adopt policies that would aid economically strapped farmers of the South. Otherwise, he promised, he would go to the White House and "poke old Grover with a pitchfork." For the rest of his colorful career, the fiery South Carolina senator would be known as "Pitchfork Ben."

After 1910, however, a series of strokes slowed his pace. His precarious medical condition led him to try various unconventional health regimens. They included deep breathing, drinking a gallon of water each day, a vegetarian diet, and avoidance of tobacco.

Concerned for his own well being, along with that of his colleagues, in the often smoke-filled chamber that he likened to a "beer garden," Tillman introduced a resolution to ban smoking there. Noting the high death rate among incumbent senators—within the previous four years 14 had died, along with the vice president and sergeant at arms—he surveyed all members. Non-smokers responded that they would like to support him, but worried that their smoking colleagues would consider this a selfish gesture.

The majority of smokers, however, responded in the Senate's best collegial tradition. They saw no reason why an old and sick senator should be driven from the chamber, his state deprived of its full and active representation, merely for the gratification of "a very great pleasure." In this spirit, the Senate adopted Tillman's resolution.

Following his death four years later, the Senate kept the restriction in force. The language of the Senate rule was drafted broadly. It prohibits not only the actual act of smoking, but also—perhaps to avoid the temptation to sneak a puff—the carrying into the chamber of "lighted cigars, cigarettes, or pipes."

Benjamin Tillman, senator from South Carolina (1895-1918).

Further Reading

Simkins, Francis Butler. *Pitchfork Ben Tillman: South Carolinian*. Baton Rouge: Louisiana State University Press, 1944.

July 2, 1915

Bomb Rocks the Capitol

A solitary figure slipped quietly into the Capitol on the Friday afternoon leading to a Fourth of July weekend. He cradled a small package containing three sticks of dynamite. The former professor of German at Harvard University, Erich Muenter, also known as Frank Holt, came to Washington to deliver an explosive message. Although the Senate had been out of session since the previous March and was not due to reconvene until December, Muenter headed for the Senate Chamber. Finding the chamber doors locked, he decided that the adjacent Senate Reception Room would serve his purposes. He worked quickly, placing his deadly package under the Senate's telephone switchboard, whose operator had left for the holiday weekend. After setting the timing mechanism for a few minutes before midnight to minimize casualties, he walked to Union Station and purchased a ticket for the midnight train to New York City.

At 20 minutes before midnight, as he watched from the station, a thunderous explosion rocked the Capitol. The blast nearly knocked Capitol police officer Frank Jones from his chair at the Senate wing's east front entrance. Ten minutes earlier, the lucky Jones had closed a window next to the switchboard. A 30-year police veteran, the officer harbored a common fear that one day the Capitol dome would fall into the rotunda. For a few frantic moments, he believed that day had come. Jones then entered the Reception Room and observed its devastation—a shattered mirror, broken window glass, smashed chandeliers, and pulverized plaster from the frescoed ceiling.

In a letter to the *Washington Evening Star,* published after the blast, Muenter attempted to explain his outrageous act. Writing under an assumed name, he hoped that the detonation would "make enough noise to be heard above the voices that clamor for war. This explosion is an exclamation point in my appeal for peace." The former German professor was particularly angry with American financiers who were aiding Great Britain against Germany in World War I, despite this country's official neutrality in that conflict.

Arriving in New York City early the next morning, Muenter headed for the Long Island estate of J. P. Morgan, Jr. Morgan's company served as Great Britain's principal U.S. purchasing agent for munitions and other war supplies. When Morgan came to the door, Muenter pulled a pistol, shot him, and fled. The financier's wounds proved superficial and the gunman was soon captured. In jail, several days later, Muenter took his own life.

Erich Muenter, a.k.a. Frank Holt, after his capture in New York.

Further Reading

U.S. Congress. Senate. *History of the United States Capitol: A Chronicle of Design, Construction, and Politics,* by William C. Allen. 106th Congress, 2d sess., 2001. S. Doc. 106-29.

March 8, 1917

Cloture Rule

Woodrow Wilson considered himself an expert on Congress—the subject of his 1884 doctoral dissertation. When he became president in 1913, he announced his plans to be a legislator-in-chief and requested that the President's Room in the Capitol be made ready for his weekly consultations with committee chairmen. For a few months, Wilson kept to that plan. Soon, however, traditional legislative-executive branch antagonisms began to tarnish his optimism. After passing major tariff, trade, and banking legislation in the first two years of his administration, Congress slowed its pace.

By 1915, the Senate had become a breeding ground for filibusters. In the final weeks of the Congress that ended on March 4, one administration measure related to the war in Europe tied the Senate up for 33 days and blocked passage of three major appropriations bills. Two years later, as pressure increased for American entry into that war, a 23-day, end-of-session filibuster against the president's proposal to arm merchant ships also failed, taking with it much other essential legislation. For the previous 40 years, efforts in the Senate to pass a debate-limiting cloture rule had come to nothing. Now, in the wartime crisis environment, President Wilson lost his patience.

Decades earlier, he had written in his doctoral dissertation, "It is the proper duty of a representative body to look diligently into every affair of government and to talk much about what it sees." On March 4, 1917, as the 64th Congress expired without completing its work, Wilson held a decidedly different view. Calling the situation unparalleled, he stormed that the "Senate of the United States is the only legislative body in the world which cannot act when its majority is ready for action. A little group of willful men, representing no opinion but their own, have rendered the great government of the United States helpless and contemptible." The Senate, he demanded, must adopt a cloture rule.

On March 8, 1917, in a specially called session of the 65th Congress, the Senate agreed to a rule that essentially preserved its tradition of unlimited debate. The rule required a two-thirds majority to end debate and permitted each member to speak for an additional hour after that before voting on final passage. Over the next 46 years, the Senate managed to invoke cloture on only five occasions.

The President's Room in the U.S. Capitol, where President Wilson hoped to meet weekly with committee chairmen.

Further Reading
U.S. Congress. Senate. *The Senate, 1789-1989*, by Robert C. Byrd, Vol. 2. 100th Congress, 1st sess., 1991. S. Doc.100-20. Chapter 5.

A Senator Attacks a Constituent

*Henry Cabot Lodge,
senator from Massachusetts
(1893-1924).*

On rare occasions throughout the Senate's history, frustrated constituents have physically attacked senators. In 1921, a man bearing a grudge about a Nevada land deal entered the Russell Building office of Nevada Senator Charles Henderson. He calmly pulled a pistol, shot the senator in the wrist, and then meekly surrendered. Henderson was not seriously hurt. In 1947, a former Capitol policeman fired a small pistol at his Senate patron, John Bricker, as the Ohio senator boarded a Senate subway car. Neither of the two shots hit Bricker, who had crouched down in the car and ordered the operator to "step on it."

There have also been rare instances of physical violence between senators. In 1902, South Carolina Senator Ben Tillman landed a blow to the face of his home-state colleague John McLaurin after the latter senator questioned his motives and integrity (see "Senate Fistfight," February 22, 1902). In 1964, South Carolina's Strom Thurmond engaged in a wrestling match outside a committee meeting room with his Texas colleague Ralph Yarborough (see "Senators Wrestle to Settle Nomination," July 9, 1964).

But only once, as far as we know, has a senator attacked a constituent. On April 2, 1917, a minor-league baseball player from Boston named Alexander Bannwart and two other antiwar demonstrators visited Massachusetts Senator Henry Cabot Lodge in his Capitol office. They had come to protest President Woodrow Wilson's request for a congressional declaration of war against Germany. They sought out Lodge because he was their senator and an influential member of the committees on Foreign Relations and Naval Affairs.

Four Boston newspapers carried accounts of that confrontation, and the accounts differed according to the respective papers' attitudes about Lodge, the war, and baseball players. They agreed only that there was an angry exchange of the words "coward" and "liar." As tempers flared and shoving began, the 67-year-old senator struck the 36-year-old ball player in the jaw. Capitol police quickly arrested the visitor.

Hours later, the senator announced that he was too busy to press charges against his constituent. And two days later, on April 4, 1917, Lodge joined the majority of his colleagues in a vote of 82 to 6 to enter World War I. Caught up in the surging tide of patriotic spirit, the constituent announced that he had changed his mind about the war and he marched off to enlist.

Further Reading
Garraty, John A. *Henry Cabot Lodge*. New York: Alfred A. Knopf, 1953.

October 6, 1917

La Follette Defends "Free Speech in Wartime"

With only 26 hours remaining in the life of the 64th Congress on March 3, 1917, Progressive Republican Senator Robert La Follette of Wisconsin launched a filibuster. At issue was whether the Senate would pass House-approved legislation to arm merchant ships against a renewed campaign of German submarine attacks. Seeing passage of this measure as taking the nation closer to intervening in World War I, La Follette sought a national referendum to demonstrate his belief that most Americans opposed that course.

A dozen senators who agreed with La Follette's tactic spoke around the clock until 9:30 on the morning of March 4. When La Follette rose to deliver the concluding remarks, the presiding officer recognized only those who opposed the filibuster. The Wisconsin insurgent erupted with white-hot rage and screamed for recognition. While Democrats swarmed around the furious senator to prevent him from hurling a brass spittoon at the presiding officer, Oregon Senator Harry Lane spotted a pistol under the coat of Kentucky Senator Ollie James. Lane quickly decided that if James reached for the weapon, he would attack him with a steel blade that he carried in his pocket. While La Follette dared anyone to carry him off the floor, the Senate ordered him to take his seat. He then blocked a series of unanimous consent agreements to take up the bill, which died at noon with the 64th Congress.

Weeks later, only six senators, including La Follette, voted against the declaration of war. As he continued to speak out against U.S. involvement, a Senate colleague called him "a pusillanimous, degenerate coward."

Following a September 20 speech, which La Follette delivered extemporaneously in Minnesota, a hostile press misquoted La Follette as supporting Germany's sinking of the *Lusitania*. His state legislature condemned him for treason. In the Senate, members introduced resolutions of expulsion.

On October 6, 1917, in response to these charges, La Follette delivered the most famous address of his Senate career—a classic defense of the right to free speech in times of war. Although this three-hour address won him many admirers, it also launched a Senate investigation into possible treasonable conduct.

Early in 1919, as the end of hostilities calmed the heightened wartime emotions, the Senate dismissed the pending expulsion resolutions and paid La Follette's legal expenses. Forty years later, when the Senate named five of its most outstanding former members, the honored group included Robert M. La Follette.

This cartoon shows Senator John Williams of Mississippi charging Senator Robert La Follette of Wisconsin with making a disloyal speech—a reference to a speech La Follette had given on September 20, 1917, in Minnesota.

Further Reading

U.S. Congress. Senate. *The Senate, 1789-1989*, Vol. 3: *Classic Speeches, 1830-1993*, by Robert C. Byrd. 100th Congress, 1st sess., 1994. S. Doc.100-20. Chapter 26.

A Vote for Women

Suffragists parading in New York City with a banner reading, "President Wilson favors votes for women."

On the morning of September 30, 1918, President Woodrow Wilson hoped that his trip to Capitol Hill would change the course of American history. In a 15-minute address to the Senate, he urged members to adopt a constitutional amendment giving American women the right to vote. The House of Representatives had approved the amendment months earlier, but Senate vote counters predicted that without the president's help, they would miss the required two-thirds majority by two votes.

Until the end of the Civil War, nearly every state prohibited women from voting. The 1868 and 1870 ratification of the 14th and 15th Amendments, which provided voting rights for African-American men, spurred women's rights advocates to seek a women's suffrage amendment.

The first such amendment was offered in the Senate in 1868, but it got nowhere. Ten years later, the Senate Committee on Privileges and Elections held hearings on a renewed proposal. As suffragists pled their cause in the packed hearing room, committee members rudely read newspapers, or stared at the ceiling. Then they rejected the amendment.

In 1882, as pressure mounted, the Senate appointed a Select Committee on Woman Suffrage, which favorably reported the amendment. Opposition forces, including a solid bloc of southern senators, derailed that proposal, and the many that followed, because of their concern that it would extend voting rights to African-American women. Others worried that newly enfranchised women temperance advocates would use their votes to outlaw the sale of alcoholic beverages.

By 1912, the number of states that allowed women to vote had risen to nine—mostly in the West. In January 1913, a delegation of suffragists presented to the Senate petitions signed by 200,000 Americans.

By 1918, President Wilson had dropped his previously indifferent attitude and fully supported the constitutional amendment. In his September 30th speech to the Senate, he cited the role of women in supporting the nation's involvement in World War I. "We have made partners of the women in this war," he said. "Shall we admit them only to a partnership of suffering and sacrifice and toil, and not to a partnership of privilege and right?" Despite his oratory, the president failed to pry loose the needed two votes and the amendment again died.

Finally, in 1919, a new Congress brought an increase in the ranks of the amendment's supporters, permitting adoption of what would become the Constitution's 19th Amendment—52 years after it was first introduced in the Senate.

Further Reading

Flexner, Eleanor. *Century of Struggle: The Woman's Rights Movement in the United States.* Cambridge, Mass.: Belknap Press of Harvard University Press, 1996.

November 5, 1918

Jeannette Rankin Runs for the Senate

No history of American representative government could properly be written without a major reference to Representative Jeannette Rankin. The Montana Republican carries the distinction of being the first woman elected to the U.S. Congress. That singular event occurred in 1916. A year later, she earned a second distinction by joining 49 of her House colleagues in voting against U.S. entry into World War I. That vote destroyed her prospects for reelection in 1918.

Over the next 20 years, Rankin tirelessly campaigned for world peace. In 1940, riding a tide of isolationism, she won her second term in the House. The December 1941 Japanese attack on Pearl Harbor put an end to isolationism, but Rankin remained true to her anti-war beliefs, becoming the only member of Congress to vote against declaring war against Japan.

What is less well known about Jeannette Rankin is that she was the first woman to organize a major campaign for a seat in the U.S. Senate. After her 1917 vote opposing World War I, she knew she stood no chance of winning a seat in a congressional district that the state legislature had recently reshaped with a Democratic majority. Instead, she placed her hopes for continuing her congressional career on being able to run state-wide as a candidate for the Senate. Narrowly defeated in the Republican primary, she launched a third-party campaign for the general election.

Although unsuccessful in her 1918 Senate race, Rankin helped destroy negative public attitudes about women as members of Congress. During her second House term in 1941, she served with six other women members, including Maine's Margaret Chase Smith. Those members carefully avoided making an issue of their gender. Rankin agreed with a colleague's famous comment, "I'm no lady. I'm a member of Congress."

Rankin and Margaret Smith followed separate paths. One promoted pacifism; the other advocated military preparedness. Rankin respected Smith as the first woman to serve in both houses of Congress. Shortly before Rankin's death in 1973, however, prospects for women in the Senate looked bleak. Margaret Smith had lost her bid for a fifth term. During the next six years, no woman served in the Senate, and not until 1992 would more than two serve simultaneously.

Three-quarters of a century separated Rankin's 1918 Senate campaign from that 1992 turning point. Since then, the slowly increasing number of women members has become the norm rather than the exception.

Jeannette Rankin became the first woman to organize a major campaign for a seat in the U.S. Senate.

Further Reading
Smith, Norma. *Jeannette Rankin: America's Conscience*. Helena: Montana Historical Society Press, 2002.

November 19, 1919

A Bitter Rejection

This Clifford Berryman cartoon, published on September 5, 1919, depicts Henry Cabot Lodge, chairman of the Senate Foreign Relations Committee, escorting the battered Treaty of Versailles out of a room labeled, "Operating Room, Senate Committee on Foreign Relations."

When members of the Senate Foreign Relations Committee learned of former President Woodrow Wilson's death in 1924, they asked their chairman, Henry Cabot Lodge, to represent them at the funeral. Informed of this plan, the president's widow sent Lodge the following note: "Realizing that your presence would be embarrassing to you and unwelcome to me, I write to request that you do not attend."

Democrat Wilson and Republican Lodge had disliked one another for years. Among the first to earn doctoral degrees from the nation's newly established graduate schools, each man considered himself the country's preeminent scholar in politics and scorned the other.

The emergency of World War I intensified their rivalry. By 1918, Wilson had been president for nearly six years, while Lodge had represented Massachusetts in the Senate for a quarter century. Both considered themselves experts in international affairs. In setting policy for ending the war, Wilson, the idealist, sought a "peace without victory," while Lodge, the realist, demanded Germany's unconditional surrender.

When the 1918 midterm congressional elections transferred control of the Senate from the Democrats to the Republicans, Lodge became both majority leader and Foreign Relations Committee chairman. Whether Wilson liked it or not, he needed Lodge's active support to ensure Senate approval of the Treaty of Versailles and its provision for a League of Nations on which he had staked so much of his political prestige.

Wilson chose to ignore Lodge. He offended the Senate by refusing to include senators among the negotiators accompanying him to the Paris Peace Conference and by making conference results public before discussing them with committee members. In a flash of anger against what he considered Senate interference, Wilson denounced Lodge and his allies as "contemptible, narrow, selfish, poor little minds that never get anywhere but run around in a circle and think they are going somewhere."

After Lodge's committee added numerous "reservations" and amendments to the treaty, the frustrated president took his campaign to the nation. During a cross-country tour in October 1919, he suffered a physical collapse that further clouded his political judgment.

In November, Lodge sent to the Senate floor a treaty with 14 reservations, but no amendments. In the face of Wilson's continued unwillingness to negotiate, the Senate on November 19, 1919, for the first time in its history, rejected a peace treaty.

Further Reading
Cooper, John Milton, Jr. *Breaking the Heart of the World: Woodrow Wilson and the Fight for the League of Nations.* New York: Cambridge University Press, 2001.

January 15, 1920

Democratic Leadership Deadlock

The death of Senate Democratic Leader Thomas Martin in November 1919 touched off a battle among Senate Democrats that revealed a deeply divided party. A year earlier, the midterm congressional elections had ended six years of Democratic control in the Senate, giving the Republicans a two-vote majority. A week after Martin's death, the Senate rejected President Woodrow Wilson's plan for U.S. participation in the League of Nations by refusing its consent to ratify the Treaty of Versailles. When acting Democratic leader Gilbert Hitchcock visited the White House to discuss a plan to revive the treaty, the bitter president—partially paralyzed following a stroke weeks earlier—refused to see him.

Leaders of both parties wanted the treaty issue resolved so that it would not dominate the 1920 presidential election. With World War I at an end, the American public was losing interest in the treaty controversy and became more focused on domestic issues. Hitchcock eventually gained access to the White House and, with other Senate Democrats, urged the president to soften his opposition in order to salvage the treaty.

In this super-charged political environment, members of the Senate Democratic caucus met on January 15, 1920, to elect a new floor leader. Preliminary headcounts indicated that the two candidates—Hitchcock of Nebraska and Oscar Underwood of Alabama—each had 19 supporters. To break this deadlock, Underwood's allies sought a ruling that would allow Treasury Secretary Carter Glass to vote. The governor of Virginia had recently appointed Glass to fill Martin's seat but Glass was not immediately free to leave the cabinet. Sensing that such an arrangement would taint his claim to the leadership, Underwood agreed to postpone the election for several months.

This situation further aggravated the treaty fight and deepened ill feelings among the Democrats. Lacking the status of elected floor leader, neither Hitchcock nor Underwood was in a position to unite the party to forge a compromise.

This stalemate produced a second defeat for the treaty in March 1920. By the time the Democratic caucus assembled in April to choose its leader, Hitchcock had tired of the battle. He withdrew in favor of Underwood, who won by acclamation. Secretary of State Robert Lansing knew both men well and offered an assessment that may have explained Underwood's victory. "Hitchcock will obey orders. Underwood prefers to give them. One is a lieutenant, the other a commander."

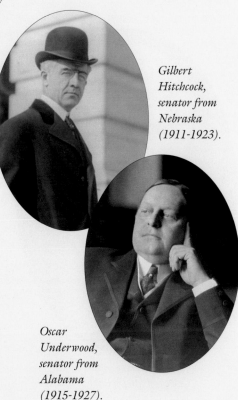

Gilbert Hitchcock, senator from Nebraska (1911-1923).

Oscar Underwood, senator from Alabama (1915-1927).

Further Reading
Cooper, John Milton, Jr. *Breaking the Heart of the World: Woodrow Wilson and the Fight for the League of Nations.* New York: Cambridge University Press, 2001.

Spring Comes to the Senate

In recent times, the Senate has noted the arrival of spring with a poetic speech of welcome by Senator Robert C. Byrd. While Senator Byrd faithfully follows the calendar, senators in the early 20th century heralded that season by following the habits of a junior senator from Colorado named Charles Thomas.

A native of Georgia, Thomas had moved in 1871 to Colorado where he built a successful practice as an attorney for lead mining interests. Although he became chairman of the Colorado Democratic party, Thomas' acerbic manner and unconventional views frustrated his highest political ambition: a seat in the United States Senate. Refusing to be discouraged, he ran in three contests over a period of 24 years, losing each one. Finally, in 1913, at the age of 63, he achieved his goal.

When Thomas reached Washington in January, his new colleagues took note of his rich, full head of hair. Then, several months later, as the month of April brought the year's first spring-like weather, Thomas did something that shocked many senators. He appeared in the Senate quite bald.

As a young man, Thomas had become prematurely bald. Sensitive to cold drafts, he donned a lush toupee during winter months, retiring the headpiece when the weather turned warm. On what he considered the right day in April 1913, Thomas packed his toupee in mothballs and headed off to work. When he reached the Senate Chamber, a doorkeeper blocked his way, explaining that only senators were allowed inside. Thomas responded, "But my friend, I have a right here. I am Senator Thomas of Colorado." "No sir, you couldn't be," said the doorkeeper. "Senator Thomas has a wonderful head of hair." At that moment, Thomas spied his state's other senator, who readily vouched for him.

As Thomas entered the chamber, Illinois Senator J. Hamilton Lewis rose to call attention to an event on a par with the sighting of the first robin of spring. Others joined in, establishing a tradition that lasted for the remainder of Thomas' years in the Senate.

Each spring, newspapers ran accounts similar to one that appeared in the May 12, 1920, *New York Times*. "At two minutes past twelve o'clock noon today, Spring arrived in the Senate Chamber. At that hour, Senator Thomas of Colorado came in without his wig." After that, senators could safely go out and purchase their Palm Beach suits and straw hats.

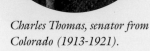

Charles Thomas, senator from Colorado (1913-1921).

Further Reading
"Omen of Spring in Senate," *New York Times*, May 12, 1920, 4.

May 27, 1920

The Senate Eliminates 42 Committees

When Wisconsin's crusading reformer Robert La Follette arrived in the Senate in 1906, he received a form letter from the Republican Committee on Committees inviting him to submit a list of the panels on which he wished to serve. He responded that he had only one preference, the Committee on Interstate Commerce. Aware of La Follette's recent success as Wisconsin's governor in regulating railroads, party leaders saw no reason to place this firebrand on that influential committee. Instead, they awarded him seats on several lesser panels.

In 1906, the Senate maintained 66 standing and select committees—eight more committees than members of the majority party. Although the minority party traditionally received a share of those chairmanships, a majority party freshman like La Follette also had reason to expect one. The large number of committees and the manner of assigning their chairmanships suggests that many of them existed solely to provide office space in those days before the Senate acquired its first permanent office building.

The Committee on Committees did find a chairmanship for La Follette. Years later, he looked back on his appointment to lead the Committee to Investigate the Condition of the Potomac River Front at Washington. "I had immediate visions of cleaning up the whole Potomac River front. Then I found that in all its history, the committee had never had a bill referred to it for consideration, and had never held a meeting." He continued, "My committee room was reached by going down into the sub-cellar of the Capitol, along a dark winding passage lighted by dim skylights that leaked badly, to the room carved out of the terrace on the west side of the Capitol."

Fourteen years later, in 1920, the Senate responded to a post-World War I mood to modernize all levels of governmental operations and decided to do something about its large number of obsolete and redundant committees. That year's *Congressional Directory* listed nearly 80 committees. Among them were the Committee on the Disposition of Useless Papers in the Executive Departments, and the Committee on Revolutionary War Claims—still in business 137 years after the conclusion of that conflict.

On May 27, 1920, with all members assigned private quarters in the 11-year-old office building, the Senate acknowledged that governmental efficiency could extend even to the halls of Congress by quietly abolishing 42 obsolete committees.

The newly opened Senate Office Building (today's Russell Building) featured office space for senators, as well as committee rooms such as this one used for Senate hearings.

Further Reading

McConachie, Lauros G. *Congressional Committees: A Study of the Origins and Development of Our National and Local Legislative Methods.* New York: Thomas Y. Crowell & Co., 1898.
Smith, Steven S., and Christopher J. Deering. *Committees in Congress.* 3rd ed. Washington, DC: CQ Press, 1997.

A Senator Becomes President

What are the chances of being elected president directly from a seat in the Senate? History's answer, at best, is "slim." While 15 of the nation's 43 presidents served in the Senate at some point in their public careers, only two—Warren Harding and John F. Kennedy—won their presidential races as incumbent senators.

In 1832, Henry Clay became the first senatorial incumbent to run. He lost to presidential incumbent Andrew Jackson. Four years later, Daniel Webster tried his luck, but came in a poor fourth against Vice President Martin Van Buren. The campaigns of 1848, 1852, and 1860 included incumbent senators, but we look in vain on the list of that era's presidents for the names of Lewis Cass, John Hale, or Stephen Douglas.

The 1850s opened up another possible route to the White House for incumbent senators—the vice-presidency. In 1852, Democratic Senator William King of Alabama—Franklin Pierce's running mate—became the first incumbent to gain his party's vice-presidential nomination. Soon after he won the election, however, he became ill and went to Cuba to recover. Too ill to return to Washington, he took his vice-presidential oath in Cuba and died soon thereafter.

Since William King's day, 24 incumbent senators have gained major party vice-presidential nominations. Of this number, 13 won the vice-presidency, but only three—Harry Truman, Richard Nixon, and Lyndon Johnson—subsequently became president.

In 1920 Warren Harding, an Ohio Republican, won his party's nomination as a compromise candidate on the 10th ballot. Harding fit a popular image of what a president should look like. Tall and handsome with silver hair and dark eyebrows, he had easily won a Senate seat six years earlier. A cheerful and friendly party loyalist, he seemed to get along well with everyone. While in the Senate, Harding developed a talent for speaking so vaguely on major issues that he was able to appeal to people on both sides of any political question. This served him well in the 1920 presidential campaign. Although his speeches make little sense when read today, they soothed a war-weary nation.

While the Democratic ticket of James Cox and Franklin Roosevelt campaigned frantically throughout the nation, Harding conducted his campaign from his front porch, ever careful to avoid sensitive subjects. On November 2, 1920, the American people rewarded his promise for "a return to normalcy" with the largest margin of victory in any presidential election to that time.

Warren G. Harding, senator from Ohio and Republican nominee for president, posing in the shade of his front porch for Louis Keila, noted sculptor, on October 22, 1920.

Further Reading

Schlesinger, Arthur M., Jr., ed. *Running for President: The Candidates and their Images.* 2 vols. New York: Simon & Schuster, 1994.

CHAPTER V

ERA OF INVESTIGATIONS

1921-1940

Newberry "Condemned"

The 1918 election to fill one of Michigan's U.S. Senate seats proved to be one of the most bitter and costly contests of that era. Its spending excesses prompted widespread calls for campaign finance reform.

To bolster his party's slim Senate majority, President Woodrow Wilson convinced automaker Henry Ford to run in the Michigan Democratic senatorial primary. Trying to improve his chances of victory, the super-rich Ford also entered that state's Republican primary. Although he lost the Republican contest to industrialist Truman Newberry, Ford captured the Democratic nomination and set out to crush Newberry in the general election. In Newberry, Ford had a tough opponent with similarly unlimited financial resources. Making effective use of campaign advertising, Newberry charged Ford with pacifism, anti-Semitism, and favoritism in his efforts to help his son Edsel avoid military service in World War I.

Senate Committee on Privileges and Elections engaged in counting the Ford-Newberry vote.

Newberry narrowly defeated Ford, but charges that he had intimidated voters and violated campaign-spending laws limiting the amount of personal funds candidates could spend on their races clouded his claim to the seat.

The Senate provisionally seated him in May 1919, pending the outcome of an investigation. As that inquiry got underway, a federal grand jury indicted Newberry on several counts of campaign law violations. Despite the senator's assertions that he knew nothing of illegal contributions and disbursements, massive evidence, gathered with the help of agents financed by Henry Ford, indicated otherwise. Found guilty on those charges in March 1920, Newberry launched an appeal that resulted in a May 1921 Supreme Court reversal of his conviction.

The Senate Committee on Privileges and Elections investigated the matter and conducted a recount of the general election ballots. The committee determined that the large amounts spent on Newberry's behalf were not his own funds but were contributed by relatives and friends without his solicitation or knowledge. Consequently, it recommended that the Michigan senator retain his seat.

On January 12, 1922, a narrowly divided Senate affirmed that Newberry had been duly elected, but it nonetheless "severely condemned" his excessive campaign expenditures as "harmful to the honor and dignity of the Senate." In the face of continuing controversy, Newberry resigned from the Senate later that year. The Newberry case led Congress in 1925 to enact a new Federal Corrupt Practices Act, but this statute proved ineffective in containing congressional campaign financial irregularities in the decades ahead.

Further Reading

U.S. Congress. Senate. *United States Senate Election, Expulsion and Censure Cases, 1793-1990*, by Anne M. Butler and Wendy Wolff. 103rd Congress, 1st sess., 1995. S. Doc.103-33.

April 15, 1922

The Senate Investigates "Teapot Dome"

On April 15, 1922, Wyoming Democratic Senator John Kendrick introduced a resolution that set in motion one of the most significant investigations in Senate history. On the previous day, the *Wall Street Journal* had reported an unprecedented secret arrangement in which the secretary of the interior, without competitive bidding, had leased the U.S. naval petroleum reserve at Wyoming's Teapot Dome to a private oil company. Wisconsin Republican Senator Robert La Follette arranged for the Senate Committee on Public Lands to investigate the matter. His suspicions deepened after someone ransacked his quarters in the Senate Office Building.

Expecting this to be a tedious and probably futile inquiry, the committee's Republican leadership allowed the panel's most junior minority member, Montana Democrat Thomas Walsh, to chair the panel. Preeminent among the many difficult questions facing him was, "How did Interior Secretary Albert Fall get so rich so quickly?"

Edward B. McLean, publisher of the *Washington Post,* and personal friend of President Harding, claimed that he had lent Secretary Fall $100,000. Senator Walsh traveled to Florida to question McLean, who pleaded illness as an excuse for not returning to Washington to testify. McLean's testimony revealed that Fall had returned his checks uncashed. When Fall refused to explain the true source of his sudden wealth, the investigation became front-page news.

Eventually, the investigation uncovered Secretary Fall's shady dealings. He had received large sums from Harry Sinclair, president of Mammoth Oil Company, which leased Teapot Dome, and from Edward Doheny, whose Pan-American Petroleum Company had been awarded drilling rights in the naval oil reserve at Elk Hills, California. Senator Walsh became a national hero; Fall became the first former cabinet officer to go to prison.

This and a subsequent Senate inquiry triggered several court cases testing the extent of the Senate's investigative powers. One of those cases resulted in the landmark 1927 Supreme Court decision *McGrain* v. *Daugherty* that, for the first time, explicitly established Congress' right to compel witnesses to testify before its committees.

Edward B. McLean before the Senate committee investigating naval oil leases on March 12, 1924.

Further Reading

Diner, Hasia. "Teapot Dome, 1924." In *Congress Investigates: A Documented History, 1792-1974*, edited by Arthur M. Schlesinger, Jr. and Roger Bruns. 5 vols. New York: Chelsea House Publishers, 1975.

U.S. Congress. Senate. *The Senate, 1789-1989*, Vol. 1, by Robert C. Byrd. 100th Cong., 1st sess., 1988. S. Doc. 100-20.

First Woman Senator

The governor faced a serious political dilemma. He wanted to run for the U.S. Senate, but his earlier opposition to ratification of the Constitution's equal suffrage amendment seriously alienated many of his state's women voters. How could he gain their allegiance?

Rebecca L. Felton, seated, first woman appointed to the U.S. Senate, being greeted by prominent political women in Washington, D.C.

On October 3, 1922, Georgia's Democratic Governor Thomas Hardwick made history by appointing the first woman to a Senate vacancy. He believed this act would appeal to the newly enfranchised women of Georgia. Taking no chances of creating a potential rival for the seat in the upcoming general election, he chose 87-year-old Rebecca Felton. His appointee had led a long and active political life. A well-known suffragist and temperance advocate, she was also an outspoken white supremacist and advocate of racial segregation.

At the time, the Senate was out of session and not expected to convene until after the election, when the appointed senator would have to step aside for her elected replacement. Felton's supporters deluged President Warren Harding with requests that he call a special session of Congress before the November election so that she could be legitimately seated. Harding ignored these pleas. Thus there was little chance that Felton would actually become a senator by taking the required oath in open session.

On election day, despite his political calculations, Hardwick lost to Democrat Walter George. When the Senate convened on November 21, 1922, George astutely stepped aside so that Felton could claim the honor of being the first female senator—if only for a day.

In her address the following day to a capacity audience, the Georgia senator described a cartoon she had received showing the Senate in session. "The seats seemed to be fully occupied, and there appeared in the picture the figure of a woman who had evidently entered without sending in her card. The gentlemen in the Senate took the situation variously," she continued. "Some seemed to be a little bit hysterical, but most of them occupied their time looking at the ceiling," without offering the newcomer a seat. Felton concluded with the following prediction. "When the women of the country come in and sit with you, though there may be but very few in the next few years, I pledge you that you will get ability, you will get integrity of purpose, you will get exalted patriotism, and you will get unstinted usefulness."

Further Reading
Talmadge, John E. "The Seating of the First Woman in the United States Senate." *Georgia Review* 10 (Summer 1956): 168-74.

Senate Majority Elects Minority Chairman

On January 9, 1924, "one of the most stubborn fights over a chairmanship in the history of the Senate" reached a bitter and exhausting conclusion. For the first time, a minority-party senator won election as chairman of a major committee over the majority party's determined opposition. At stake was leadership of the powerful Senate Interstate Commerce Committee.

This event occurred at a time of great political volatility. Several months earlier, President Warren Harding's unexpected death had abruptly placed Calvin Coolidge in the White House. Senate Republican Majority Leader Henry Cabot Lodge of Massachusetts, in the Senate since 1893, and that body's most senior member, hated Coolidge, his bitter home-state party rival. The 1922 mid-term elections had reduced his party's majority by eight seats, leaving 51 Republicans—whose ranks included seven independent-minded members—and 45 Democrats. Aging and irritable, Lodge showed little interest by 1924 in working for unity in a party already deeply divided between conservative and progressive factions. With that year's presidential election campaign just ahead, prospects for enacting a substantive legislative program seemed remote.

When the 68th Congress convened in December 1923, Iowa's conservative Republican senator, Albert Cummins, expected to continue serving as Interstate Commerce Committee chairman and Senate president pro tempore—posts that he had held since the Republicans took control of the Senate in 1919. As president pro tempore at a time when there was no vice president, Cummins stood to gain both prestige and the vice president's higher salary. Deeply opposed to Cummins, Progressive Republicans hoped to gain the Interstate Commerce Committee's chairmanship for that panel's second most senior member, Wisconsin progressive Robert La Follette. To accomplish this, they threatened to shift their vital seven votes to another candidate for president pro tempore unless Cummins stepped aside as committee chair. Conservative and mainstream Republicans, however, feared La Follette's influence as committee chair and encouraged Cummins to drop his bid for the president pro tempore's post in order to preserve his chairmanship. For his part, Cummins decided to fight for both positions.

The resulting struggle kept the Senate in turmoil for more than a month into the new session. Neither Cummins nor the committee's ranking Democrat, South Carolina's Ellison Smith, could muster the necessary majority. On January 9, 1924, after 32 ballots, the Progressive Republicans, in their desperation to block Cummins, reluctantly provided the votes necessary to elect Democrat Smith.

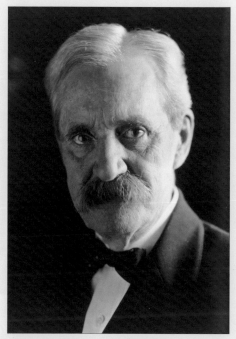

Albert Baird Cummins, senator from Iowa (1908-1926).

Further Reading

"Senate's 32d Vote Elects E. D. Smith ," *New York Times*, January 10, 1924, 2.

Radio Days

"It will profoundly change the Senate." "It will benefit media-savvy members and force the retirement of those who are uncomfortable with the new technology." These concerns were commonly heard during the early 1980s debate over whether to permit the televising of Senate floor proceedings, but they originated 60 years earlier in response to another media innovation—radio.

World War I produced significant advances in the field of radio technology. In the aftermath of that conflict, commercial radio stations began operation throughout the nation and radio pioneers explored the public service and entertainment potential of this new medium.

In the Senate, it took a new member with a background in radio to grasp possibilities for applying this emerging technology to the chamber operations. Soon after Nebraska Republican Robert Howell took his seat in 1923, he proposed establishment of a joint army-navy commission to examine the use of radio in the Senate. Howell had served as a naval submarine officer during World War I and later conducted a survey of radio uses in Europe.

Senators Joseph T. Robinson of Arkansas (1913-1937), left, and Charles Curtis of Kansas (1907-1913, 1915-1929), rehearse for a 1928 talk on Congress to be delivered over radio.

The first part of Howell's proposal addressed the problem of chronically poor acoustics in the Senate Chamber by requesting technical advice on placement of an "apparatus" there to allow each senator at his desk to "individually and clearly hear, without the use of a head receiver, the proceedings of the Senate at all times in whatever tone of voice conducted." The proposal's second portion sought information on broadcasting Senate proceedings to the nation through the radio facilities of the war and navy departments.

Freshman Howell immediately ran into opposition from Republican Majority Leader Henry Cabot Lodge, a 30-year veteran. Citing the cost and disruption of equipment installation, Lodge concluded, "I do not at all know whether or not the Senate desires to have everything which is said here broadcasted." Other senators treated Howell's proposal as a joke, with one promising support only if the Senate voted to install a radio transmitter in the White House "so we can hear what is going on down there." Another warned about extended sessions. "We stay here twice too long as it is. If we put in a radio, we'd never adjourn."

Although the Senate eventually agreed to Howell's resolution on May 2, 1924, it took no follow-up action. Decades passed before the installation in 1971 of an effective voice amplification system in the chamber and the inauguration in 1986 of regular radio and television coverage of floor proceedings.

Further Reading
U.S. Congress. *Congressional Record*, 68th Congress, 1st sess., pp. 5122-24, 7666.

January 28, 1925

The Senate Judiciary Committee Grills a Nominee

On January 5, 1925, President Calvin Coolidge nominated Attorney General Harlan Fiske Stone to a vacancy on the U.S. Supreme Court. Commentators around the nation readily agreed that Stone's character, learning, and temperament perfectly suited him to the job.

Within days, however, a complication arose that threatened Stone's chances for an easy Senate confirmation. The source of the trouble was Senator Burton K. Wheeler, a progressive Democrat—and former U.S. attorney—from Montana. The previous year, Wheeler had launched an investigation to determine why Stone's predecessor, Attorney General Harry Daugherty, had failed to prosecute government officials implicated in the Teapot Dome oil-leasing scandal. As a result of Wheeler's probe, Daugherty resigned in March 1924. A month later, with Stone settling in as attorney general, a federal grand jury in Montana indicted Senator Wheeler on charges related to the conduct of his private law practice. Seeing the indictment as an effort to discredit his continuing investigation of the Justice Department, Wheeler asked the Senate to examine the charges against him. Following a two-month inquiry, and without waiting for the Montana court to dispose of the case, the Senate overwhelmingly exonerated Wheeler.

The Wheeler case tormented Attorney General Stone for months. Influential friends of Wheeler urged Stone to drop both the Montana case and new information that led Wheeler's opponents to seek a second indictment. Stone explained that he felt honor bound to pursue the second indictment, even though it involved a sitting senator whom the Senate had recently investigated and cleared. The Senate, he said, "is just not the place to determine the guilt or innocence of a man charged with crime."

On January 24, 1925, five days after the Senate Judiciary Committee had recommended Stone's confirmation, Senator Thomas Walsh—Wheeler's Montana colleague and legal counsel—convinced the Senate to return the nomination to committee for further review. Although President Coolidge refused to withdraw the nomination, he agreed to an unprecedented compromise. He would allow Stone to become the first Supreme Court nominee in history to appear before the Senate Judiciary Committee. On January 28, 1925, Stone's masterful performance during five hours of public session testimony cleared the way for his quick confirmation.

Senator Wheeler soon won acquittal of all charges. Not until 1955, however, did the Senate Judiciary Committee routinely adopt the practice, based on the precedent established by the Stone nomination, of requiring all Supreme Court nominees to appear in person.

From left to right, *Senator Albert B. Cummins of Iowa, Attorney General Harlan Fiske Stone, and Senator Thomas J. Walsh of Montana, on the day of Stone's public testimony before the Senate Judiciary Committee.*

Further Reading

Abraham, Henry J. *Justices, Presidents and Senators: A History of the U.S. Supreme Court Appointments from Washington to Clinton.* 4th ed. Lanham, MD: Rowman & Littlefield Publishers, 1999.

Wheeler, Burton K. *Yankee from the West: The Candid Story of the Freewheeling U.S. Senator from Montana.* Garden City, N.Y.: Doubleday & Company, 1962.

June 1, 1926

The American Senate Published

Until the 1930s, newly elected vice presidents tradition-ally went to the Senate Chamber on inauguration day to deliver a brief speech. They generally took this occasion to ask the senators over whom they would preside for the next four years to forgive them for not knowing much about parliamentary procedure and to bear with them while they tried to learn. This polite tradition sustained a major jolt in 1925. On that occasion, Vice President Charles Dawes, a conser-vative Republican, unleashed a blistering attack on a small group of progressive Republican senators who had filibustered legislation at the end of the previous session.

Eight years earlier, the Senate had adopted its first cloture rule, which allowed two-thirds of the senators present and voting to take steps to end debate on a particular measure. Dawes thought the Senate should revise that rule, making it easier to apply by allowing a simple majority to close debate. The existing two-thirds rule, he thundered, "at times enables Senators to consume in oratory those last precious minutes of a session needed for momentous decisions," thereby placing great power in the hands of a few senators. Unless Rule 22 was liberal-ized, it would "lessen the effectiveness, prestige, and dignity of the United States Senate." Dawes' unexpected diatribe infuriated senators of all philosophical leanings, who believed that the chamber's rules were none of the vice president's business.

On June 1, 1926, Columbia University professor Lindsay Rogers published a book entitled *The American Senate*. His purpose was to defend the Senate tradition of virtually unlimited debate, except in times of dire national emergency. Professor Rogers fundamentally disagreed with Vice President Dawes. In his memorably stated view, the "undemocratic, usurping Senate is the indispensable check and balance in the American system, and only complete freedom of debate allows it to play this role." "Adopt [majority] cloture in the Senate," he argued, "and the character of the American Government will be profoundly changed."

Written in a breezy journalistic style, Rogers' *The American Senate* encompassed issues beyond debate limitation. For example, he believed members spent too much time on trivial issues and that professional investigators—not members—should handle congressional inquiries. Although now long forgotten, his work set the agenda for other outside scholarly observers and became one of the most influential books about the Senate to appear during the first half of the 20th century.

Vice President Charles Dawes wanted the Senate to change its cloture rule, as depicted in this cartoon, which shows Dawes as a circus ringmaster trying to get an elephant labeled "Senate Majority" to jump through a hoop labeled "Rules Revision."

Further Reading
Rogers, Lindsay. *The American Senate*. New York: A.A. Knopf, 1926.

May 11, 1928

Senators Vote to Knock Out Walls

It was predictable. Elect a former public health commissioner to the United States Senate and wait for the recommendations about an unhealthy working environment. Royal Copeland entered the Senate in 1923 after a five-year term as commissioner of the New York City board of health. A practicing physician and a medical educator, the New York senator wasted little time in reaching a conclusion about the quality of the air in the Senate Chamber. He cited the deaths of 34 incumbent senators over the past 12 years and suggested that their lives had probably been shortened by having to work in that chamber. In the winter, the dry heated air was blamed for the spread of influenza, bronchitis, and the common cold; in the summer, excessive heat and humidity sapped members' energy and tested their tempers.

In June 1924, as the increasingly warm late spring days again called attention to this perennial problem, the Senate adopted Senator Copeland's resolution directing Capitol officials to consult with leading architects to develop a plan that would improve the "living conditions of the Senate Chamber."

The firm of Carrere & Hastings, which had designed the Russell Senate Office Building a generation earlier, quickly produced the requested plan. The architects proposed converting the chamber's configuration to that of a semi-circular amphitheater, lowering the ceiling for improved hearing, and removing several walls to extend the room to the Capitol's northern wall.

In removing these interior walls, the Senate would have to sacrifice the Marble Room, the President's Room, and the vice president's formal office. To brighten the chamber's dreary interior, Carrere & Hastings proposed the addition of three two-story-high windows in the outer wall, along with a ventilating apparatus to draw fresh air into the quarters.

On May 11, 1928, the Senate approved funding of $500,000 to accomplish the project. Five days later, however, Senator Copeland abruptly requested that his proposal be "indefinitely postponed" because it was "no longer necessary." The reason for this sudden reversal lay in a separate appropriation of $323,000 to produce a ventilation system that had been endorsed by a team of public health experts. Tests demonstrated that the chamber could be made comfortable and healthy—without the cost and disruption of knocking down walls—through an innovation, designed by the Carrier Corporation, known as "manufactured weather." Work began early the following year and, by August 1929, the Senate had in place its first air conditioning system.

Senator Royal S. Copeland of New York (1923-1938), left, advocate for better air quality in the Senate, inspecting one of the ventilating fans that supply air to the Senate Chamber.

Further Reading

U.S. Congress. Senate. *History of the United States Capitol: A Chronicle of Design, Construction, and Politics*, by William C. Allen. 106th Congress, 2d sess., 2001. S. Doc. 106-29.

Senator Censured in Lobbyist Case

When former Senator Hiram Bingham died in 1956, one obituary writer observed that the Connecticut Republican "had crammed [many] careers into his lifetime, any one of which might have sufficed for most men."

Over the course of his 80 years, Bingham had been a scholar, explorer, aviator, businessman, and politician. Born in 1875, he earned degrees from Yale, Berkeley, and Harvard. With a doctorate in South American history, he traveled that continent extensively. In 1911, he became the first explorer to uncover the fabulous Incan ruins of Machu Picchu. Bingham taught at Harvard, Yale, and Princeton and wrote more than a dozen books related to South American geography and history. In the early 1920s, he entered Connecticut politics and won races for lieutenant governor, governor, and U.S. senator.

This genial and accomplished man appeared destined for a distinguished Senate career. Then he made a poor decision. As a member of the Senate Finance Committee in September 1929, Bingham asked the Connecticut Association of Manufacturers to detail one of its lobbyists to his office during the committee's consideration of tariff legislation. When the Finance Committee closed its deliberations to the public, Bingham placed the lobbyist on the Senate payroll so he could attend those sessions as a Senate staffer. He neglected, however, to tell other committee members that the lobbyist also remained on the association's payroll. As he had salary funds for only one staff position, Bingham executed a plan that was irregular even by the murky standards of his day. His own clerk, although still performing his duties, went off the Senate payroll for the duration of the hearings. The lobbyist then passed his Senate salary on to the clerk.

When an ongoing Senate Judiciary subcommittee investigation discovered this arrangement, Bingham defended it by saying that the association's representative was not the kind of lobbyist who visited members "trying to get them to do something they did not want to do." The subcommittee condemned this relationship, but recommended no formal Senate action. The matter would have died there but for Bingham's decision to attack the subcommittee's inquiry as a partisan witch hunt. This awakened the Senate's interest and resulted in a resolution of censure. On November 4, 1929, the Senate voted 54 to 22 to censure Bingham. After leaving the Senate following the 1932 Democratic electoral landslide, he explored new careers, including that of lobbyist.

Senator Hiram Bingham of Connecticut (1924-1933), left, lands in an autogiro on the Capitol Plaza in 1931.

Further Reading

Bingham, Alfred M. *Portrait of an Explorer: Hiram Bingham, Discoverer of Machu Picchu*. Ames: Iowa State University Press, 1989.

Bingham, Woodbridge. *Hiram Bingham: A Personal History*. Boulder: Bin Lan Zhen Publishers, 1989.

U.S. Congress. Senate. *United States Senate Election, Expulsion and Censure Cases, 1793-1990* by Anne M. Butler and Wendy Wolff. 103rd Cong., 1st sess., 1995. S. Doc. 103-33.

November 24, 1929

Senator Francis Warren, Last Union Vet, Dies

Just before Thanksgiving Day in 1929, the Senate mourned the loss of one of its best-known members. When he died on November 24, 1929, Wyoming's Francis E. Warren had served in the Senate longer than any person in history—37 years. Warren held two other distinctions. He was the last senator to have served on the Union side in the Civil War and among the first to have hired a woman staff member.

Born in Massachusetts in 1844, Warren enlisted in a home-state regiment at the start of the Civil War. During the siege of Port Hudson, Louisiana, in 1863, a Confederate bombardment killed most of his squad's members, but left Warren with a scalp wound and the Congressional Medal of Honor.

After the war, he moved to Wyoming, where he invested successfully in livestock and real estate. Warren's career in Republican politics blossomed along with his financial success. When Wyoming entered the Union in 1890, he became its first governor and, weeks later, one of its first two U.S. senators.

The freshman senator landed choice legislative assignments, including chairmanship of the Committee on Irrigation and Reclamation. From that panel, the shrewd, hard-working, behind-the-scenes operator shaped land-use policies vital to the arid West.

In 1905, the year Warren became chairman of the Senate's Military Affairs Committee, his daughter married an aspiring young army captain named John Pershing. The following year, President Theodore Roosevelt promoted the chairman's son-in-law from captain to general, jumping him ahead of nearly 900 more senior officers. Tragically, in 1915, Warren's daughter and three of his four grandchildren died in a fire at a military base.

The widowed General Pershing went on to become commander of American forces in World War I. As chair or ranking minority member of the Appropriations Committee from 1911 to 1929, Warren had a major role in funding the war effort.

Earlier, in 1900, Warren set a controversial precedent when he hired Leona Wells as one of the first female Senate clerical staff members. The idea that a woman secretary would sit behind a committee's closed doors, listening in on confidential proceedings, scandalized his colleagues. Over the next nearly three decades, Wells demonstrated the groundlessness of those concerns, displaying a competence equal to that of the best male secretaries. By the time of Warren's death, more than 200 women had joined Wells on the Senate payroll, assuming responsibilities that few would have imagined possible in 1900.

General John J. Pershing escorting the widow and son of the late Senator Francis E. Warren of Wyoming following his funeral rites at the Capitol.

Further Reading
"Warren of Wyoming, Dean of Senate, Dies," *New York Times*, November 25, 1929, 1.

Supreme Court Nominee Rejected

The Senate rejected he nomination of Judge John Parker of North Carolina to the Supreme Court by a vote of 39 to 41.

On the seventh of May 1930, the Senate rejected a Supreme Court nominee. What makes this action worth noting today is that it was the Senate's only rejection of a Supreme Court candidate in the 74-year span between 1894 and 1968. Throughout most of the 19th century, the Senate had shown no such reticence, rejecting or otherwise blocking nearly one out of every three high court nominees.

Early in 1930, death claimed two Supreme Court justices. Republican President Herbert Hoover chose former associate justice Charles Evans Hughes to fill the vacant position of chief justice. As the deepening economic depression eroded the president's clout on Capitol Hill, a coalition of southern senators and progressives from other regions sought to block Hughes' confirmation. Some opposed the nominee for his close ties to large corporations, while others believed that his resignation from the court years earlier to run as the 1916 Republican presidential nominee disqualified him from a second chance. After only several days of debate, the Senate confirmed his appointment, but with many members deeply resentful of the manner in which the administration had handled the nomination.

Three weeks after the Hughes confirmation, a second justice died. Hoover believed he had an easily confirmable candidate when he nominated John Parker, a prominent North Carolina Republican and chief judge of the Fourth Circuit Court of Appeals.

Unfortunately for Judge Parker, two actions from his past doomed his chances. Several years earlier, he had delivered a strongly anti-labor opinion that infuriated the American Federation of Labor. The NAACP also joined the opposition in response to remarks Parker had made a decade before. In the midst of a 1920 campaign for governor of North Carolina, Parker had responded to a race-baiting prediction by his opponents that, if elected, he would encourage political participation by black citizens. "The participation of the Negro in politics," said Parker, "is a source of evil and danger to both races and is not desired by the wise men in either race or by the Republican Party of North Carolina." That comment, his anti-labor opinion, and senatorial resentment against the Hoover administration, led to his rejection by a vote of 39 to 41.

Hoover's next nominee, Owen Roberts, cleared the Senate without controversy. Over the following 38 years, until 1968, the Senate approved all high court nominees, conducting roll call votes on only 7 of 24 candidates.

Further Reading

Abraham, Henry J. *Justices, Presidents and Senators: A History of U.S. Supreme Court Appointments From Washington to Clinton.* 4th ed. Lanham, MD: Rowman & Littlefield, 1999.

June 25, 1930

The Senate Considers Banning Dial Phones

The Senate acquired its first operator-assisted telephone in 1881. Over the next half century, telephone operators gradually supplemented telegraph operators in helping senators send their messages. In the spring of 1930, reflecting further advances in communications technology, the following resolution came before the Senate:

Whereas dial telephones are more difficult to operate than are manual telephones; and Whereas Senators are required, since the installation of dial phones in the Capitol, to perform the duties of telephone operators in order to enjoy the benefits of telephone service; and Whereas dial telephones have failed to expedite telephone service; Therefore be it resolved that the Sergeant at Arms of the Senate is authorized and directed to order the Chesapeake and Potomac Telephone Co. to replace with manual phones within 30 days after the adoption of this resolution, all dial telephones in the Senate wing of the United States Capitol and in the Senate office building.

Sponsored by Virginia's Carter Glass, the resolution passed without objection when first considered on May 22, 1930. Arizona's Henry Ashurst praised its sponsor for his restrained language. *The Congressional Record* would not be mailable, he said, "if it contained in print what Senators think of the dial telephone system." When Washington Senator Clarence Dill asked why the resolution did not also ban the dial system from the District of Columbia, Glass said he hoped the phone company would take the hint.

One day before the scheduled removal of all dial phones, Maryland Senator Millard Tydings offered a resolution to give senators a choice. It appeared that some of the younger senators actually preferred the dial phones. This angered the anti-dial senators, who immediately blocked the measure's consideration.

Finally, technology offered a solution. Although the telephone company had pressed for the installation of an all-dial system, it acknowledged that it could provide the Senate with phones that worked both ways. But Senator Dill was not ready to give up. In his experience, the dial phone "could not be more awkward than it is. One has to use both hands to dial; he must be in a position where there is good light, day or night, in order to see the number; and if he happens to turn the dial not quite far enough, then he gets a wrong connection."

Senator Glass, the original sponsor, had the last word before the Senate agreed to the compromise plan. "Mr. President, so long as I am not pestered with the dial and may have the manual telephone, while those who want to be pestered with [the dial] may have it, all right."

Vice President Charles Curtis' secretarial staff. The woman on the left uses a manual phone.

Further Reading

U.S. Congress. *Congressional Record*, 71st Congress, 1st sess., pp. 9341, 11269, 11648-49.

Cotton Tom's Last Blast

This cartoon depicting Senator Thomas Heflin of Alabama (1920-1931), as a shabby vaudeville actor with a sword and spear labeled "Religious Bigotry" was published in April 1928 after Heflin tried to organize a rally in North Carolina against Al Smith, the Catholic governor of New York, who was campaigning for the Democratic nomination for president.

On only the most extraordinary occasions has the Senate permitted a former member to come before the body to address senators. One of those occasions took place on April 26, 1932. Over the fierce objection of the majority leader, the Senate, by a one-vote margin, extended this unusual privilege to former Alabama Senator James Thomas Heflin.

Known as "Cotton Tom" because of his devotion to Alabama's leading agricultural commodity, the flamboyant Heflin built a political career as an unremitting opponent of equal rights for black Americans, women, and Roman Catholics.

In 1908, while a member of the U.S. House of Representatives, he had shot and seriously wounded a black man who confronted him on a Washington streetcar. Although indicted, Heflin succeeded in having the charges dismissed. In subsequent home-state campaigns, he cited that shooting as one of his major career accomplishments.

While firmly against giving the vote to women, Heflin believed they would be grateful for his role in establishing Mother's Day as a national holiday.

Elected to the Senate in 1920, Cotton Tom opposed federal child labor legislation, in part, because it might create a serious shortage of agricultural field hands. His anti-Catholicism and his support for Prohibition led him to oppose his party's 1928 presidential candidate, New York Governor Al Smith.

Heflin's endorsement of Republican Herbert Hoover outraged Alabama's Democratic leaders, who denied him their party's nomination in 1930 to another Senate term. Unstoppable, he ran as an independent, but lost decisively to John Bankhead. When he returned to Washington for a post-election session, he demanded a Senate investigation of voting fraud in hopes of overturning Bankhead's election. The inquiry lasted 15 months and cost $100,000.

In April 1932, with Heflin's term expired and Bankhead seated, the Senate prepared to vote on a committee recommendation against Heflin. At that point, the former senator got his chance to put his case to the full Senate. Originally given two hours, he took five. His face crimson, Heflin punctuated his remarks with vehement gestures and offensive racist jokes. As he thundered to a conclusion, the gallery audience, packed with his supporters, jumped to its feet with a roar of approval and was immediately ordered out of the chamber. Two days later, the Senate overwhelmingly dismissed Heflin's claim. Cotton Tom had delivered his last blast.

Further Reading

U.S. Congress. *Congressional Record*, 72nd Congress, 1st sess., pp. 8918-45.

U.S. Congress. Senate. *United States Senate Election, Expulsion and Censure Cases, 1793-1990*, by Anne M. Butler and Wendy Wolff. 103rd Congress, 1st sess., 1995. S. Doc.103-33.

June 17, 1932

Capitol Besieged

For as long as representative assemblies have existed, in nations throughout the world, images of rebellious troops marching on legislative chambers to enforce their demands have disturbed the sleep of lawmakers. The framers of the U.S. Constitution had those images in mind in 1787 as they convened at Independence Hall in Philadelphia. Just four years earlier, mutinous Revolutionary War soldiers had surrounded that same building during a meeting of the Continental Congress. Seeking immediate congressional action to provide back pay and pensions, the angry militiamen stuck their muskets through open windows and pointed them at the likes of James Madison and Alexander Hamilton. Congress responded to this threat by fleeing Philadelphia and moving the capital to Princeton, New Jersey. Memories of this incident caused the framers to include a provision in the Constitution guaranteeing federal control over the national seat of government.

A century and a half later, on June 17, 1932, another army massed outside the halls of Congress. While the soldiers of that army carried no muskets, they came to pressure Congress to award them a bonus the government had promised in legislation passed eight years earlier for their service in World War I. Under that 1924 law, however, the bonus was not to be paid until 1945. Adjusted to the military record of individual veterans, the award was expected to average $1,000. Desperate and penniless in the depths of the Great Depression, this self-styled Bonus Expeditionary Force of 25,000 veterans came to the nation's capital to lobby for an immediate payment. Two days earlier, the House of Representatives, over its own leadership's objections, bowed to the protestors' demands and passed the necessary legislation.

Now, as the Senate prepared to vote, thousands of veterans rallied outside its chamber on the east front plaza. Capitol police, armed with rifles, took up positions at the building's doors. Despite Democratic Leader Joe Robinson's support for the legislation, most members favored a remedy that would benefit not only the veterans but all economically distressed Americans. The Senate overwhelmingly rejected the bonus bill. Hearing the news, the marchers dispersed peacefully, but remained in Washington at makeshift campsites near Capitol Hill.

A month later, heavily armed federal troops, led by General Douglas MacArthur and Majors Dwight Eisenhower and George Patton, torched and gassed the veterans' camps, killing several and wounding many. Anarchy, both military and civilian, seemed a real possibility in those very dark times.

Bonus army on the Capitol lawn, Washington, D.C., July 13, 1932.

Further Reading

Daniels, Roger. *The Bonus March: An Episode of the Great Depression*. Westport, Conn.: Greenwood Publishers, 1971.
Dickson, Paul and Thomas B. Allen. *The Bonus Army: An American Epic*. New York: Walker & Co., 2004.

The Senate Sacks its Sergeant at Arms

It was every Senate staffer's worst nightmare: to be called to the Senate Chamber to explain a personal action considered disrespectful of the institution. On a cold winter's afternoon in 1933, that is what happened to Sergeant at Arms David Barry. The Senate's chief law enforcement officer, responsible for carrying out orders to arrest others sought by the Senate, was himself commanded to appear before the body. The widely respected official had held his office for nearly 14 years, making him—even today—the third longest-serving sergeant at arms in Senate history. In February 1933, however, Barry faced immediate dismissal and possible trial in federal court on charges of libel.

The 73-year-old Republican had spent most of his life associated with the Senate, previously serving as a page, a secretary to several members, and a newspaper correspondent. Barry's term would have ended four weeks later with the start of the 73rd Congress, when control passed to the Democrats. But members believed that his transgression was so outrageous that it deserved an immediate response.

Late in 1932, Barry drafted an article to be published soon after his retirement. Unfortunately for him, the journal printed it while Barry was still in office. In the article, he criticized reformers who called for major changes in Senate operations. He explained, "there are not many crooks in Congress, that is, out and out grafters; there are not many Senators or Representatives who sell their vote for money, and it is pretty well known who those few are; but there are many demagogues of the kind that will vote for legislation solely because they think that it will help their political and social fortunes."

On February 3, hours after accounts of the article appeared in the morning papers, the Senate summoned Barry to its chamber. The deeply upset sergeant at arms told the assembled senators that he had written the article, "carelessly and thoughtlessly." "My idea was to defend the Senate from the [mistaken] popular belief that there are crooks and grafters here. . . . I do not know of any such men and did not mean to imply that I did." On February 7, 1933, after waiting several days to avoid giving the impression of a hasty judgment, the Senate fired Barry. Thus ended an otherwise distinguished Senate career.

David S. Barry, Senate sergeant at arms (1919-1933).

Further Reading
Barry, David S. "Over the Hill to Demagoguery." *New Outlook* 161 (February 1933): 40-59.
U.S. Congress. *Congressional Record*, 72nd Congress, 2nd sess., pp. 3511-3530.
U.S. Congress. Senate. Committee on the Judiciary. *David S. Barry*. Hearings, 72nd Congress, 2d sess., pp. 1-40.

September 4, 1934

"Merchants of Death"

On a hot Tuesday morning following Labor Day in 1934, several hundred people crowded into the Caucus Room of the Senate Office Building to witness the opening of an investigation that journalists were already calling "historic." Although World War I had been over for 16 years, the inquiry promised to reopen an intense debate about whether the nation should ever have gotten involved in that costly conflict.

The so-called "Senate Munitions Committee" came into being because of widespread reports that manufacturers of armaments had unduly influenced the American decision to enter the war in 1917. These weapons' suppliers had reaped enormous profits at the cost of more than 53,000 American battle deaths. As local conflicts reignited in Europe through the early 1930s, suggesting the possibility of a second world war, concern spread that these "merchants of death" would again drag the United States into a struggle that was none of its business. The time had come for a full congressional inquiry.

To lead the seven-member special committee, the Senate's Democratic majority chose a Republican—42-year-old North Dakota Senator Gerald P. Nye. Typical of western agrarian progressives, Nye energetically opposed U.S. involvement in foreign wars. He promised, "when the Senate investigation is over, we shall see that war and preparation for war is not a matter of national honor and national defense, but a matter of profit for the few."

Over the next 18 months, the "Nye Committee" held 93 hearings, questioning more than 200 witnesses, including J. P. Morgan, Jr., and Pierre du Pont. Committee members found little hard evidence of an active conspiracy among arms makers, yet the panel's reports did little to weaken the popular prejudice against "greedy munitions interests."

The investigation came to an abrupt end early in 1936. The Senate cut off committee funding after Chairman Nye blundered into an attack on the late Democratic President Woodrow Wilson. Nye suggested that Wilson had withheld essential information from Congress as it considered a declaration of war. Democratic leaders, including Appropriations Committee Chairman Carter Glass of Virginia, unleashed a furious response against Nye for "dirt-daubing the sepulcher of Woodrow Wilson." Standing before cheering colleagues in a packed Senate Chamber, Glass slammed his fist onto his desk until blood dripped from his knuckles.

Although the Nye Committee failed to achieve its goal of nationalizing the arms industry, it inspired three congressional neutrality acts in the mid-1930s that signaled profound American opposition to overseas involvement.

The "Dough" Boy (*pencil drawing by Harold M. Talburt*) *depicts international arms traffickers who were believed by some to have been instrumental in drawing the nation into World War I.*

Further Reading

Wiltz, John Edward. "The Nye Munitions Committee, 1934." In *Congress Investigates: A Documented History, 1792-1974*, edited by Arthur M. Schlesinger, Jr. and Roger Bruns. 5 vols. New York: Chelsea House, 1975.

Huey Long Filibusters

Huey P. Long, senator from Louisiana (1932-1935).

Described as "the most colorful, as well as the most dangerous, man to engage in American politics," Louisiana's Huey Pierce Long served in the Senate from 1932 until his assassination less than four years later. Today, visitors to his six-foot, eight-inch bronze likeness in the U.S. Capitol's Statuary Hall see this master of the Senate filibuster captured in mid-sentence.

Long gave the Senate's official reporters of debates a Bible because his wife wanted the reporters to "take those supposed quotations you are making from the Bible and fit them into your speeches exactly as they are in the Scripture." She might also have suggested donating a copy of the U.S. Constitution, for he loved to quote his version of that document as well.

On June 12, 1935, the fiery Louisiana senator began what would become his longest and most dramatic filibuster. His goal was to force the Senate's Democratic leadership to retain a provision, opposed by President Franklin Roosevelt, requiring Senate confirmation for the National Recovery Administration's senior employees. His motive was to prevent his political enemies in Louisiana from obtaining lucrative N.R.A. jobs.

Huey Long spoke for 15 hours and 30 minutes—the second-longest Senate filibuster to that time. As day turned to night, he read and analyzed each section of the Constitution—a document he claimed the president's New Deal programs had transformed to "ancient and forgotten lore."

Looking around the chamber at several of his colleagues dozing at their desks, the Louisiana populist suggested to Vice President John Nance Garner, who was presiding, that every senator should be forced to listen to him until excused. Garner replied, "That would be unusual cruelty under the Bill of Rights." Finished with the Constitution, Long asked for suggestions. "I will accommodate any senator on any point on which he needs advice," he threatened. Although no senator took up his offer, reporters in the press gallery did by sending notes to the floor. When these ran out, he provided his recipes for fried oysters and potlikker. At four in the morning, he yielded to a call of nature and soon saw his proposal defeated. Two days later, however, he was back, refreshed and ready to fight for a liberalization of a controversial new plan—the Social Security Act.

Further Reading
White, Richard D., Jr. *Kingfish*. New York: Random House, 2006.
Williams, T. Harry. *Huey Long*. New York: Knopf, 1969.

First Official Parliamentarian Named

In January 1955, the Senate briefly suspended its proceedings to honor seven staff members. Never before had there been such an occasion. The seven employees shared one characteristic: Each had worked for the Senate for more than half a century.

The best known among this honored group was Charles Watkins. Twenty years earlier, in July 1935, Watkins had been appointed the Senate's first official parliamentarian.

Charles Watkins had arrived in the Senate in 1904 from Arkansas to work as a stenographer. Blessed with a photographic memory, and a curiosity about Senate procedures, he eventually transferred to the Senate floor as journal clerk. In 1919, he started what became a 45-year search of the *Congressional Record*, back to the 1880s, for Senate decisions that interpreted the body's individual standing rules to the legislative needs of the moment.

In 1923, Watkins replaced the ailing assistant secretary of the Senate as unofficial advisor on floor procedure to the presiding officer. From that time, he became the body's parliamentarian, in fact if not in title. Finally, in 1935, at a time when an increased volume of New Deal-era legislation expanded opportunities for procedural confusion and legislative mischief, he gained the actual title.

By 1949, when Watkins reached the age of 70, the Senate authorized hiring of an assistant parliamentarian to give him some relief during the all-night filibusters of that era. On one occasion in the 1950s, he worked a round-the-clock filibuster for 48 unrelieved hours.

In 1964, still on the job after 60 years, Watkins' legendary memory began to fail, causing problems with the advice he gave to presiding officers. At the end of that year's grueling session, Majority Leader Mike Mansfield reluctantly informed the 85-year-old "Charlie" Watkins that his tenure as parliamentarian had come to an end.

At that 1955 tribute to long-serving staff, South Dakota Senator Francis Case praised Watkins' command of parliamentary procedure. "Once his mind clasps a point, it sets like a vise. He is as a seeing-eye dog to guide the newcomers through parliamentary mazes and a rod and a staff to those who preside. It might be said that he sits only a little lower than the angels and dispenses wisdom like an oracle."

Today, the book known as *Riddick's Senate Procedure*, based on the research Watkins began in 1919, and continued by his successor Floyd Riddick, serves as a perfect memorial to this dignified and kindly man of the Senate.

Charles L. Watkins, Senate parliamentarian (1935-1964).

Further Reading

Ritchie, Donald A. "Charles Lee Watkins." In *Arkansas Biography*, edited by Nancy A. Williams. Fayetteville: University of Arkansas Press, 2000.

"Senate Aide Ends A 59-Year Career," *New York Times,* December 31, 1964, 5.

Hugo Black Lobby Investigation

Hugo Lafayette Black, one of the nation's great senators and Supreme Court justices, was born in 1886 in rural central Alabama. When he was only six years old, little Hugo decided that listening to lawyers argue cases in a local courthouse was more fun than playing school-yard games. He loved politics and declared himself a Democrat almost before he could pronounce the word. Upon graduation from the University of Alabama Law School, Black became a police court judge and then a noted labor lawyer.

In 1923, when the Ku Klux Klan controlled the voting machinery in nearly every Alabama county, the politically ambitious Black made a decision that he spent the rest of his life regretting. He joined the Klan. With many Alabama lawyers and jurors members of the Klan, Black equated membership with courtroom success. Realizing his error, he soon resigned, but he enlisted help from Klan leaders in his successful race for the U.S. Senate in 1926.

When the Democrats took control of the Senate in 1933, at the beginning of the New Deal, Hugo Black drew on his skills as a prosecuting attorney to become nationally famous as a congressional investigator. In his aggressive questioning style, he gave witnesses the impression he already had the facts and wished them only to confirm them for the record.

On July 11, 1935, the Senate authorized a special Senate investigation of public utility company lobbyists. Black gained headlines as chairman of the special committee. Congress was then considering legislation designed to break up the giant "power trusts." The Senate inquiry unleashed on members' offices a blizzard of protesting telegrams. Black suspected that the utility lobbyists had orchestrated the campaign. In response, he introduced a bill that required all lobbyists to register their names, salaries, expenses, and objectives with the secretary of the Senate. By subpoenaing lobbyists, company officials, and telegraph office records, he was able to prove that of some 15,000 telegrams sent to Capitol Hill, only three were paid for by private citizens. The rest, he said, were the work of a "high-powered, deceptive, telegram-fixing, letter-framing, Washington-visiting $5 million lobby."

Black's investigation resulted in the first congressional system of lobbyist registration. It also helped him win Franklin Roosevelt's first appointment to the Supreme Court. Despite lingering controversy over his early Klan membership, the former police court judge, between 1937 and 1971, compiled a record as the Court's greatest civil libertarian and defender of the Bill of Rights.

Hugo L. Black, senator from Alabama (1927-1937).

Further Reading

Newman, Roger K. *Hugo Black: A Biography*. New York: Pantheon Books, 1994.

U.S. Congress. Senate. *The Senate, 1789-1989*, Vol. 2, by Robert C. Byrd. 100th Congress, 1st sess., 1991. S. Doc. 100-20. Chapter 22.

U.S. Congress. Senate. Special Committee to Investigate Lobbying Activities. *Investigation of Lobbying Activities: Hearings before a Special Committee to Investigate Lobbying Activities*. 75th Cong., 1st sess., July 12, 1935-April 17, 1936, 6 vols.

Republican Leader Front and Center

At the opening of the 75th Congress on January 5, 1937, Senate Republican Leader Charles McNary anticipated a difficult session. The 1936 congressional elections had produced a Senate with the lopsided party ratio of 76 Democrats to 16 Republicans. On that first day, McNary counted only one advantage—minor though it may have seemed at the time. He had become the first Republican floor leader to occupy a front-row, center-aisle seat in the Senate Chamber.

Until the early 20th century, the Senate operated without majority and minority leaders. In 1885, political scientist Woodrow Wilson wrote, "No one is the Senator. No one may speak for his party as well as for himself; no one exercises the special trust of acknowledged leadership."

In the Senate's earliest decades, leadership came principally from the president pro tempore and chairmen of major committees.

The modern system of Senate party leadership emerged slowly in the years from the 1880s to the 1910s. During this period, both parties organized formal caucuses and selected caucus chairmen who began to assume many of the agenda-setting roles of the modern floor leader.

Struggles with increasingly powerful presidents, the crisis of World War I, and the battle over the League of Nations spurred the further evolution of Senate floor leadership. While party caucuses began formally to designate their floor leaders, they gave little thought to where those leaders should be located within the Senate Chamber. If the leaders had desired to claim the front-row, center-aisle desks that have become the modern symbol of their special status, the presence of senior members comfortably lodged in those places dashed their hopes.

Finally, in 1927, the senior member who had occupied the prime desk on the Democratic side retired and party leader Joseph Robinson readily claimed the place. Republican leaders had to wait another decade, however, before retirement opened up the corresponding seat on their side. Finally, on January 5, 1937, Republican Leader McNary took his seat across from Robinson.

Later that year, Vice President John Nance Garner announced a policy—under the Senate rule requiring the presiding officer to "recognize the Senator who shall first address him"—of giving priority recognition to the majority leader and then the minority leader before all other senators seeking to speak. By 1937, Senate floor leadership had assumed its modern form.

Charles McNary, senator from Oregon (1917-1944), served as Republican leader of the Senate from 1933 to 1944.

Further Reading

Baker, Richard A. and Roger H. Davidson, eds. *First Among Equals: Outstanding Senate Leaders of the Twentieth Century.* Washington, D.C.: Congressional Quarterly Press, 1991.

Historical Records Saved

Bound copies of the Senate Journal *are stored on shelves at the National Archives.*

Word reached the Capitol on a sweltering summer's afternoon that invading forces had swept aside the defending American army at Bladensburg and would occupy Washington by dusk. While the president and his cabinet consulted demoralized commanders at a military outpost, the first lady packed a portrait of the nation's first president into her carriage and left town. Despite the wartime emergency of this 1814 summer, Congress had been in recess for four months.

Since 1789, Secretary of the Senate Samuel Otis had safeguarded the Senate's ever-expanding collection of records, including bills, reports, handwritten journals, Washington's inaugural address, and the Senate markup of the Bill of Rights. But Otis had died two days after the Senate adjourned in April 1814.

With the secretary's position vacant, a quick-thinking Senate clerk hastily loaded boxes of priceless records into a wagon and raced to the safety of the Virginia countryside. Nearly five years later, when the Senate returned to the reconstructed Capitol from temporary quarters, a new Senate secretary moved the rescued records back into the building. With space always at a premium in the Capitol, these founding-era documents, as well as those created throughout the remaining decades of the 19th century, ended up in damp basements and humid attics.

In 1927, a young Senate clerk named Harold Hufford entered a basement storeroom to find disordered papers and surprised mice. Under his foot lay an official-looking document that bore two large markings: the print of his rubber heel and the signature of John C. Calhoun. Hufford reported, "I knew who Calhoun was; and I knew the nation's documents shouldn't be treated like that."

For the next decade Hufford inventoried Senate records in more than 50 locations throughout the Capitol. Unfortunately, others had preceded him. Autograph seekers had routinely harvested signatures from presidential messages. Some notable state papers, such as Woodrow Wilson's message to the Senate on the outbreak of World War I, had simply vanished.

The opening of the National Archives building in the mid-1930s provided the opportunity to correct this dire situation. On March 25, 1937, the history-conscious Senate launched a rescue mission, perhaps less dramatic than that of 1814, but equally monumental, as it agreed to transfer these records—and all others no longer needed for current operations—to the National Archives.

Further Reading

U.S. Congress. Senate. *The Senate, 1789-1989*, Vol. 2, by Robert C. Byrd. 100th Congress, 1st sess., 1991. S. Doc.100-20. Chapter 16.

U.S. Congress. Senate. *Guide to the Records of the United States Senate at the National Archives, 1789-1989, Bicentennial Edition.* 100th Congress, 2d sess., 1989. S. Doc. 100-42.

July 14, 1937

Death of Senate Majority Leader

On the morning of July 14, 1937, a maid entered the Methodist Building, across the street from the Capitol. When she turned the key to the apartment of her client, the Senate majority leader, a terrible sight awaited her. There sprawled on the floor, a copy of the previous day's *Congressional Record* lying near his right hand, was the pajama-clad body of Arkansas Senator Joseph Taylor Robinson. At the height of his powers, with hopes of a Supreme Court appointment as his reward for services to a grateful president, the grievously over-worked 64-year-old Robinson had succumbed to heart disease.

Today, Robinson's portrait hangs just outside the Senate Chamber's south entrance. It suggests the warm and gentle demeanor he displayed when relaxing with friends. Another artist, however, might have captured a different side of his personality—the one that he occasionally displayed as Democratic floor leader. "When he would go into one of his rages," reported a close observer, "it took little imagination to see fire and smoke rolling out of his mouth like some fierce dragon. Robinson could make senators and everyone in his presence quake by the burning fire in his eyes, the baring of his teeth as he ground out his words, and the clenching of his mighty fists as he beat on the desk before him."

Joe Robinson entered the Senate in 1913, weeks before the Constitution's 17th Amendment took effect, as the last senator who owed his office to election by a state legislature. In 1923, his Senate Democratic colleagues elected him their floor leader, a post he retained for the next 14 years. Iron determination, fierce party loyalty, and willingness to spend long hours studying Senate procedures and legislative issues allowed Robinson, more than any predecessor, to define and expand the role of majority leader.

In 1933, at the head of a large and potentially unruly Democratic majority, he helped President Franklin Roosevelt push New Deal legislation through the Senate in record time. In the blistering hot summer of 1937, he rallied to the president's call a final time. Ignoring doctors' orders to avoid stress, he labored to salvage Roosevelt's legislative scheme to liberalize the Supreme Court by expanding its membership to as many as 15, adding one new position for every sitting justice over the age of 70. Robinson's death cost the president his "court-packing" plan and deprived the Senate of a towering leader.

Funeral service for Joseph T. Robinson in the Senate Chamber.

Further Reading

Bacon, Donald C. "Joseph Taylor Robinson." In *First Among Equals: Outstanding Senate Leaders of the Twentieth Century,* edited by Richard A Baker, and Roger H. Davidson. Washington, D.C.: Congressional Quarterly, Inc., 1991.

"Mr. Smith" Comes to Washington

From a back-row desk on the Democratic side of a crowded Senate Chamber, the idealistic freshman member labored into the 24th hour of a one-man filibuster. His secretary sat in the gallery frantically signaling which rules would keep him from losing the floor. The vice president was in his place and so was every senator. No one moved. Finally the freshman's leading antagonist, a cynical old-timer, rose to seek a unanimous consent agreement. He asked the Senate's permission to bring into the chamber 50,000 telegrams, from all sections of the nation, demanding that the young senator end his futile crusade. Distraught, but vowing to continue his fight against an entrenched political establishment, the exhausted senator then collapsed.

A scene from Mr. Smith Goes to Washington.

As overturned baskets of telegrams cascaded paper over the junior member's prone body, the senior senator suddenly changed course. Shaken by what he had just seen, he dramatically confessed to corrupt deeds and demanded that the Senate expel him instead of his idealistic younger colleague. Recognizing the freshman senator's vindication, the chamber erupted with joyful shouts as the vice president lamely tried to restore order.

The credits rolled and the lights came on. The audience that packed Washington's Constitution Hall on October 17, 1939, included 45 real-life senators and 250 House members. They had come to a world premiere of the Columbia Pictures film, *Mr. Smith Goes to Washington.* The film starred 30-year-old Jimmy Stewart as the noble-minded "Mr. Smith," Claude Rains as the corrupt-but-redeemed senior senator, and Jean Arthur as Smith's loyal secretary.

Paramount Pictures and MGM had previously turned down offers to purchase the story, fearing that its unflattering portrayal of the Senate might be interpreted as a "covert attack on the democratic form of government."

Most of the senators attending the premiere responded with good humor to the Hollywood treatment, with its realistic reproduction of the Senate Chamber. Several, however, were not amused. Majority Leader Alben Barkley described the film as "silly and stupid," adding that it made the Senate look like "a bunch of crooks." Years later, producer Frank Capra alleged that several senators had actually tried to buy up the film to prevent its release.

Mr. Smith was an immediate hit, second only to *Gone with the Wind* in 1939 box office receipts. A congressional spouse named Margaret Chase Smith particularly enjoyed the premiere. Friends suggested that perhaps the time had come for a real-life story entitled "Mrs. Smith Goes to Washington." Within eight months, the death of her husband and the voters of Maine's Second Congressional District allowed the 42-year-old Mrs. Smith to begin writing that script.

Further Reading

"Capra Picture Blasts Myth of Capital as a Stage," *Washington Evening Star,* October 18, 1939.

"The Screen in Review: Frank Capra's 'Mr. Smith Goes to Washington' at the Music Hall Sets a Seasonal High in Comedy," *New York Times,* October 20, 1939.

U.S. Congress. Senate. *The Senate, 1789-1989,* Vol. 2, by Robert C. Byrd. 100th Congress, 1st sess., 1991. S. Doc.100-20. Chapter 21.

January 22, 1940

"Lion of Idaho" Laid to Rest

On a cold morning in January 1940, crowds lined the Capitol's corridors hoping for admission to the Senate Chamber galleries. Shortly after noon, as senators took their seats, several hundred House members filed into the chamber, followed by the Supreme Court, the cabinet, diplomats, and President Franklin Roosevelt. All had come for the funeral service of the 33-year Senate veteran whom *Time* magazine anointed as the "most famed senator of the century"—the progressive Republican from Idaho, William E. Borah.

A bronze statue of Borah now stands outside the Senate Chamber. It captures a large kindly man, with a sharply chiseled face and a head of hair resembling the mane of a lion.

William Borah began his Senate career in 1907. His deeply resonant voice, his natural skills as an actor, and his rich command of the English language at once marked him as a gifted orator. A third of a century later, at his Senate funeral, no one delivered a eulogy because no one could match his eloquence.

Affectionately known as the "Lion of Idaho," Borah took fiercely independent views that kept him at odds with his party's leaders. A progressive reformer, he attacked business monopolies, worked to improve the lot of organized labor, promoted civil liberties, and secured passage of constitutional amendments for a graduated income tax and direct election of senators.

Borah is best remembered for his influence on American foreign policy in the years between World Wars I and II. From his senior position on the Senate Foreign Relations Committee, he sought to keep the nation free of entangling foreign alliances, defeating American efforts to join the League of Nations and the World Court. Concerned at evidence of America's increasing desire to become an imperial power, Borah believed that other nations should be left free to determine their own destinies guided only by the rule of law and public opinion.

Other senators envied Borah's saturation press coverage. Reporters routinely gathered in his office for informal mid-afternoon conversations. His pronouncements on the issues of the day appeared in print so frequently that one newspaper quipped, "Borah this and Borah that, Borah here and Borah there, Borah does and Borah doesn't—until you wish that Borah wasn't."

The hundreds who filed past his coffin in the Senate Chamber displayed just how glad they were that Borah was.

Bronze statue of Senator William Edgar Borah of Idaho (1907-1940), by Bryant Baker, located near the Senate Chamber's entrance in the Capitol.

Further Reading

McKenna, Marian C. *Borah*. Ann Arbor: University of Michigan Press, 1961.

CHAPTER VI

WAR AND REORGANIZATION

1941-1963

March 1, 1941

The Truman Committee

No senator ever gained greater political benefits from chairing a special investigating committee than did Missouri's Harry S. Truman.

In 1940, as World War II tightened its grip on Europe, Congress prepared for eventual U.S. involvement by appropriating $10 billion in defense contracts. Early in 1941, stories of widespread contractor mismanagement reached Senator Truman. In typical fashion, he decided to go take a look. During his 10,000-mile tour of military bases, he discovered that contractors were being paid a fixed profit no matter how inefficient their operations proved to be. He also found that a handful of corporations headquartered in the East were receiving a disproportionately greater share of the contracts.

Convinced that waste and corruption were strangling the nation's efforts to mobilize itself for the war in Europe, Truman conceived the idea for a special Senate Committee to Investigate the National Defense Program. Senior military officials opposed the idea, recalling the Civil War-era problems that the congressional Joint Committee on the Conduct of the War created for President Lincoln. Robert E. Lee had once joked that he considered the joint committee's harassment of Union commanders to be worth at least two Confederate divisions. Truman had no intention of allowing that earlier committee to serve as his model.

Congressional leaders advised President Franklin Roosevelt that it would be better for such an inquiry to be in Truman's sympathetic hands than to let it fall to those who might use it as a way of attacking his administration. They also assured the president that the "Truman Committee" would not be able to cause much trouble with a budget of only $15,000 to investigate billions in defense spending.

By unanimous consent on March 1, 1941, the Senate created what proved to be one of the most productive investigating committees in its entire history.

During the three years of Truman's chairmanship, the committee held hundreds of hearings, traveled thousands of miles to conduct field inspections, and saved millions of dollars in cost overruns. Earning nearly universal respect for his thoroughness and determination, Truman erased his earlier public image as an errand-runner for Kansas City politicos. Along the way, he developed working experience with business, labor, agriculture, and executive branch agencies that would serve him well in later years. In 1944, when Democratic Party leaders sought a replacement for controversial Vice President Henry Wallace, they settled on Truman, thereby setting his course directly to the White House.

Senator Harry Truman of Missouri (1935-1945), fourth from left, *with members of the Senate Committee to Investigate the National Defense Program, at the Ford Motor Company in 1942.*

Further Reading

Riddle, Donald H. *The Truman Committee*. New Brunswick, N.J.: Rutgers University Press, 1964.

Wilson, Theodore. "The Truman Committee, 1941." In *Congress Investigates: A Documented History, 1792-1974*, edited by Arthur M. Schlesinger, Jr., and Roger Bruns. 5 vols. New York: Chelsea House Publishers, 1975.

December 26, 1941

Churchill Addresses Congress

Outside the U.S. Capitol Building, platoons of soldiers and police stood at high alert. Shortly after noon, British Prime Minister Winston Churchill entered the Senate Chamber to address a joint meeting of Congress. He took his place at a lectern bristling with microphones. Above his head, large, powerful lamps gave the normally dim room the brilliance of a Hollywood movie set. Motion picture cameras began to roll.

The 1941 Christmas holiday had thinned the ranks of senators and representatives still in town, and had dictated moving the joint meeting from the House to the smaller Senate Chamber to avoid the embarrassment of empty seats. Yet, all 96 desks were filled with members, justices of the Supreme Court, and cabinet officers—minus the secretaries of state and war. The overflow gallery audience consisted largely of members' wives, certain that they would never again witness such an event.

Less than three weeks after the Japanese attack on Pearl Harbor, and as that nation's submarines appeared off the coast of California, Churchill had arrived in Washington to begin coordinating military strategy with the president and leaders of Congress.

The eloquent prime minister began his address on a light note. He observed, "If my father had been an American, and my mother British, instead of the other way around, I might have gotten here [as a member] on my own. In that case, this would not have been the first time you would have heard my voice." He then grimly predicted that Allied forces would require at least 18 months to turn the tide of war and warned that "many disappointments and unpleasant surprises await us."

Regarding the Japanese aggressors, he asked, "What kind of a people do they think we are? Is it possible that they do not realize that we shall never cease to persevere against them until they have been taught a lesson which they and the world will never forget?" As for the German forces, "With proper weapons and proper organization, we can beat the life out of the savage Nazi." These "wicked men" who have brought evil forces into play must "know they will be called to terrible account if they cannot beat down by force of arms the peoples they have assailed."

When Churchill concluded his 30-minute address, he flashed a "V" for victory sign and departed to thunderous applause. One journalist described this historic address as "full of bubbling humor, biting denunciation of totalitarian enemies, stern courage—and hard facts."

Winston Churchill addressing the U.S. Congress in the Senate Chamber on December 26, 1941.

Further Reading

"Churchill Promises We Will Be Able to Take Initiative 'Amply' in 1943," *New York Times,* December 27, 1941, 1.

Gilbert, Martin. *Churchill and America.* New York: Free Press, 2005.

Senate Elects Rev. Frederick Harris Chaplain

Frederick B. Harris, Senate Chaplain (1942-1947, 1949-1969).

When the Senate of 1789 convened in New York City, members chose as their first chaplain the Episcopal bishop of New York. When the body moved to Philadelphia in 1790, it awarded spiritual duties to the Episcopal bishop of Pennsylvania. And when it reached Washington in 1800, divine guidance was entrusted to the Episcopal bishop of Maryland.

During its first 20 years, the Senate demonstrated a decided preference for Episcopalians. Among the initial 12 chaplains were one Presbyterian, one Baptist, and 10 Episcopalians.

Through the 19th century, Senate chaplains rarely held office for more than several years, as prominent clergymen actively contended for even a brief appointment to this prestigious office. With the 20th century, however, came year-round sessions and the need for greater continuity. The office became less vulnerable to changes in party control. Appointed by a Republican Senate in 1927, Reverend Z. T. Phillips—the Senate's 19th Episcopalian—continued after Democrats gained control in 1933, serving a record 14 years until his death in May 1942.

On October 10, 1942, the Senate elected its 56th chaplain, the Reverend Frederick Brown Harris. The highly regarded pastor of Washington's Foundry Methodist Church, Harris failed to survive the 1947 change in party control that led to the election of the Reverend Peter Marshall. When Marshall died two years later, however, the Senate invited Reverend Harris to resume his Senate ministry. With his retirement in 1969, Harris set the as-yet-unchallenged service record of 24 years.

More than any of his predecessors, Frederick Brown Harris shaped the modern Senate chaplaincy. Members appreciated the poetic quality of his prayers. In November 1963, when word of President John F. Kennedy's assassination reached him, Harris went immediately to the Senate Chamber. He later recalled, "The place was in an uproar. Senate leaders Mike Mansfield and Everett Dirksen asked me to offer a prayer. I called upon the senators to rise for a minute of silence, partly because of the gravity of the tragedy, but partly to give me a minute more time to think of something to say."

Borrowing from the poet Edwin Markham, he said, "This sudden, almost unbelievable, news has stunned our minds and hearts as we gaze at a vacant place against the sky, as the President of the Republic, like a giant cedar green with boughs, goes down with a great shout upon the hills, and leaves a lonesome place against the sky."

Further Reading

Harris, Frederick Brown. *Senate Prayers and Spires of the Spirit*. Edited by J. D. Phelan. St. Louis: Bethany Press, 1970.

Whittier, Charles H. *Chaplains in Congress*. Washington, DC: Congressional Research Service, Library of Congress, Report 90-65 GOV. 1990.

November 14, 1942

Arrests Compel a Senate Quorum

In November 1942, a full-scale civil rights filibuster threatened to keep the Senate in session until Christmas. For five days, southern senators conducted a leisurely examination of legislation to outlaw the poll taxes that their states used to disenfranchise low-income voters, including many African Americans.

The 1942 filibuster took place just days after mid-term congressional elections had cost Senate Democrats nine seats. Frustrated, Democratic Majority Leader Alben Barkley decided the time had come to cut off the debate. During a Saturday session on November 14, Barkley obtained an order directing Sergeant at Arms Chesley Jurney to round up the five absent southern members needed to provide a quorum.

Jurney sent Deputy Sergeant at Arms Mark Trice to the Mayflower Hotel apartment of Tennessee Senator Kenneth McKellar, the Senate's third most senior member. In his book on Tennessee senators, Senator Bill Frist describes McKellar as an "extraordinarily shrewd man of husky dimensions with a long memory and a short fuse." When Trice called from the lobby, McKellar refused to answer his phone. The deputy then walked up to the apartment and convinced the senator's maid to let him in.

When Trice explained that McKellar was urgently needed back at the Capitol, the 73-year-old legislator agreed to accompany him. As they approached the Senate wing, McKellar

suddenly realized what was up. An aide later recalled, "His face grew redder and redder. By the time the car reached the Senate entrance, McKellar shot out and barreled through the corridors to find the source of his summons."

Barkley got his quorum, but McKellar got even. He later convinced President Franklin Roosevelt not to even consider Barkley's desire for a seat on the Supreme Court. Such a nomination, he promised, would never receive Senate approval.

When Senate Democrats convened the following January to elect officers, a party elder routinely nominated Sergeant at Arms Jurney for another term. McKellar countered with the nomination of a recently defeated Mississippi senator. An ally of McKellar strengthened the odds against Jurney's reelection by suggesting that he had been involved in financial irregularities. As the Democratic caucus opened an investigation, Jurney withdrew his candidacy.

While no documentation of "financial irregularities" survives, Jurney had the misfortune of being caught between a frustrated majority leader and an unforgiving filibuster leader. The poll tax issue continued to spark episodes of protracted debate until finally put to rest in 1964 by the 24th Amendment to the U.S. Constitution.

Mark Trice, deputy sergeant at arms (1932-1946), secretary of the Senate (1953-1955).

Further Reading

Frist, William H, with J. Lee Annis, Jr. *Tennessee Senators, 1911-2001: Portraits of Leadership in a Century of Change*. Lanham, MD: Madison Books, 1999.

Riedel, Richard Langham. *Halls of the Mighty: My 47 Years at the Senate*. Washington, D.C.: Robert B. Luce, 1969.

July 25, 1943

Combat Tour for Senators

On July 25, 1943, shortly after Allied forces invaded Sicily and bombed Rome, five United States senators set out on a unique and controversial mission. They boarded a converted bomber at National Airport to begin a 65-day tour of U.S. military installations around the world. Each senator wore a dog tag and carried one knife, one steel helmet, extra cigarettes, emergency food rations, manuals on jungle survival, and two military uniforms. The senators were to wear the military uniforms while flying over enemy territory and visiting U.S. field operations in the fragile hope that, if captured, they would be treated humanely as prisoners of war.

The idea for this inspection trip originated among members of the Senate Committee on Military Affairs and the Senate Special Committee to Investigate the National Defense Program. The latter panel, chaired by Senator Harry Truman, had spent two years examining waste and corruption at military construction facilities around the United States. Both committees wished to expand their investigations to onsite overseas visits. Majority Leader Alben Barkley at first opposed the idea of senators taking up the time of military commanders. With the encouragement of Senator Truman and President Franklin Roosevelt, however, he reluctantly agreed to create a small committee, chaired by Georgia Democrat Richard Russell, composed of two members from the Truman Committee and two from Military Affairs.

The committee's main task was to observe the quality and effectiveness of war materiel under combat conditions. As laudable as this mission seemed, departing members received a good deal of criticism both from colleagues and constituents. At a time of stringent gasoline rationing, a constituent wrote Russell that it would be wiser to allocate his aircraft's fuel to the needs of "your Georgia people."

The senators' first stop was England, where they bunked with the Eighth Air Force, dined with the king and queen, and interviewed Winston Churchill. They moved on to North Africa, the Persian Gulf, India, China, and Australia, before returning home on September 18.

Russell had planned to brief the Senate at a secret session set for October 7. Before that briefing, however, committee member Henry Cabot Lodge, Jr., upstaged the chairman by giving his own account in public session. Although this, and leaks by other members, infuriated Russell, his committee's report framed the key issues of postwar reconstruction and set a firm precedent for future overseas travel by inquiring senators.

Senate Military Affairs Committee members inspect the operating room of Helgafel Hospital in Iceland, July 30, 1943.

Further Reading
Fite, Gilbert C. *Richard B. Russell, Jr., Senator from Georgia*. Chapel Hill: University of North Carolina Press, 1991.

October 19, 1943

A Woman Presides over the Senate

It occurred without ceremony. On October 19, 1943, for the first time, a woman formally took up the gavel as the Senate's acting president pro tempore. In the absence of the vice president and the president pro tempore, the secretary of the Senate read a letter assigning the duties of the chair to Arkansas Democrat Hattie Caraway.

By 1943, Senator Caraway had become accustomed to breaking the Senate's gender barriers. Twelve years earlier, on January 12, 1932, she became the first woman elected to the Senate. In 1933, she became the first woman to chair a Senate committee.

Hattie Caraway entered the Senate in November 1931, by gubernatorial appointment, following the death of her husband, Senator Thaddeus Caraway. She then ran successfully for election to the remaining months of her husband's term, assuring state party leaders that she had no interest in running for the subsequent full term.

Senator Caraway rarely spoke on the Senate floor and soon became known as "Silent Hattie." Tourists in the Senate galleries always noticed the woman senator in the dark Victorian-style dress, sitting quietly at her desk knitting or completing crossword puzzles. When asked why she avoided speeches, she quipped, "The men have left nothing unsaid."

In May 1932, she changed her mind and declared her candidacy for a full term. Several of her five male competitors joked that she would be lucky to attract 1 percent of the vote. What they failed to consider was the budding interest of her Senate seatmate, Louisiana's Huey Long. Long detested Caraway's Arkansas colleague, Senate Democratic Leader Joseph T. Robinson, and deeply appreciated her inclination to vote with him rather than with Robinson.

Senator Long expressed his gratitude by joining Caraway for an extraordinary one-week, 2,000-mile, 40-speech campaign tour through 37 Arkansas communities. Their seven-vehicle caravan included two sound trucks allowing him to proclaim, "We're here to pull a lot of pot-bellied politicians off a little woman's neck." Caraway won the election with double the vote of her nearest rival. Her diligent Senate service and effective advocacy of New Deal legislative initiatives won her another term in 1938. That path-breaking career concluded in 1945, following a primary defeat by Representative J. William Fulbright. On her final day in office, the Senate tendered Hattie Caraway the high honor of a standing ovation.

Hattie Caraway, senator from Arkansas (1931-1945).

Further Reading

Kincaid, Diane, ed. *Silent Hattie Speaks: The Personal Journal of Senator Hattie Caraway.* Westport, Conn.: Greenwood Press, 1979.

Malone, David. *Hattie and Huey: An Arkansas Tour.* Fayetteville: University of Arkansas Press, 1989.

Senate Majority Leader Resigns

Never before had a Senate majority leader resigned his office in disgust at the actions of a president of his own party. In his first seven years as Democratic majority leader, Kentucky's Alben Barkley had earned a reputation among his colleagues for his loyalty to President Franklin Roosevelt. It was Roosevelt, after all, who had twisted enough Democratic senatorial arms in 1937 to ensure Barkley's election to that post—by a margin of just one vote.

In January 1944, Roosevelt sent to Congress draft legislation for a $10 billion increase in taxes to help pay the cost of American involvement in World War II. When the bill emerged from the Senate Finance Committee, however, it included only 20 percent of what the president had requested. Concluding that the scaled-back authorization was about all that the Senate was likely to pass, Majority Leader Barkley met twice with the president to plead that he approve the measure. Ignoring his party's Senate leader, Roosevelt vetoed the bill, blasting its inadequate funding and its language, "which not even a dictionary or thesaurus can make clear."

In a "cold fury," Barkley announced that he planned to make a speech "without regard for the political consequences." In that speech, delivered the following day before a packed chamber with most senators at their desks, he denounced the president for his "deliberate and unjustified misstatements," which placed on Congress "the blame for universal dissatisfaction with tax complexities." Barkley branded the president's statement that the bill provided "relief not for the needy, but for the greedy" a "calculated and deliberate assault upon the legislative integrity of every Member of Congress."

On the following morning, Barkley convened the Democratic caucus in its Russell Building meeting room. Tears streaming down his face, he resigned as party leader and left the conference. Moments later, Texas Senator Tom Connally burst from the room, booming, "Make way for liberty! Make way for liberty!" With that, he led a jovial delegation of senators down the hall to Barkley's office to inform him of his unanimous reelection. As one Democratic senator commented, "Previously, he spoke to us for the president; now he speaks for us to the president."

Two days later, the Senate joined the House in overriding the president's veto. When the Democratic Convention met that summer, Barkley's break with the president probably cost him the vice-presidential nomination and, with Roosevelt's death the following spring, the presidency.

Senator Alben Barkley of Kentucky (1927-1949, 1955-1956), right, *welcomes President Franklin D. Roosevelt upon his return from Tehran on December 17, 1943. Barkley served as Democratic leader of the Senate from 1937 to 1949.*

Further Reading

Drury, Allen. *A Senate Journal: 1943-1945*. New York: McGraw-Hill, 1963.

September 2, 1944

Death of a "Gentle Knight"

In 1955, the Senate established a special committee to select five outstanding former senators who were no longer living for the special honor of having their portraits permanently displayed in the Capitol's Senate Reception Room. The committee chairman, Senator John F. Kennedy, asked 160 nationally prominent scholars with special knowledge of Senate operations and American political history to nominate five candidates. When committee staff tallied the experts' recommendations, the senator at the top of their list was Nebraska progressive Republican George Norris—best remembered as the father of the Tennessee Valley Authority and author of the Constitution's 20th Amendment, which changed the starting date of congressional and presidential terms from March to January.

Born in 1861, Norris grew up in Ohio and Indiana, but moved to Nebraska in his early 20s to establish a law practice. In 1902, he won a seat in the U.S. House of Representatives and quickly gained a reputation for his independence. He instigated a revolt in 1910 of insurgent Republicans and Democrats against the powerful House Speaker Joseph Cannon. These reformers won a vote to deny the Speaker membership on the House Rules Committee and thereby democratized the process of committee appointments.

Norris began his 30-year Senate career in 1913. Although he supported many of Woodrow Wilson's progressive domestic policies, he was a vocal opponent of that president's foreign policies before and after the First World War, and joined other "irreconcilables" in opposing the Treaty of Versailles. During the Republican administrations of the 1920s, Norris pressed for a progressive agenda that included farm relief, improved labor conditions, conservation of natural resources, and rural electrification. He persistently advocated a federal program to build dams on the Tennessee River in order to provide affordable electricity and economic planning along the river valley, a goal that he finally achieved in 1933. During the Great Depression, Norris worked closely with President Franklin D. Roosevelt, who referred to him as "the very perfect gentle knight of American progressive ideals." Defeated for a sixth term in 1942, he retired to Nebraska, where he died on September 2, 1944.

Today, no portrait of George Norris adorns the Senate Reception Room. Despite Chairman Kennedy's active support, a rule of his committee that required the choices to be unanimous and the persistence of Norris's political adversaries still in the Senate blocked his selection. While denied this singular honor, Norris subsequently gained another commendable distinction in becoming one of the few senators in history to be the subject of scholarly biography that filled *three* volumes.

George Norris, senator from Nebraska (1913-1943).

Further Reading

Lowitt, Richard. *George W. Norris: The Triumph of a Progressive, 1933-1944.* Urbana: University of Illinois Press, 1978.

A Senate Journal, 1943-1945

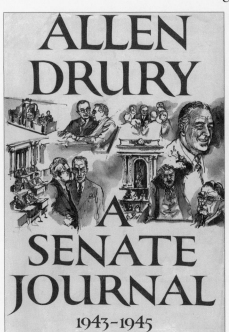

In 1963, United Press correspondent Allen Drury published the diary he had kept from 1943 to 1945.

One of the best books ever written about the Senate took the form of a diary. Published in 1963, its title is *A Senate Journal, 1943-1945*. Here is what its author, United Press correspondent Allen Drury, had to say about a May 28, 1945, session in which the Senate rejected, for its own members, a politically explosive $2,500 congressional expense allowance. "The Senate decided today that Representatives are worth $2,500 more than Senators. It was an unhesitating decision, endorsed by an overwhelming vote. It . . . left the House out on a limb. Each house got something. The Senate got the glory and the House got the cash. It was quite a lively afternoon."

Assigned to cover the wartime Senate in December 1943, Drury immediately began to keep a diary. He hoped its eventual publication would enlighten Americans about the Senate. "There is," he concluded, "a vast area of casual ignorance concerning this lively and appealing body." Drury later used his diary notes to compose his 1960 Pulitzer-Prize-winning novel *Advise and Consent*.

As a journalist, Drury had the good fortune to arrive in the Senate at a time of obvious and dramatic change—from the crisis of World War II to the challenges of the postwar era. He met and observed a handful of the old-time senators, "delightful characters, one or two of them still in tail-coats and possessed of flowing hair, all filled with a lively awareness of their own egos, all imbued with a massive sense of the dignity and power of being a Senator of the United States." As he later wrote to the Senate Historical Office, "I've always regretted I abandoned 'Senate Journal' after a year. I could have gone on cannibalizing myself for years to come, had I but had the foresight."

A Senate Journal is packed with brilliant character sketches. Here is Drury's April 1944 evaluation of Vice President Henry Wallace. "Wallace is a man foredoomed by fate. No matter what he does, it is always going to seem faintly ridiculous, and no matter how he acts, it is always going to seem faintly pathetic. He looks like a hayseed, talks like a prophet."

Allen Drury set high standards for future Senate diarists.

Further Reading
Drury, Allen. *A Senate Journal, 1943-1945*. New York: McGraw-Hill, 1963.

September 18, 1945

Truman Nominates a Republican Senator to the Supreme Court

The prospect of a vacancy on the Supreme Court generally stirs speculation about which incumbent members of the Senate might be eligible candidates. Given the increasing contentiousness of the Senate review process for high court vacancies, some believe that selecting one of the Senate's own members might smooth the road to a speedy confirmation. This raises the question: "How often are senators nominated to be justices?"

In all of the Senate's history, only seven incumbent members have moved directly to the Supreme Court—the most recent being in 1945. Seven others were seated within a few years of leaving the Senate—the most recent being in 1949. The first incumbent was Connecticut's Oliver Ellsworth, who in 1796 became chief justice. As a senator, Ellsworth had shaped the 1789 Judiciary Act, which put in place the federal court system. The only former senator to enter the Court as chief justice was Salmon Chase of Ohio. Chase had left the Senate to serve as Abraham Lincoln's treasury secretary prior to his appointment in 1864.

In the summer of 1945, the retirement of Justice Owen Roberts presented a political challenge to Harry Truman, who had been president for only three months. The seven remaining associate justices had gained their seats as Democratic appointees

of President Franklin Roosevelt. In a gesture designed to improve relations with Republican congressional leaders, the new Democratic president decided to appoint a Republican.

In making his decision, President Truman consulted with Chief Justice Harlan Stone, the court's only Republican, to see if Ohio Republican Senator Harold Burton would be acceptable. Truman and Burton had become friends when they served together on the Senate Special Committee to Investigate the National Defense Program. Chief Justice Stone welcomed the appointment on the theory that Burton's Senate experience would be useful in helping the Court determine legislative intent as it reviewed statutes.

Truman's decision was not entirely altruistic. In sending a Republican to the Court, the president knew that the Democratic governor of Ohio was prepared to replace Burton in the Senate with a Democrat.

President Harry S. Truman, left, congratulates new Associate Justice of the Supreme Court, former Senator Harold Burton of Ohio.

Further Reading

Abraham, Henry. *Justices, Presidents, and Senators: A History of the U.S. Supreme Court Appointments from Washington to Clinton.* 4th ed. Lanham, MD: Rowman & Littlefield, 1999.

"Senator Burton is Named a Supreme Court Justice," *New York Times*, September 19, 1945, 1.

July 18, 1947

Congress Revises Presidential Succession Act

On July 18, 1947, President Harry Truman signed the Presidential Succession Act. The original act of 1792 had placed the Senate president pro tempore and Speaker of the House in the line of succession, but in 1886 Congress had removed them. The 1947 law reinserted those officials, but placed the Speaker ahead of the president pro tempore.

Throughout most of the 19th century, the Senate assumed it was empowered to elect a president pro tempore only during the absence of a vice president. But what should senators do at the end of a session? Since Congress was customarily out of session for half of each year, what would happen in that era of high mortality rates if both the president and vice president died during the adjournment period and there was no designated president pro tempore? For decades, the Senate relied upon an elaborate charade in which the vice president would voluntarily leave the chamber before the end of a session to enable the Senate to elect a president pro tempore. Fearing that the presidency might thus accidentally slip into the hands of the opposition, vice presidents occasionally refused to perform this little courtesy when the opposing party held the Senate majority.

In 1886 Congress replaced the two congressional officials in the line of succession with cabinet officers, in the order of their agencies' creation. Proponents of this change argued that the Senate elected its presidents pro tempore based on parliamentary rather than executive skills. No president pro tempore had ever served as president, while six former secretaries of state had been elected to that office.

When the 1945 death of Franklin Roosevelt propelled Vice President Truman into the presidency, Truman urged placing the Speaker, as an elected representative of his district, as well as the chosen leader of the "elected representatives of the people," next in line to the vice president. Since one could make the same argument for the president pro tempore, Truman's decision may have reflected his strained relations with 78-year-old President pro tempore Kenneth McKellar and his warm friendship with 65-year-old House Speaker Sam Rayburn. After all, it was in Rayburn's hideaway office, where he had gone for a late afternoon glass of bourbon, that Truman first learned of his own elevation to the presidency.

President pro tempore Kenneth McKellar of Tennessee (1917-1953), left, receives the Senate gavel from then Vice President Harry Truman.

Further Reading
Feerick, John D. *From Falling Hands: The Story of Presidential Succession.* New York: Fordham University Press, 1965.

Member's Death Ends a Senate Predicament

In late July 1947, the Senate adjourned for the year without resolving a serious complaint against one of its members. Seven months earlier, facing charges of personal corruption and civil rights violations, Mississippi Democrat Theodore Bilbo presented his credentials for a new Senate term. Idaho Democrat Glen Taylor immediately demanded that the Senate delay Bilbo's swearing in until it could review the recently received findings of two special investigating committees. Angry at Taylor's action, several of Bilbo's southern colleagues launched a filibuster, which threatened to block the Senate's efforts to organize for the new Congress. They argued that the Mississippi senator should be allowed to take his seat while the Senate looked into the matter. A day later, on January 4, Senate Democratic Leader Alben Barkley temporarily broke the impasse by announcing that Bilbo was returning to Mississippi for cancer surgery and would not insist on being sworn in until he had recovered and returned to Washington.

Theodore Bilbo had been a highly controversial figure in Mississippi politics for 40 years. After two terms as governor, he entered the Senate in 1935. During the early 1940s, a growing national focus on civil rights issues spurred Bilbo to amplify his long-held views on white supremacy. As large numbers of black voters returned home to Mississippi at the conclusion of their World War II military service, Bilbo's racist utterances dominated his 1946 reelection campaign and drew national media attention.

Following his victory in the July Democratic primary, which guaranteed reelection in November, the Senate received a petition from a group of that state's African American residents protesting the senator's campaign tactics. The petition charged that Bilbo's "inflammatory appeals" to the white population had stirred up racial tensions, provoked violence, and kept many black citizens away from polling places.

Late in 1946, two special Senate committees investigated Bilbo's conduct. One looked into his campaign activities. A slim majority of that panel concluded that although he ran a crude and tasteless campaign, he should be seated. A second committee uncovered evidence that he had converted thousands of dollars of campaign contributions to his personal use. Both reports lay before the Senate as it convened in January 1947.

Following a series of unsuccessful medical procedures throughout early 1947, Theodore Bilbo died on August 21. Although his death ended the Senate's predicament over his seating, it marked only the beginning of an extended postwar struggle to protect the voting rights of all Americans.

Theodore Bilbo, senator from Mississippi (1935-1947).

Further Reading
Green, Adwin Wigfall. *The Man Bilbo*. 1963. Reprint. Westport, Conn.: Greenwood Press, 1976.

Truman Calls for "Turnip Day" Session

President Harry Truman was desperate. With fewer than four months remaining before election day, his public approval rating stood at only 36 percent. Two years earlier, Congress had come under Republican control for the first time in a quarter century. His opponent, New York Governor Thomas Dewey, seemed already to be planning his own move to the White House. In search of a bold political gesture, the president turned to the provision in the Constitution that allows the president "on extraordinary occasions" to convene one or both houses of Congress.

On 27 occasions, presidents have called both houses into "extraordinary session" to deal with urgent matters of war and economic crisis. The most recent of these extraordinary sessions convened in July 1948.

On July 15, several weeks after the Republican-controlled Congress had adjourned for the year, leaving much business unfinished, Truman took the unprecedented step of using his presidential nomination acceptance speech to call both houses back into session. He delivered that speech under particularly trying circumstances. Without air conditioning, delegates sweltered in the Philadelphia convention hall's oven-like atmosphere. By the time the president finally stepped before the cameras in this first televised Democratic national convention, organizers had lost all hope of controlling the schedule.

At 1:45 a.m., speaking only from an outline, Truman electrified the soggy delegates. In announcing the special session, he challenged the Republican majority to live up to the pledges of their own recently concluded convention to pass laws to ensure civil rights, extend Social Security coverage, and establish a national health-care program. "They can do this job in 15 days, if they want to do it," he challenged. That two-week session would begin on "what we in Missouri call 'Turnip Day'," taken from the old Missouri saying, "On the twenty-fifth of July, sow your turnips, wet or dry."

Republican senators reacted scornfully. To Michigan's Arthur Vandenberg, it sounded like "a last hysterical gasp of an expiring administration." Yet, Vandenberg and other senior Senate Republicans urged action on a few measures to solidify certain vital voting blocs. "No!" exclaimed Republican Policy Committee chairman Robert Taft of Ohio. "We're not going to give that fellow anything." Charging Truman with abuse of a presidential prerogative, Taft blocked all legislative action during the futile session. By doing this, Taft amplified Truman's case against the "Do-nothing Eightieth Congress" and contributed to his astounding November come-from-behind victory.

President Harry S. Truman delivering his acceptance speech following his nomination for the presidency at the Democratic National Convention on July 15, 1948.

Further Reading

Hamby, Alonzo L. *Man of the People: A Life of Harry S. Truman.* New York: Oxford University Press, 1995.

September 13, 1948

First Woman Elected to Both Houses

Is the Senate any place for a woman? This question dominated the 1948 U.S. Senate Republican primary in the state of Maine. Contesting for the seat of retiring Senate Majority Leader Wallace White were the current governor, a former governor, and four-term member of the U.S. House of Representatives Margaret Chase Smith.

Unlike her wealthy opponents, who enjoyed strong statewide political connections, Margaret Smith initially had neither adequate funding nor name recognition among the two-thirds of Maine's population living outside her congressional district. She also faced deeply ingrained prejudice against women serving in elective office. As the wife of one of her opponents put it, "Why [send] a woman to Washington when you can get a man?"

While a member of the House, Smith had built a record of left-leaning independence that irritated her party's more conservative leaders. Seemingly hopeless at its beginning, her primary campaign made a virtue of her independence and her pioneering efforts to provide equal status for women in the military during World War II. Eventually, she gained extensive national media coverage, attracting the admiring attention of prominent journalists, including widely read women writers such as May Craig and Doris Fleeson.

Sensitive to being considered a feminist, Smith said, "I want it distinctly understood that I am not soliciting support because I am a woman. I solicit your support wholly on the basis of my eight years in Congress."

In the June 1948 primary, Smith polled twice as many votes as all of her challengers combined. Her opponents' attacks against the capacity of women to hold public office, in a state where two-thirds of the registered voters were women, proved unwise.

In the general election, held in mid-September, she overwhelmed her Democratic opponent—a dermatologist who argued that since it was a sick world, the nation needed doctors in government.

In winning the September 13, 1948, election, Margaret Chase Smith launched a successful 24-year Senate career, becoming the first woman to serve in both houses of Congress.

Margaret Chase Smith, senator from Maine (1949-1973).

Further Reading
Sherman, Janann. *No Place for a Woman: A Life of Senator Margaret Chase Smith.* New Brunswick, N.J.: Rutgers University Press, 2000.

Supreme Court Nominee Refuses to Testify

S herman Minton. An unfamiliar name today, perhaps, but in the fall of 1949, it was on the lips of all 96 U.S. senators.

An Indiana Democrat, Minton had won election to the Senate in 1934, joining a 13-member all-Democratic freshman class. That class included Missouri's Harry Truman, who was assigned a desk next to Minton's in the Senate Chamber. Minton rose rapidly in his Senate party's ranks. In 1937, as assistant Senate majority whip, Minton vigorously defended President Franklin Roosevelt's ill-fated legislative plan to expand the membership of the Supreme Court, packing it with liberal justices to undercut that tribunal's conservative course. He also proposed a constitutional amendment requiring a vote of seven of the nine justices to declare a federal law unconstitutional. Two years later, Senate Democrats elected the gregarious Hoosier their assistant leader. Defeated in 1940 for a second Senate term, partly because his call for American entry into World War II did not play well in isolationist Indiana, Minton worked briefly as an assistant to President Roosevelt. The president subsequently appointed him to a federal appeals court. In September 1949, President Harry Truman named his former Senate seatmate to the Supreme Court.

When Judge Minton's nomination reached the Senate Judiciary Committee, several members recalled his earlier views on restructuring the high court. The committee decided to summon the nominee to explain his views. Minton refused. He contended that as a Senate leader in the 1930s, he had the right to advocate his party's views to the best of his ability. But, now, as a federal judge, he had moved from player to referee. The sympathetic committee then withdrew its request and the Senate quickly confirmed his appointment.

Two Senate customs, both in decline by the late 1940s, reinforced Minton's unwillingness to testify. The first was that when a senator received a presidential nomination, the Senate would immediately proceed to its consideration without referral to a committee. On Supreme Court nominations, the Senate had followed this practice, with one exception, until the late 1930s. The second custom, closely observed until 1925, held that Supreme Court nominees, regardless of their prior occupations, were not expected to testify before the Judiciary Committee.

During his seven years on the high court, Justice Minton occasionally visited the Senate floor to listen to debate. Today, he is remembered as the last member of Congress—incumbent or former—to receive a Supreme Court appointment.

Sherman Minton leaving the White House on October 5, 1949, after visiting President Truman to thank him for the Supreme Court nomination.

Further Reading

Gugin, Linda C., and James E. St. Clair. *Sherman Minton: New Deal Senator, Cold War Justice*. Indianapolis: Indiana Historical Society, 1997.

Thorpe, James A. "The Appearance of Supreme Court Nominees Before the Senate Judiciary Committee." *Journal of Public Law* 18 (1969): 371-402.

"Communists in Government Service"

"Today we are engaged in a final, all-out battle between communistic atheism and Christianity. The modern champions of communism have selected this as the time. And, ladies and gentlemen, the chips are down—they are truly down."

On February 9, 1950, the junior senator from Wisconsin thundered this warning in a Lincoln's birthday address to the Women's Republican Club of Wheeling, West Virginia.

Joseph R. McCarthy had come to the Senate three years earlier after unseating 22-year incumbent Robert La Follette, Jr., who had devoted more energies to passage of his landmark 1946 Legislative Reorganization Act than to that year's Republican senatorial primary.

The *Saturday Evening Post* heralded McCarthy's arrival with an article entitled "The Senate's Remarkable Upstart." For the next three years, McCarthy searched for an issue that would substantiate his remarkableness. As one of his many biographers

has observed, McCarthy's initial years in the Senate were characterized by his impatient disregard of the body's rules, customs, and procedures. Another scholar noted the ease with which he rearranged the truth to serve his purposes. "Once he got going, logic and decorum gave way to threats, personal attacks, and multiple distortions."

In the Wheeling speech, among the most significant in American political history, McCarthy's recklessness finally merged with his search for a propelling issue. He explained that home-grown traitors were causing America to lose the cold war. "While I cannot take the time to name all the men in the State Department who have been named as members of the Communist Party and members of a spy ring, I have here in my hand a list of 205." Until his Senate censure four years later, Joseph R. McCarthy would be that body's most controversial member.

Joseph R. McCarthy, senator from Wisconsin (1947-1957).

Further Reading
Griffith, Robert. *The Politics of Fear: Joseph McCarthy and the Senate*. Rochelle Park, N.J.: Hayden Book Company, Inc., 1970.

Kefauver Crime Committee Launched

In April 1950, the body of a Kansas City gambling kingpin was found in a Democratic club-house, slumped beneath a large portrait of President Harry S. Truman. His assassination intensified national concerns about the post World War II growth of powerful crime syndicates and the resulting gang warfare in the nation's larger cities.

On May 3, 1950, the Senate established a five-member Special Committee to Investigate Organized Crime in Interstate Commerce. Sensitive to the desire of several standing committees to conduct the investigation, Senate party leaders selected the special committee's members from the committees on Interstate Commerce and the Judiciary, including each panel's senior Republican. As chairman, the Democratic majority designated an ambitious freshman— Tennessee Senator Estes Kefauver.

The committee visited 14 major cities in 15 months, just as increasing numbers of Americans were purchasing their first television sets. When the panel reached New Orleans in January 1951, a local television station requested permission to televise an hour of testimony, perhaps to compete with a radio station that was carrying the entire proceedings. As the committee moved on to Detroit, a television station in that city preempted the popular children's show, *Howdy Doody*, to broadcast senators grilling mobsters.

Like a theater company doing previews on the road, the committee headed for Broadway, where the independent television station of the *New York Daily News* provided live feed to the networks. When the notorious gambler Frank Costello refused to testify on camera, the committee ordered the TV not to show his face. The cameras instead focused on the witness' nervously agitated hands, unexpectedly making riveting viewing. As the Associated Press explained, "Something big, unbelievably big and emphatic, smashed into the homes of millions of Americans last week when television cameras, cold-eyed and relentless, were trained on the Kefauver Crime hearings."

The Committee received 250,000 pieces of mail from a viewing audience estimated at 30 million. Although the hearings boosted Chairman Kefauver's political prospects, they helped to end the 12-year Senate career of Democratic Majority Leader Scott Lucas. In a tight 1950 reelection race against former Illinois Representative Everett Dirksen, Lucas urged Kefauver to keep his investigation away from an emerging Chicago police scandal until after election day. Kefauver refused. Election-eve publication of stolen secret committee documents hurt the Democratic Party in Cook County, cost Lucas the election, and gave Dirksen national prominence as the man who defeated the Senate majority leader.

Members of the Kefauver Committee. Left to right: Senator Charles Tobey of New Hampshire (1939-1953), Senator Herbert O'Conor of Maryland (1947-1953), committee counsel Rudolph Halley, Senator Estes Kefauver of Tennessee (1949-1963), and Senator Alexander Wiley of Wisconsin (1939-1963).

Further Reading

Moore, William Howard. *The Kefauver Committee and the Politics of Crime, 1950-1952.* Columbia: University of Missouri Press, 1974.

June 1, 1950

A "Declaration of Conscience"

Senator Joseph R. McCarthy encountered Maine Senator Margaret Chase Smith in the Capitol subway. He asked her why she looked so serious. Smith responded that she was on her way to the Senate Chamber to make a speech, and that he would not like what she had to say. McCarthy followed her into the chamber and watched as she began her remarks—her "Declaration of Conscience"—in a soft and trembling voice. As the freshman Republican proceeded, the color drained from McCarthy's face.

"Mr. President," she said on June 1, 1950, "I would like to speak briefly and simply about a serious national condition. It is a national feeling of fear and frustration that could result in national suicide and the end of everything that we Americans hold dear." She continued, "The United States Senate has long enjoyed the worldwide respect as the greatest deliberative body in the world. But recently that deliberative character has too often been debased to the level of a forum of hate and character assassination sheltered by the shield of congressional immunity."

When Smith completed her 15-minute address, McCarthy silently left the chamber. He explained his silence to an associate, "I don't fight with women senators." In a characteristically scornful manner, he privately referred to Smith and the six other senators who had endorsed her "Declaration" as "Snow White and her Six Dwarfs."

Initially, Smith had shared McCarthy's concerns, but she grew angry at the ferocity of his attacks and his subsequent defamation of those whom she knew to be above suspicion. Without mentioning McCarthy by name, she decided to take a stand against her colleague and his tactics.

The speech triggered a public explosion of support and outrage. *Newsweek* ran her photo on its cover and touted her as a possible vice-presidential candidate. Within weeks, however, the nation's attention shifted to the invasion of South Korea that launched the United States into a hot war against Communist aggression. For the time being, her remarks were forgotten. Four years would pass before Smith gained the satisfaction of voting with the Senate to censure McCarthy, thereby ending his campaign of falsehood and intimidation.

This cartoon, published in 1953 and reflecting McCarthy's hunt for Communists in the State Department, depicts a dismayed Secretary of State John Foster Dulles finding McCarthy hiding in his desk drawer.

Further Reading

Sherman, Janann. *No Place for a Woman: A Life of Senator Margaret Chase Smith*. New Brunswick, N.J.: Rutgers University Press, 2000.

September 22, 1950

The Senate Donates a Historic Desk

In the summer of 1938, a structural engineer climbed to the roof over the Senate Chamber. After completing a thorough examination of the 90-ton iron and glass-paneled ceiling, he concluded that its beams and supports, installed 80 years earlier, were obsolete, over-stressed, and a direct danger to those below. Discussion of his finding quickly expanded to the related problems of the chamber's inadequate ventilation, acoustics, and lighting. By the time additional studies were completed, however, World War II had engulfed Europe. Facing a wartime emergency and the need to divert inventories of steel to military use, Congress deferred reconstruction of both its legislative chambers and provided for temporary supports that some senators likened to "barn rafters."

With the war over, both houses accepted consulting architects' design plans for a complete renovation of their chambers. These new plans abandoned the Victorian-style Senate Chamber of the late 1850s in favor of the current chamber's neoclassical theme.

The reconstruction took place in two phases. On July 1, 1949, the Senate vacated its chamber to allow for the ceiling's construction and moved down the hall to its pre-1859 quarters for that session's remaining 14 weeks. Owing to the old chamber's smaller capacity, members moved without their desks. A year later, they again returned to those cramped quarters so that the chamber's lower portion could be refashioned.

No longer needed in the Senate Chamber's new design scheme was the historic walnut presiding officer's desk that Capitol Architect Thomas U. Walter had designed in 1858. This gave Senate Chief Clerk Emery Frazier an idea. A student of the Senate's history and a proud native of Kentucky, Frazier devised a plan to have the Senate present the surplus desk to its last user—at that time the nation's most famous Kentuckian—Vice President and former Senate Majority Leader Alben Barkley. Frazier noted that the desk's first occupant 90 years earlier—Vice President John Breckinridge—had also represented Kentucky in the Senate.

On September 22, 1950, the Senate agreed unanimously to present the desk to Barkley as "an expression of high appreciation." Today, it resides at the University of Kentucky in Lexington.

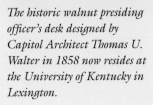

The historic walnut presiding officer's desk designed by Capitol Architect Thomas U. Walter in 1858 now resides at the University of Kentucky in Lexington.

Further Reading

"U.S. Senate Clerk's Desk Is Presented to Kentucky," *Louisville* [Ky.] *Courier-Journal*, August 2, 1951.

February 3, 1951

Attending Physician Offers Advice to Lawmakers

In December 1928, one House member dropped dead and two others collapsed from causes attributed to overwork. Although officials in each case immediately summoned medical assistance from city hospitals, several hours passed before a physician arrived to render aid. In 1928 alone, incumbent members of the Senate and House were dying at the appalling rate of almost 20 per year.

On December 5, 1928, the House passed a resolution directing the secretary of the navy to detail a medical officer to be present near the House Chamber while that body was in session. The secretary assigned Dr. George Calver, who initially took up residence in the House Democratic cloakroom. Not to be outdone by the House in a gesture of concern for the well-being of its members, the Senate in April 1930 adopted a concurrent resolution extending Dr. Calver's jurisdiction to its premises. Although the House subsequently ignored that concurrent resolution, the navy secretary, on the strength of the Senate's action, directed Dr. Calver to "look after both houses." Thus was born the Office of Attending Physician, which moved to two ground-floor rooms in its current location near the midpoint of the Capitol's west-front corridor. Within several months, both houses recognized the office's existence by providing funding for its operations.

Soon after he took office in the darkest days of the Great Depression, Dr. Calver earned national headlines with a stern warning to members. Following the collapse of the House Ways and Means Committee chairman during an influenza outbreak, and the sidelining of dozens of senators and representatives, Calver cautioned against overdoing committee work.

The Congress that began in December 1931 suffered a particularly large toll. Before it was four months old, that body witnessed the deaths of four senators and 16 representatives. Many others took to their beds under a legislative strain that long-serving members considered unprecedented.

For the next 35 years, until his retirement in 1966, Dr. Calver routinely captured national media attention with his advice to hardworking members. On February 3, 1951, the *New York Times Magazine* reported on his "nine commandments of health," which were printed on large placards and displayed throughout the Capitol. They included: "Eat wisely, drink plentifully (of water!). Play enthusiastically, and relax completely. Stay out of the Washington social whirl—go out at night twice a week at most." His ultimate advice: "Don't let yourself get off-balance, nervous, and disturbed over things."

George C. Calver, attending physician for Congress, photographed soon after his appointment in 1928.

Further Reading
New York Times Magazine, February 3, 1951.

April 18, 1951

Arthur Vandenberg Dies

The April 1951 death of Arthur H. Vandenberg removed from the Senate one of its undisputed 20th-century giants. Although his death saddened his colleagues and admirers, it did not surprise them, for he had been away from the Senate for most of the 19 months since undergoing surgery for lung cancer. His son acknowledged that the senator had known of his condition for more than a year before that surgery in October 1949, but had been too busy with his Senate duties to seek timely treatment.

In 1945, Arthur Vandenberg delivered a celebrated "speech heard round the world," announcing his conversion from isolationism to internationalism. In so doing, he became the embodiment of a bipartisan American approach to the cold war.

Born in Michigan, he studied law at the University of Michigan but chose a career in journalism. Vandenberg served as editor and publisher of the *Grand Rapids Herald* from 1906 until 1928, when he was appointed to fill a vacancy in the U.S. Senate. Running as a Republican, Vandenberg then won election to the seat, which he held until his death.

During the 1930s, Senator Vandenberg became a leading proponent of isolationism, determined to keep the United States out of another world war, but the Japanese attack on Pearl Harbor ended his isolationism. During the Second World War, he grappled with the potential international role for the United States in the postwar world. On January 10, 1945, he delivered his most memorable speech in the Senate, confessing that prewar isolationism was the wrong course, calling on America to assume the responsibilities of world leadership, and endorsing the creation of the United Nations.

In 1947, at the start of the cold war, Vandenberg became chairman of the Senate Foreign Relations Committee. In that position, he cooperated with the Truman administration in forging bipartisan support for the Truman Doctrine, the Marshall Plan, and NATO—the first mutual defense treaty that the United States had entered since its alliance with France during the American Revolution. When Vandenberg spoke, the Senate Chamber filled with senators and reporters, eager to hear what he had to say. His words swayed votes and won national and international respect for his nonpartisan, consensus-building, statesman-like approach to foreign policy.

In September 2004, the Senate formally recognized Arthur Vandenberg's singular contributions by adding his portrait image to the permanent gallery of outstanding former senators in the Senate Reception Room.

Arthur Vandenberg, senator from Michigan (1928-1951).

Further Reading

"Vandenberg Dies; Michigan's GOP Senior Senator," *Washington Post,* April 19, 1951, 1.

"Vandenberg, Wagner Take Places of Honor," *Roll Call,* September 15, 2004.

May 3, 1951

A Constitutional Crisis Averted

Consider the dangers for a constitutional democracy of this potentially explosive mixture: a stalemated war, an unpopular president, and a defiant general with a plan for victory and a huge public following. In the somber spring of 1951, Senators Richard Russell and Tom Connally sought to diffuse this brewing crisis by arranging for the committees they chaired—Armed Services and Foreign Relations—to conduct a series of joint hearings.

The target of their inquiry was General Douglas MacArthur. Three weeks before the hearings began on May 3, President Harry Truman had fired MacArthur as commander of United Nations' forces in the Korean War. Truman had rejected the general's view that the only way to end the stalemate in Korea was to launch an attack on China. When MacArthur then publicly criticized his commander in chief, a furious Truman sacked him for insubordination. Instantly, MacArthur became a national hero—a potential presidential candidate. After he delivered his "farewell address" to a tumultuous joint meeting of Congress and rode in a massive hero's parade in New York City, senators received two million pieces of mail in his favor.

As chairman of the joint hearings, Senator Russell conducted the proceedings with great deliberation, providing for a full exchange of views. Realizing that the testimony would include highly sensitive war-related testimony, but also aware of the value of making these discussions quickly available to avoid trouble-causing leaks, he arranged a compromise. The joint committee would conduct the sessions in secret, but release immediately sanitized transcripts every 30 minutes to reporters crowded outside the Caucus Room's heavily guarded doors.

In three days of testimony, MacArthur weakened his own case with vague and over-stated responses. He observed that his troubles came from the politicians in Washington who had introduced "a new concept into military operations—the concept of appeasement." When MacArthur was asked whether he thought his plan for bombing China might trigger another world war, he observed that this was not his area of responsibility. His case was fatally weakened with testimony from senior military leaders who strongly disagreed with MacArthur's plan. After seven weeks of exhaustive testimony, the public lost interest. By fully airing this dangerous issue, Chairman Russell had avoided a political conflagration and brilliantly demonstrated the Senate's proverbial role as the saucer into which the hot tea is poured to be safely cooled.

A cartoonist's view of Richard Russell's 1951 inquiry into the MacArthur dismissal.

Further Reading

Fite, Gilbert C. *Richard B. Russell, Jr., Senator from Georgia*. Chapel Hill: University of North Carolina Press, 1991.

Wayne Morse Sets Filibuster Record

His admirers called him "The Tiger of the Senate." His many enemies, including five presidents, called him a lot worse. Today he is remembered as a gifted lawmaker and principled maverick who thrived on controversy.

Wayne Morse was born in Wisconsin in 1900. In his early years, he fell under the influence of that state's fiery progressive senator, Robert M. La Follette, a stem-winding orator and champion of family farmers and the laboring poor. In the 1930s, Morse became the nation's youngest law school dean and a skilled labor arbitrator. In 1944, despite his New Deal sympathies, he won election as a Republican to an Oregon U.S. Senate seat.

During the 1952 presidential campaign, Morse broke ranks with Republican leaders over the party's platform and Dwight Eisenhower's choice of Richard Nixon as his running mate. Claiming the Republican Party had left him, Morse announced his switch to Independent status.

Wayne Morse, senator from Oregon (1945-1969), lying on a cot in the Senate cloakroom during a continuous debate over atomic energy.

In January 1953, Morse arrived at the opening session of the 83rd Congress with a folding chair and a comment. "Since I haven't been given any seat in the new Senate, I decided to bring my own." Although he was placed on the majority Republican side, that party's caucus stripped him of his choice committee assignments.

Against this backdrop, Wayne Morse rose on the Senate floor on April 24, 1953. Described as "a lean trim man, with a clipped mustache, sharp nose, and bushy black eyebrows," he began a filibuster against Tidelands Oil legislation. When he concluded after 22 hours and 26 minutes, he had broken the 18-hour record set in 1908 by his mentor, Robert La Follette. Morse kept that distinction until 1957, when Strom Thurmond logged the current record of 24 hours and 18 minutes.

In 1955, Morse formally changed his party allegiance, giving Senate Democrats the one-vote margin that returned them to the majority. Majority Leader Lyndon Johnson gave him his choice of committee assignments. In 1968, Morse, a resolute critic of the war in Vietnam, lost his Senate seat to Robert Packwood by less than 3,000 votes. He died six years later in the midst of a campaign to regain that seat. This blunt-spoken, iconoclastic populist is remembered today with many colorful stories. For example, Clare Boothe Luce was forced to resign her newly confirmed ambassadorship after commenting that her troubles with Senator Morse went back to the time when he had been kicked in the head by a horse.

Further Reading

Drukman, Mason. *Wayne Morse: A Political Biography.* Portland: Oregon Historical Society Press, 1997.

June 9, 1954

"Have You No Sense of Decency?"

Wisconsin Republican Senator Joseph R. McCarthy rocketed to public attention in 1950 with his allegations that hundreds of Communists had infiltrated the State Department and other federal agencies. These charges struck a particularly responsive note at a time of deepening national anxiety about the spread of world communism.

McCarthy relentlessly continued his anticommunist campaign into 1953, when he gained a new platform as chairman of Senate Permanent Subcommittee on Investigations. He quickly put his imprint on that subcommittee, shifting its focus from investigating fraud and waste in the executive branch to hunting for Communists. He conducted scores of hearings, calling hundreds of witnesses in both public and closed sessions.

A dispute over his hiring of staff without consulting other committee members prompted the panel's three Democrats to resign in July 1953. Republican senators also stopped attending, in part because so many of the hearings were called on short notice or held away from the nation's capital. As a result, McCarthy and his chief counsel Roy Cohn largely ran the show by themselves, relentlessly grilling and insulting witnesses. Harvard law dean Erwin Griswold described McCarthy's role as "judge, jury, prosecutor, castigator, and press agent, all in one."

In the spring of 1954, McCarthy picked a fight with the U.S. Army, charging lax security at a top-secret army facility. The army responded that the senator had sought preferential treatment for a recently drafted subcommittee aide. Amidst this controversy, McCarthy temporarily stepped down as chairman for the duration of the three-month nationally televised spectacle known to history as the Army-McCarthy hearings.

The army hired Boston lawyer Joseph Welch to make its case. At a session on June 9, 1954, McCarthy charged that one of Welch's attorneys had ties to a Communist organization. As an amazed television audience looked on, Welch responded with the immortal lines that ultimately ended McCarthy's career: "Until this moment, Senator, I think I never really gauged your cruelty or your recklessness." When McCarthy tried to continue his attack, Welch angrily interrupted, "Let us not assassinate this lad further, senator. You have done enough. Have you no sense of decency, sir, at long last? Have you left no sense of decency?"

Overnight, McCarthy's immense national popularity evaporated. Censured by his Senate colleagues, ostracized by his party, and ignored by the press, McCarthy died three years later, 48 years old and a broken man.

Army lawyer Joseph Welch, left with head in hand, *and Senator Joseph McCarthy,* standing, *at the Army-McCarthy hearings in 1954.*

Further Reading

U.S. Congress. Senate. *Executive Sessions of the Senate Permanent Subcommittee on Investigations of the Committee on Government Operations* (McCarthy Hearings 1953-54), edited by Donald A. Ritchie and Elizabeth Bolling. Washington: GPO, 2003. S. Prt. 107-84.

Senator Elected on a Write-in Ballot

Strom Thurmond, senator from South Carolina (1954-2003).

On the first day of September 1954, South Carolina Democratic Senator Burnet Maybank died unexpectedly. Earlier that year, Maybank had won his party's primary nomination for a third full Senate term. With time running short before the November general election, the Democratic Party's state executive committee, on a divided vote, decided not to hold a special primary. Instead, the committee unanimously designated its own nominee—66-year-old state senator Edgar Brown. Known in state circles as "Mr. Democrat," Brown had long and effectively served the party. No one seriously questioned his right to the seat, but many questioned the process by which he appeared about to claim it. The executive committee badly miscalculated the depth of public feeling that such decisions should be made in the voting booth.

At that point, 51-year-old former Governor Strom Thurmond announced his intention to run as a write-in candidate. Capitalizing on public outrage, he denounced the state party hierarchy for its high-handed decision and promised voters that although he would be running as an Independent, he would, if elected, participate in the Senate Democratic Caucus and vote as a Democrat to organize the Senate. (In 1954, Republicans controlled the Senate by a one-vote majority.)

On November 2, 1954, Strom Thurmond won with 63 percent of the vote and thereby became the only person ever elected to the Senate on a write-in. During his abbreviated 1954 campaign, he had pledged that if elected, he would resign prior to the 1956 primary so that voters rather than the party executive committee could make that crucial choice. True to his word, Senator Thurmond resigned in April 1956. He won that primary and the November general election. He once again took his Senate oath on November 7, 1956. Although he changed his party allegiance in September 1964 to become a Republican, Thurmond went on to establish two significant service records. On March 8, 1996, he became the oldest person to serve in the Senate at the age of 93 years and 94 days, breaking the record set by Rhode Island Democrat Theodore F. Green on January 3, 1961. A year later, on May 25, 1997, Thurmond became the longest-serving member in Senate history to that time when he reached 41 years and 10 months.

Further Reading

Bass, Jack and Marilyn W. Thompson. *Strom: The Complicated Personal and Political Life of Strom Thurmond*. New York: Public Affairs, 2005.

Clymer, Adam. "Strom Thurmond, Foe of Integration, Dies at 100," *New York Times,* June 27, 2003, A1.

Cohodas, Nadine. *Strom Thurmond & the Politics of Southern Change*. Macon, Ga.: Mercer University Press, 1993.

November 17, 1954

The Senate's New Gavel

A visitor sitting in the Senate Chamber gallery on November 17, 1954, could have been excused for wondering what exactly was happening on the floor below. Just after 2 p.m., the Senate declared a recess. Instead of members heading away from the floor, many arrived and took their seats. Through the center doors appeared Majority Leader William Knowland and Minority Leader Lyndon Johnson, followed by the vice president of India. The leaders guided their guest to the rostrum and introduced him to the vice president of the United States, Richard Nixon.

In his remarks, the Indian vice president noted that his recently independent nation had modeled its democratic institutions on those of the United States. As presiding officer of his nation's upper house, he welcomed the opportunity to present to the Senate an instrument without which a presiding officer would be ineffectual—a gavel. He hoped the gavel would inspire senators to debate "with freedom from passion and prejudice."

In replying, Vice President Nixon explained that the donated gavel would replace the Senate's old gavel—a two-and-one-half-inch, hour-glass-shaped piece of ivory, which, he said, had begun "to come apart" recently. What Nixon failed to mention was that the gavel had begun "to come apart" thanks to his own heavy hand.

Vice President John Adams may have used that gavel in 1789, although he seems to have preferred the attention-getting device of tapping his pencil on a water glass. By the 1940s, the old gavel had begun to deteriorate; in 1952 the Senate had silver pieces attached to both ends to limit further damage. During a heated, late-night debate in 1954, Nixon shattered the instrument. Unable to find a replacement through commercial sources, the Senate turned to the Embassy of India. The replacement gavel duplicated the original with the addition of a floral band carved around its center.

There may have been no more effective wielder of that legislative instrument than Charles Fairbanks, vice president from 1905 to 1909. According to one witness, "He wouldn't hit it very hard, but when things started to get noisy on the floor, he'd lean over the desk and just tap-tap-tap a few times on the thin part of the desk. He used to say," according to the observer, "it wasn't loud noise that attracted the senators' attention, it was just a different noise."

The new Senate gavel, right, replaced the old cracked gavel in 1954.

Further Reading
Bedini, Silvio. "The Mace and the Gavel: Symbols of Government in America." *Transactions of the American Philosophical Society* 87 (1997): 63-70.

Alben Barkley Delivers Immortal Farewell Address

It was perhaps the best exit line in all of American political history. Never has a United States senator bid farewell with such timing and drama.

Kentucky's Alben Barkley served in the U.S. House from 1913 until 1927, when he moved to the Senate. In 1937, Senate Democrats chose him as their majority leader. At the 1948 Democratic convention, the 70-year-old Barkley won the vice-presidential nomination. The following January, after 12 years of leading the Senate from the floor, Vice President Barkley became its constitutional presiding officer. His young grandson considered the formal title of "Mr. Vice President" to be a mouthful and invented an abbreviated alternative, by which Barkley was known for the rest of his life: "The Veep."

Barkley loved the Senate and became the last vice president to preside more than half the time the Senate was in session. He was also the last vice president not to have an office in or near the White House. Despite the honor of his vice-presidential position, Barkley missed being a senator. He enjoyed telling the story of the mother who had two sons. One went to sea; the other became vice president; and neither was heard from again. When his vice-presidential term ended in 1953, Barkley happily ran for Kentucky's other Senate seat. His 1954 defeat of an incumbent Republican returned Senate control to the Democrats by a one-vote margin and made Lyndon Johnson majority leader.

On April 30, 1956, the 78-year-old Kentucky senator traveled to Virginia's Washington and Lee University. There he gave one of his trademark rip-snorting, Republican-bashing speeches. At its conclusion, he reminded his audience that after 42 years in national politics he had become a freshman again and had declined a front-row chamber seat with senior senators. "I am glad to sit on the back row," he declared, "for I would rather be a servant in the House of the Lord than to sit in the seats of the mighty." Then, with the applause of a large audience ringing in his ears, he dropped dead.

For an old-fashioned orator, there could have been no more appropriate final stage exit.

Alben W. Barkley, senator from Kentucky (1927-1949, 1955-1956).

Further Reading

Barkley, Alben W. "The Majority Leader in the Legislative Process." In *The Process of Government*, edited by Simeon S. Willis, et al. Lexington: Bureau of Government Research, University of Kentucky, 1949.

Barkley, Alben W. *That Reminds Me*. Garden City, NY: Doubleday & Co., 1954.

Barkley, Jane R. *I Married the Veep*. New York: Vanguard Press, 1958.

Ritchie, Donald A. "Alben W. Barkley: The President's Man." In *First Among Equals: Outstanding Senate Leaders of the Twentieth Century*, edited by Richard A. Baker and Roger H. Davidson. Washington, D.C.: Congressional Quarterly, 1991.

July 13, 1956

Dirksen Building Cornerstone Laid

The search for adequate office space proved to be a major theme in the institutional history of Congress during the 20th century. The first permanent Senate office building, later named to honor Georgia Senator Richard Russell, opened in 1909. In 1941, congressional officials acknowledged that this facility—despite an addition built along its First Street side in the 1930s—had reached its capacity. Faced with the option of leasing expensive space in nearby private buildings, they began planning for a second building. World War II intervened, however, and delayed action until 1948. By that time, the demand for additional quarters had reached a critical point.

Until the 1940s, Senate staff positions had been mostly clerical and custodial. The shock of the wartime experience convinced congressional leaders of the need to expand Hill staffs to include experts on a growing list of complex policy issues.

Soon after the war ended, Congress passed the Legislative Reorganization Act of 1946. This landmark statute allowed Congress to hire professional staffs in ranges of competence and salary equal to those employed within the executive branch. Each committee gained four professional and six clerical aides.

This surge of newly arriving staff intensified the need for a second building—one intended primarily to accommodate committees. In a departure from committee arrangements in the Russell Building, where members and witnesses sat around a common table, the new building would feature large hearing rooms with raised platforms for members and facilities suitable for the newly emerging medium of television.

In 1948, the Senate acquired land across First Street from the Russell Building. The block—known as "Slum's Row"—contained substandard housing considered an unsightly backdrop to the Capitol. When construction crews cleared the land, 500 people were left to find other homes.

As architects completed their drawings in 1949, a dispute among key senators over the building's size and cost delayed the project for another five years. Finally, the Senate agreed to a scaled back plan and officials laid the cornerstone on July 13, 1956.

When the new facility, later named in memory of Illinois Senator Everett Dirksen, opened in October 1958, few might have predicted that 14 years later a proposal for yet another building would begin its journey through the legislative pipeline. In 1982, this third structure opened as the Philip Hart Senate Office Building.

The new Senate Office Building, later named the Dirksen Senate Office Building, under construction in December 1956.

Further Reading

U.S. Congress. Senate. *History of the United States Capitol: A Chronicle of Design, Construction, and Politics,* by William C. Allen. 106th Congress, 2d sess., 2001. S. Doc. 106-29.

July 27, 1956

Escaping Summer's Heat

On July 27, 1956, Congress completed work on its appropriations bills and adjourned for the year. In doing this at a time when the new fiscal year began on July 1, members followed the traditional practice of concluding the year's session before the truly sultry "dog-days" of August set in. The end to the 1956 session came at midnight, as Majority Leader Lyndon Johnson and his colleagues boisterously applauded the chamber's presiding officer, Vice President Richard Nixon.

As senators left town, none could have realized that day's history-making significance. Never again in the 20th century, owing to increased congressional workload and better air conditioning, would Congress adjourn for the year as early as July.

For years, diplomats received hardship pay for enduring Washington's oppressive summer heat. Members of Congress received no such bonus. Consequently, unless the demands of war or other national emergencies kept them in session, they tried to adjourn before high temperatures and humidity overwhelmed the Capitol's primitive air-conditioning system.

When the Senate moved to its current chamber in 1859, members paid particular attention to that room's steam-powered ventilation apparatus. In their first summer session there, during June 1860, senators complained of the

Two women fry eggs on a cement wall near the Capitol in the hot summer of 1929.

hot, stale air. Only the looming crisis of the Civil War kept them from authorizing reconstruction of the chamber adjacent to the building's outside walls so that they could at least open some windows for cross-ventilation.

Another 70 years passed before the 1929 installation of a cooling system grandly advertised as "manufactured weather." That system also proved inadequate on the hottest days. Although some improvement came with the renovation of the chamber in 1950, members at mid-century still had to contend with the city's summertime climate.

There were other reasons for the 1956 July adjournment. Four days earlier, the House of Representatives had overwhelmingly passed a major civil rights bill. Georgia Senator Richard Russell, who opposed the legislation, convinced Majority Leader Johnson that bringing up that bill in the Senate would trigger a filibuster guaranteed to keep them in session until the mid-August Democratic national convention. The bitterness sure to result from a prolonged debate, Russell warned, would weaken the party at its convention and destroy any hope Johnson might have had of gaining a future presidential nomination.

Perhaps departing senators had in mind House Speaker John Nance Garner's advice about summer sessions: "No good legislation ever comes out of Washington after June."

Further Reading
White, William S. "Congress Quits After Approving Foreign Aid Fund." *New York Times,* July 28, 1956.

Citadel

On January 10, 1957, the chief congressional correspondent of the *New York Times*, William S. White, published a book entitled *Citadel: The Story of the U.S. Senate*. An immediate bestseller, *Citadel* soon became one of the most influential books ever written about the Senate.

In promoting this book, William White enjoyed several advantages. First, he admired the Senate, which he characterized as "the one touch of authentic genius in the American political system." He had covered Congress for more than a decade and had recently won a Pulitzer Prize for his biography of the late Republican Majority Leader Robert Taft. As pressures for passage of the first civil rights act since the Reconstruction era focused the public's attention on the Senate, one book reviewer commented that *Citadel* would help Americans understand the "mysterious ways of senators and the baffling behavior of the Senate."

By any standard, William White was a Senate insider. A native Texan, White had known and admired Democratic Majority Leader Lyndon Johnson for 25 years. He proudly counted himself among Johnson's inner circle of advisers.

Employing a light and breezy style, White takes the reader into his confidence to explain what was really happening behind the public face of the Senate. An extended essay, rather than a scholarly treatise, *Citadel* remains worth reading decades later.

White popularized the notion of the Senate as a gentlemen's club, run by a small inner circle of intuitively skilled legislators. He described the model senator of his day as a "sensitive soul," with the temperament of an artist rather than a person in business. He characterized each major Senate committee as an "imperious force," whose chairman, "unless he is a weak and irresolute man, is emperor."

Thirty years after publishing *Citadel,* White looked back fondly at the Senate of the mid 1950s. "My old Senate had a full complement of big egos, but on the whole those who thought extremely well of themselves had good reason so to think."

Both *Citadel* and Senator John F. Kennedy's Pulitzer-Prize-winning *Profiles in Courage*, published within months of each other, enhanced the Senate's popular image. This did not go unnoticed on the House side of the Capitol. One day White ran into Speaker Sam Rayburn. Rayburn acknowledged him coolly and asked why he was visiting the House. White responded, "Do I need a passport?" Rayburn shot back, "Yes, hereafter you do."

CITADEL
★
The Story of the U. S. Senate by William S. White

Author of
THE TAFT STORY
PULITZER PRIZE BIOGRAPHY

Told in human terms, illustrated with anecdotes of drama and wit, here is a unique study of a place upon whose vitality and honor will at length rest the whole issue of the kind of society we are to maintain.

An immediate bestseller, Citadel *soon became one of the most influential books ever written about the Senate.*

Further Reading
White, William S. *Citadel: The Story of the U.S. Senate.* New York: Harper & Brothers, 1957.

March 12, 1959

The "Famous Five"

J ust after noontime on March 12, 1959, a festive crowd jammed the Capitol's Senate Reception Room to induct five former members into a senatorial "hall of fame."

Four years earlier, the Senate had formed a special committee to identify outstanding former members, no longer living, whose

Republican Leader Everett Dirksen delivers remarks at the reception honoring the five outstanding former senators whose portraits would hang in the Senate Reception Room.

likenesses would be placed in five vacant portrait spaces in the Reception Room.

Leading the five-member committee was a 38-year-old freshman who had recently written a book about courageous senators. That book, published in January 1956 under the title *Profiles In Courage,* earned Senator John F. Kennedy the 1957 Pulitzer Prize in biography. The committee also included Democrats Richard Russell (GA) and Mike Mansfield (MT), and Republicans Styles Bridges (NH) and John Bricker (OH).

The Kennedy committee struggled to define senatorial greatness. Should they apply a test of "legislative accomplishment"? Perhaps, in addition to positive achievement there should be recognition of, as they put it, "courageous negation." What about those senators who consistently failed to secure major legislation, but in failing, opened the road to success for a later generation?

Personal integrity? That might exclude the chronically indebted Daniel Webster. National leadership? That would knock out great regional leaders like John C. Calhoun. The unanimous respect of one's colleagues? That would doom the antislavery leader Charles Sumner. The Kennedy committee's established criteria nicely evaded these questions. It agreed to judge candidates "for acts of statesmanship transcending party and State lines" and to define "statesmanship" to include "leadership in national thought and constitutional interpretation as well as legislation." The committee further agreed that it would not recommend a candidate unless all its members agreed to that choice.

An advisory committee of 160 scholars offered 65 candidates. Sixty-five names for five spaces! Senator Kennedy quipped that sports writers choosing entrants to the Baseball Hall of Fame had it easy by comparison. As its top choice, the scholars' committee named Nebraska's Progressive Republican George Norris, a senator from 1913 to 1943. Senate panel member Styles Bridges disagreed and, along with Nebraska's two incumbent senators, consequently blocked his further consideration.

On May 1, 1957, the Kennedy Committee reported to the Senate its choices: Henry Clay (KY), John C. Calhoun (SC), Daniel Webster (MA), Robert Taft (OH), and Robert La Follette, Sr. (WI). In 2004, the Senate added Arthur Vandenberg (MI) and Robert Wagner (NY) to this distinguished company.

Further Reading

Kennedy, John F, "Search for the Five Greatest Senators," *The New York Times Magazine,* April 14, 1957.

U.S. Congress. Senate. *Senate Reception Room.* 85th Cong., 1st sess., 1957. S. Rep. 85-279.

April 14, 1959

Taft Bell Tower Dedicated

The Taft family of Cincinnati, Ohio, has inspired two major Capitol Hill landmarks. William Howard Taft, the nation's 27th president and 10th chief justice, successfully campaigned for construction of the Supreme Court Building, allowing the Court to move out of its cramped Capitol quarters in 1935. His son, Robert Alphonso Taft, who represented Ohio in the U.S. Senate from 1939 until his death in 1953, is the subject of the Taft Memorial, located one block north and west of the Capitol.

On April 14, 1959, a crowd of 5,000 braved a morning chill as President Dwight Eisenhower dedicated the Taft Memorial to the Republican Senate majority leader whose presidential hopes he had extinguished in the 1952 Republican primaries. Following Eisenhower's brief remarks, and a eulogy by former President Herbert Hoover, Vice President Richard Nixon accepted the structure on behalf of the Senate.

The memorial, authorized in 1955, includes a 100-foot bell tower of Tennessee marble resting on a base 15 feet above ground level. A 10-foot bronze statue of Robert Taft stands on that base, along the tower's west side. Incised in the marble above his head are words paying tribute to "the honesty, indomitable courage and high principles of free government symbolized by his life." The bell tower's unadorned design reflects Taft's "simple strength and quiet dignity."

The tower's carillon includes 27 matched bronze bells ranging in weight from 126 pounds to 6 tons. The large central bell strikes on the hour, while the smaller fixed bells chime on the quarter-hour. By resolution of Congress, they play the Star Spangled Banner at 2 p.m. on the Fourth of July.

A month before the tower's dedication, a portrait of Robert Taft had been unveiled in a Senate Reception Room ceremony honoring five outstanding former senators.

These memorial activities sparked great interest, over the next quarter century, in naming office buildings and Capitol rooms after esteemed former members.

The Robert A. Taft Memorial and Carillon, located on Constitution Avenue between New Jersey Avenue and First Street, NW.

Further Reading

U.S. Congress. House. *Dedication Ceremony: Robert A. Taft Memorial, Tuesday, April 14, 1959.* 86th Congress, 1st sess., 1959. H. Doc. 121.

Cabinet Nomination Defeated

Over its more than two centuries of existence, the Senate has formally rejected only nine cabinet nominees. The 64-year period between 1925 and 1989 produced just one rejection. It occurred on June 19, 1959.

President Dwight Eisenhower called it "the second most shameful day in Senate history," second only to Andrew Johnson's impeachment trial. *Time* magazine pronounced it a "stinging personal slap . . . U.S. history's bitterest battle over confirmation of a presidential nomination." Others debated whether it was a "legislative lynching or political suicide."

When Eisenhower gave Admiral Lewis Strauss a recess appointment as secretary of commerce two weeks before the 1958 midterm congressional elections, neither man expected the cataclysm that awaited the Republican Party on election day. Strauss had served for the past four years as chairman of the Atomic Energy Commission. His tenure there had been particularly stormy. On one occasion, he angrily stated that New Mexico's Democratic Senator Clinton Anderson, chairman of the Joint Committee on Atomic Energy, had "a limited understanding of what is involved" in cold-war atomic energy policy. Although Anderson never forgave Strauss for that remark, he told the White House he would not stand in the way of his confirmation to the lower-profile post as commerce secretary.

The 1958 elections, however, dramatically changed the Senate's composition and outlook. An economic recession, White House influence-peddling scandals, and concerns over Soviet breakthroughs in outer space produced the largest transfer of seats from one party to another in the Senate's history. Democrats gained 13 Republican seats, plus two seats from the new state of Alaska. This added up to 64 Democrats and 34 Republicans.

With the 1960 elections nearing, congressional Democrats sought issues on which they could conspicuously oppose the Republican administration. The Strauss nomination proved tailor made. During confirmation hearings that quickly turned sour, Strauss displayed a condescending and disdainful attitude toward members of the Senate. His insistence on remaining at the witness table to cross-examine hostile witnesses—and senators—angered his supporters and delighted opponents. Anderson abandoned his earlier hands-off pledge and vigorously lobbied his Senate colleagues to reject the imperious admiral.

At 35 minutes past midnight, on June 19, 1959, in a packed Senate Chamber, the Strauss nomination died on a cliff-hanging roll-call vote of 46 in favor, 49 opposed. The Strauss rejection heralded a period of legislative stalemate for the remaining 18 months of the Eisenhower presidency.

Clinton P. Anderson, left, *senator from New Mexico (1949-1973), shakes hands with Admiral Lewis Strauss, President Eisenhower's nominee for secretary of commerce.*

Further Reading
Baker, Richard A. "A Slap at the 'Hidden-Hand Presidency': The Senate and the Lewis Strauss Affair." *Congress and the Presidency* 14 (Spring, 1987): 1-15.

November 8, 1959

"Wild Bill"

North Dakota Republican William Langer was one of the 20th century's most colorful United States senators. In 1959, he was described as "tempestuous," "swashbuckling," and "thoroughly unpredictable in his actions and attitudes."

"Wild Bill" Langer, as he came to be known, began his public career in 1916 as North Dakota's hard-charging attorney general. In 1932, he won the state's governorship thanks to support from Depression-ravaged farmers. Two years later, however, he was convicted and removed from office for forcing state employees to donate 5 percent of their salaries to his political organization. Always a fighter, Langer won exoneration and another term as governor. In 1940, he gained a seat in the U.S. Senate.

On January 3, 1941, when Langer appeared in the Senate Chamber to take his oath, Majority Leader Alben Barkley announced that several citizens of North Dakota had petitioned the Senate to deny him a seat owing to his financial misconduct as governor. The Senate seated him without prejudice and referred the matter to the Committee on Privileges and Elections. That inquiry by the committee consumed an entire year.

In January 1942, the committee's 4,200-page majority report recommended Langer be denied his seat as morally unfit to be a United States senator. Allegations included jury tampering and inciting to riot. A committee minority sharply disagreed, noting that voters had been well aware of the largely unsubstantiated charges at the time of Langer's election. The minority warned against allowing the Senate to be used by a winner's opponents to overturn the results of a lawful election. In its requirements for election to the Senate, they noted, the Constitution makes no reference to moral purity.

For two weeks in March 1942, as the challenges of the nation's recent entry into World War II confronted Congress, William Langer sat in the Senate Chamber listening to colleagues debate his moral character. In the end, by a two-to-one margin, they upheld his seating.

Langer went on to win three additional Senate terms and to serve as Judiciary Committee chairman. A strict isolationist, he was one of only two senators to vote against the United Nations charter. (Henrik Shipstead of Minnesota was the other.) He won his final election in 1958 without the endorsement of his party and—refusing to leave his ailing wife's bedside—without making a single speech. Langer died on November 8, 1959. His funeral is memorable as being the most recent to have been held in the Senate Chamber.

William Langer, senator from North Dakota (1941-1959).

Further Reading

Geelan, Agnes. *The Dakota Maverick: The Political Life of William Langer, Also Known as "Wild Bill" Langer.* [Fargo? N.D.]: Geelan, 1975.

U.S. Congress. Senate. *United States Senate Election, Expulsion and Censure Cases, 1793-1990,* by Anne M. Butler and Wendy Wolff. 103rd Congress, 1st sess., 1995. S. Doc. 103-33.

U.S. Senators and Their World

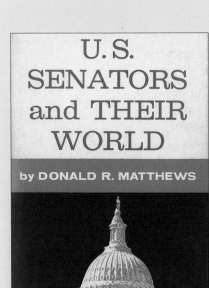

Senator John F. Kennedy called U.S. Senators and Their World *"sharp, perceptive, instructive and entertaining."*

Following World War II, scholars and journalists took a searching new look at the U.S. Senate. They saw the Senate as a counterbalance to a presidency whose powers had been sharply inflated under the guise of wartime emergency. Of the resulting books, one of the most influential was entitled *U.S. Senators and Their World*. It was published in 1960, by University of North Carolina political scientist Donald Matthews.

Matthews approached the Senate like an anthropologist discovering a new civilization. Beginning in 1947, he conducted dozens of off-the-record interviews with members. "How did senators think?" "In what ways did service in the Senate change them?" This led Matthews to explore the "unwritten rules of the game." "How do those rules affect senatorial behavior?" "Who is influential in the Senate and why?"

As Matthews developed his study, he identified six "folkways." He said, "Only those who have served in the Senate, and perhaps not even all of them, are likely to grasp its folkways in all their complexity." Here is what Professor Matthews had to say about the folkway he called "reciprocity":

Every senator, at one time or another, is in a position to help out a colleague. The folkways of the Senate hold that a senator should provide this assistance and that he should be repaid in kind. The most important aspect of this pattern of reciprocity is, no doubt, the trading of votes. [Reciprocity] demands an ability to calculate how much "credit" a senator builds up with a colleague by doing him a favor of "going along." If a senator expects too little in return, he has sold himself and his constituents short. If he expects too much, he will soon find that to ask the impossible is fruitless and that "there are just some things a senator can't do in return for help from you." Finally, this mode of procedure requires that a senator live up to his end of the bargain, no matter how implicit the bargain may have been. "You don't have to make these commitments," one senator said, "and if you keep your mouth shut you are often better off, but if you do make them, you had better live up to them."

U.S. Senators and Their World is now considered a classic. It is worth reading as a reminder of how much the Senate has changed over the last half century—and how much it has stayed the same.

Further Reading
Matthews, Donald R. *U.S. Senators and Their World*. New York: Vintage Books, 1960.

Hollywood Comes to the Hill

On March 20, 1962, 60 senators went to the movies. They traveled to Washington's Trans-Lux Theater for a sneak preview of Otto Preminger's *Advise and Consent*. Based on Allen Drury's best-selling novel involving a bitter Senate confirmation battle, the film presented a star-studded cast that included President Franchot Tone, Vice President Lew Ayres, controversial secretary of state nominee Henry Fonda (whose character had lied to a Senate subcommittee about a previous youthful flirtation with a pro-Communist political group), Senate Majority Leader Walter Pidgeon, and President pro tempore Charles Laughton, with other roles played by Peter Lawford, Burgess Meredith, and Gene Tierney. Preminger had tried unsuccessfully to get Martin Luther King to play an African American senator from Georgia.

Senators had a more than passing interest in this film. For several months in the fall of 1961 film crews had swarmed over public and private spaces within the Russell Senate Office Building, turning its corridors, offices, and especially its Caucus Room into stage sets. A patient host, the Senate drew the line at using its chamber. For scenes in that location, Preminger updated the Hollywood set used for the 1939 filming of Frank Capra's classic, *Mr. Smith Goes to Washington*. The director recruited senators to act as extras and convinced 58 of them to sponsor premieres in their home states. He also hired 400 socially prominent Washingtonians, with $25 donations to their designated charities, to participate in a party scene, filmed at the palatial Washington estate, Tregaron. Democrat Henry Jackson of Washington State seized the opportunity to invite Helen Hardin, his future wife, on a cheap but impressive date. Jackson, an extra in the party scene, got the premiere's biggest laugh from colleagues as he declined a drink from a passing waiter.

Senators offered predictably mixed reviews. Ohio Democrat Stephen Young, mindful of ongoing cold war crises, considered this "a bad time in world history to downgrade the U.S. Senate" and introduced legislation to prohibit the film's distribution outside the United States. New York Republican Kenneth Keating thought the film was "terrific." He wired Preminger that incumbent senators should henceforth "look to you for tips on how a senator should walk, dress, and posture with his hands." South Dakota Republican Karl Mundt had the final word. He pronounced the film "fictionalized entertainment with a touch of reality, while the U.S. Senate is a lot of reality with a touch of entertainment."

Actor Charles Laughton, in white suit, was filmed on location outside the Russell Senate Office Building for the movie Advise and Consent.

Further Reading

Drury, Allen. *Advise and Consent*. New York: Doubleday, 1959.

"60 Senators Caucus at 'Advise' Preview," *New York Times*, March 22, 1962.

"Consent Lacks Consensus," *The Washington Post, Times Herald*, March 22, 1962, D1.

April 2, 1962

S-207—The Mike Mansfield Room

I n the decade following the end of World War II, Congress added large numbers of professional staff to its workforce. These additional employees quickly saturated available Capitol Hill office space. As construction of a second Senate office building neared completion in 1958, Congress agreed to provide more new space by extending the Capitol's East Front.

S-207 as it appears today.

The 32-foot addition, built between 1958 and 1962, added 90 prized rooms to the overcrowded Capitol.

On April 2, 1962, 70 senators gathered in one of the largest of those new rooms to celebrate the project's completion. Known as S-207, and later named to honor Majority Leader Mike Mansfield, that room promised a convenient setting for many of the Senate's legislative and social activities. Its elegant appointments included walls paneled in American black walnut and a mantel of "Meadow White" Vermont marble. In the years ahead, it would accommodate the weekly party caucus luncheons, serve as a dormitory for senators during overnight filibusters, and host countless festive receptions.

Perhaps the most notable reception ever held in S-207 was the first one. At mid-afternoon on April 2, Senate restaurant workers set up a large bar and—according to the custom of the day—stocked it with the ingredients essential to produce an imaginative variety of mixed drinks. By 5 p.m. the room had more than reached its capacity with the arrival of dozens of senators, cabinet officers, and the guest of honor—President John F. Kennedy.

Noticeably absent from that festive gathering was the maverick Oregon senator, Wayne Morse. At that moment, Morse was conducting one of those late-afternoon Senate floor speeches that had caused those who disliked evening sessions to dub him the "Five-o'clock Shadow." As a cloud of cigarette and cigar smoke thickened over the heads of the throng in S-207, Morse suspended an attack on the privatization of communications satellites to address another issue that deeply irritated him—the serving of hard liquor at social functions in the Capitol.

Senate Republican Leader Everett Dirksen greeted President Kennedy at the door of S-207 and quietly warned him that Morse was "on the floor assailing the iniquities of drinking in the Capitol." Looking relieved at the opportunity to abandon the reception's choking ambience, the president headed for the nearly empty chamber. Glimpsing the indefatigable Morse at his late-afternoon best, he defused the tense moment by joking, "This is the way it was when I left the Senate."

Further Reading
U.S. Congress. *Congressional Record*, 87th Congress, 2nd sess., pp. 5681, 5691.

September 24, 1963

Smile: Photographing the Senate in Session

In September 1963, an irritated Senator Richard Russell exclaimed, "All senators like to have their pictures taken! When I look around and see some of my colleagues and then view my own physiognomy in the mirror, I sometimes wonder why. But," he said, "that is a weakness of mankind."

Rule IV of the rules regulating the Senate wing of the Capitol forbids "the taking of pictures of any kind" in the Senate Chamber and surrounding rooms. The Senate's suspension of this rule on September 24, 1963, for the purpose of taking the Senate's first official photograph provoked Russell's scorn.

The Senate did not formally adopt a rule limiting photography in its chamber until the 1950s. That decade's introduction of high-speed film led to a proliferation of easily concealed pocket cameras. Adventurous photographers, both amateur and professional, found the chamber a most inviting target. Several decades earlier, on June 20, 1938, *Life* magazine had published a chamber photo, which it headlined as the "first picture ever taken on the floor of the U.S. Senate in session." The magazine proudly noted, "The only previous photographs of the Senate at work have been sneak shots taken with smuggled cameras from the gallery."

In 1963, the National Geographic Society requested permission to take the first formal portrait of the Senate in session. That organization was preparing the first edition of *We the People*, an illustrated book on Congress. The book's editors insisted on photos of the Senate and House in session.

Senate Majority Leader Mike Mansfield scheduled the picture-taking session to occur just before a historic vote on the Nuclear Test Ban Treaty. Ninety-eight members took their seats at 10:15 a.m. Concerned about adequate lighting, cameraman George Mobley had set up three giant reflectors containing 21 large flashbulbs. Following each of six exposures, technicians hurriedly replaced the burned-out bulbs for the next shot. During one exposure, a bulb exploded and showered glass onto Representative Fred Schwengel, whose Capitol Historical Society had sponsored the *We the People* publication project.

The Geographic's photographers next captured the Senate in 1971 and again in 1975. These three photos, taken from the rear of the chamber, document the evolving face of the Senate. The 1963 image shows senators sitting stiffly at their desks facing the presiding officer. In the 1971 picture, some members are slyly observing the photographer. By 1975, the entire Senate, perhaps more media-savvy, had turned to embrace the camera straight on.

1963 photograph of the U.S. Senate, just prior to a historic vote on the Nuclear Test Ban Treaty.

Further Reading
"Senate Sits for its First Photograph," *Washington Post, Times Herald*, September 25, 1963, A1.

189

CHAPTER VII

THE MODERN SENATE

1964-2002

Harry Truman Visits the Senate

May 8 marks the birth anniversary of an American president who never tired of saying that the "happiest ten years" of his life were those he spent in the United States Senate. Born on May 8, 1884, Missouri's Harry S. Truman came to the Senate at the age of 50 in January 1935.

Truman quickly became popular among his Senate colleagues who appreciated his folksy personality, his modesty, and his diligence. In 1941, he took up the assignment that made his political career. Convinced that waste and corruption were strangling the nation's efforts to mobilize for the war in Europe, Truman chaired the Senate Special Committee to Investigate the National Defense Program. During the three years of his chairmanship, the "Truman Committee" held hundreds of hearings in Washington and around the country. This role erased his earlier image as a Kansas City political hack and gave him working experience with business, labor, agriculture, and executive agencies that would serve him well in later years. In 1944, when party leaders sought a replacement for controversial Vice President Henry Wallace, Truman's national stature made him an ideal compromise choice.

On May 8, 1964, Harry Truman celebrated his 80th birthday with a tumultuous return visit to the Senate Chamber. In the mid-1930s, Senator Truman had proposed that former presidents be allowed the privilege of speaking on the Senate floor, and in committees, to discuss pending legislation. He made this offer as a token of respect for Herbert Hoover, the only living former president at that time. In 1963, the Senate modified its rules to incorporate a more restrictive version of Truman's earlier proposal. In a gesture that initially applied to Truman, Hoover, and Dwight Eisenhower, the Senate agreed to allow former presidents to address the body "upon proper written notice."

Truman entered the chamber to a thunderous standing ovation. After being escorted to the front row seat of Majority Leader Mike Mansfield, he listened as 25 senators in turn rose to speak in celebration of his career and birthday. When it was his time to respond, Truman choked with emotion. Referring to the Senate's newly extended privilege, he said, "I'm so overcome that I can't take advantage of this rule right now." Then, as senators pressed in to shake his hand, he exclaimed, "You can wish me many more happy birthdays, but I'll never have another one like this."

President Harry S. Truman holds a birthday cake presented to him by the "One More Club," precursor to the White House News Photographers Association, ca. 1950.

Further Reading
McCullough, David. *Truman*. New York: Simon & Schuster, 1992.

June 10, 1964

Civil Rights Filibuster Ended

At 9:51 on the morning of June 10, 1964, Senator Robert C. Byrd completed an address that he had begun 14 hours and 13 minutes earlier. The subject was the pending Civil Rights Act of 1964, a measure that occupied the Senate for 57 working days, including six Saturdays. A day earlier, Democratic Whip Hubert Humphrey, the bill's manager, concluded he had the 67 votes required at that time to end the debate.

The Civil Rights Act provided protection of voting rights; banned discrimination in public facilities—including private businesses offering public services—such as lunch counters, hotels, and theaters; and established equal employment opportunity as the law of the land.

As Senator Byrd took his seat, House members, former senators, and others—150 of them—vied for limited standing space at the back of the chamber. With all gallery seats taken, hundreds waited outside in hopelessly extended lines.

Georgia Democrat Richard Russell offered the final arguments in opposition. Minority Leader Everett Dirksen, who had enlisted the Republican votes that made cloture a realistic option, spoke for the proponents with his customary eloquence. Noting that the day marked the 100th anniversary of Abraham

Lincoln's nomination to a second term, the Illinois Republican proclaimed, in the words of Victor Hugo, "Stronger than all the armies is an idea whose time has come." He continued, "The time has come for equality of opportunity in sharing in government, in education, and in employment. It will not be stayed or denied. It is here!"

Never in history had the Senate been able to muster enough votes to cut off a filibuster on a civil rights bill. And only once in the 37 years since 1927 had it agreed to cloture for any measure.

The clerk proceeded to call the roll. When he reached "Mr. Engle," there was no response. A brain tumor had robbed California's mortally ill Clair Engle of his ability to speak. Slowly lifting a crippled arm, he pointed to his eye, thereby signaling his affirmative vote. Few of those who witnessed this heroic gesture ever forgot it. When Delaware's John Williams provided the decisive 67th vote, Majority Leader Mike Mansfield exclaimed, "That's it!"; Richard Russell slumped; and Hubert Humphrey beamed. With six wavering senators providing a four-vote victory margin, the final tally stood at 71 to 29. Nine days later the Senate approved the act itself—producing one of the 20th century's towering legislative achievements.

Senators Everett Dirksen and Hubert Humphrey and Speaker of the House John McCormick watch as President Lyndon Johnson signs the 1964 Civil Rights Act, July 2, 1964.

Further Reading

Graham, Hugh Davis. *The Civil Rights Era: Origins and Development of National Policy.* New York: Oxford University Press, 1990.

Mann, Robert. *The Walls of Jericho: Lyndon Johnson, Hubert Humphrey, Richard Russell and the Struggle for Civil Rights.* New York: Harcourt Brace, 1996.

The Senate's "Taj Mahal"

The practice of naming Capitol rooms to honor distinguished Americans who served in the Senate began very quietly on June 25, 1964. On that day, workmen affixed a 10-by-14-inch bronze plaque to the south wall of a sumptuously appointed second-floor room known as "S-211." No press coverage; no fanfare. The honoree was the former Senate majority leader, and current president of the United States, Lyndon Johnson.

When Johnson became the Senate majority leader in 1955, he appropriated from the Joint Economic Committee a third-floor room that today serves as the inner office of the assistant Democratic leader. Offering a working fireplace and a spectacular view of the mall, that room presented one drawback. Its location, one floor above the Senate Chamber, proved increasingly inconvenient for a leader who needed to move quickly and frequently between both places.

In 1958, the Senate opened a new office building designed especially to house committees, including those that had been occupying prime space in the Capitol. Johnson seized his opportunity to acquire office space that was both conveniently located and suitably appropriate to his leadership post—S-211. But the room—

originally designed as the Senate Library, but never used for that purpose—had grown shabby during its three-quarter-century occupancy by the Senate District of Columbia Committee. Johnson arranged for its restoration, with a color scheme vibrant in royal greens and golds, and the ultimate status symbol of that day—a private bathroom. Some dared label the majority leader's refurbished quarters the "Taj Mahal."

When Johnson moved to the vice-presidency in 1961, he kept S-211, causing his successor, Mike Mansfield, to relocate the leader's office across the hall. When the vice-presidency fell vacant with Johnson's move to the White House in November 1963, control of S-211 reverted to the Senate's leadership.

Several days after the 1964 installation of the Johnson plaque, at the initiative of Majority Leader Mansfield, workers attached a similar marker to Room S-210, across the hall. The plaque honors Senator John F. Kennedy's 1960 presidential campaign occupancy of that space, conveniently adjacent to his running mate's office.

In 1987, S-211 underwent a second redecoration to return it to the ornate Victorian appearance intended by its 19th-century architect. Yet, one central feature of the 1958 restoration remained untouched until its removal in 2006—Lyndon Johnson's bathroom.

Vice President Lyndon B. Johnson presiding at the rostrum of the Senate Chamber in 1961.

Further Reading

U.S. Congress. Senate. *Constantino Brumidi: Artist of the Capitol,* by Barbara A. Wolanin. 103rd Congress, 2d sess., 1998. S. Doc. 103-27.

July 9, 1964

Senators Wrestle to Settle Nomination

Soon after he signed the Civil Rights Act of 1964, President Lyndon Johnson sent the Senate a particularly significant nomination. Sensitive to southern concerns about the scope and implementation of that landmark statute, Johnson considered carefully whom he would name to the newly established Community Relations Service, designed to mediate local racial disputes. He selected a white southerner, former Florida Governor LeRoy Collins.

The Senate referred the Collins nomination to its Commerce Committee, whose most senior southern member was South Carolina Senator Strom Thurmond. Collins had angered Thurmond with a speech in the senator's home state in which he charged that southern leaders' "harsh and intemperate" language unnecessarily provoked racial unrest. Thurmond, an opponent of the Civil Rights Act when it was before the Senate, pointed out that Collins had openly supported segregation in the 1950s. Collins responded, "We all adjust to new circumstances."

Commerce Committee Chairman Warren Magnuson of Washington State knew he had the votes to favorably report the Collins nomination to the full Senate. For two days, however, he had tried unsuccessfully to obtain a quorum so that the committee could act. Knowing of the chairman's difficulty, Thurmond stationed himself outside the committee's room in the Dirksen Senate Office Building on July 9, 1964, hoping to block action by turning away late-arriving senators.

At that moment, Texas Senator Ralph Yarborough appeared. Yarborough had been the only southern senator to vote for the Civil Rights Act. The Texan laughingly said, "Come on in, Strom, and help us get a quorum." In a similarly light-hearted manner, Thurmond responded, "If I can keep you out, you won't go in, and if you can drag me in, I'll stay there." Both men were 61 years old, but Thurmond was 30 pounds lighter and in better physical condition.

After a few moments of light scuffling, each senator removed his suit jacket. Thurmond then wrestled the increasingly out-of-breath Yarborough to the floor. "Tell me to release you, Ralph, and I will," said Thurmond. Yarborough refused. Another senator approached and suggested that both men stop before one of them suffered a heart attack. Finally, Chairman Magnuson appeared and growled, "Come on, you fellows, let's break this up."

Recognizing a great exit line, Yarborough grunted, "I have to yield to the order of my chairman." The combatants did their best to compose themselves and entered the committee room.

Although Thurmond had won the match, he lost that day's vote: 16 to 1.

Senator Strom Thurmond of South Carolina (1954-2003), left, and Senator Ralph Yarborough of Texas (1957-1971) after an impromptu wrestling match.

Further Reading

Cohodas, Nadine. *Strom Thurmond & the Politics of Southern Change*. Macon, Ga.: Mercer University Press, 1993.

Filibuster Derails Supreme Court Nominee

Associate Justice of the Supreme Court Abe Fortas, whose nomination as chief justice was filibustered by the Senate.

In June 1968, Chief Justice Earl Warren informed President Lyndon Johnson that he planned to retire from the Supreme Court. Concern that Richard Nixon might win the presidency later that year and get to choose his successor dictated Warren's timing.

In the final months of his presidency, Johnson shared Warren's concerns about Nixon and welcomed the opportunity to add his third appointee to the Court. To replace Warren, he nominated Associate Justice Abe Fortas, his longtime confidant. Anticipating Senate concerns about the prospective chief justice's liberal opinions, Johnson simultaneously declared his intention to fill the vacancy created by Fortas' elevation with Appeals Court Judge Homer Thornberry. The president believed that Thornberry, a Texan, would mollify skeptical southern senators.

A seasoned Senate vote-counter, Johnson concluded that despite filibuster warnings, he just barely had the support to confirm Fortas. The president took encouragement from indications that his former Senate mentor, Richard Russell, and Republican Minority Leader Everett Dirksen would support Fortas, whose legal brilliance both men respected.

The president soon lost Russell's support, however, because of administration delays in nominating his candidate to a federal judgeship. Johnson urged Senate leaders to waste no time in convening Fortas' confirmation hearings. Responding to staff assurances of Dirksen's continued support, Johnson told an aide, "Just take my word for it. I know [Dirksen]. I know the Senate. If they get this thing drug out very long, we're going to get beat. Dirksen will leave us."

Fortas became the first sitting associate justice, nominated for chief justice, to testify at his own confirmation hearing. Those hearings reinforced what some senators already knew about the nominee. As a sitting justice, he regularly attended White House staff meetings; he briefed the president on secret Court deliberations; and, on behalf of the president, he pressured senators who opposed the war in Vietnam. When the Judiciary Committee revealed that Fortas received a privately funded stipend, equivalent to 40 percent of his Court salary, to teach a college course, Dirksen and others withdrew their support. Although the committee recommended confirmation, floor consideration sparked the first filibuster in Senate history on a Supreme Court nomination.

On October 1, 1968, the Senate failed to invoke cloture. Johnson then withdrew the nomination, privately observing that if he had another term, "the Fortas appointment would have been different."

Further Reading

Abraham, Henry J. *Justices, Presidents and Senators: A History of U.S. Supreme Court Appointments from Washington to Clinton.* 4th ed. Lanham, MD: Rowman & Littlefield, 1999.

Kalman, Laura. *Abe Fortas: A Biography.* New Haven: Yale University Press, 1990.

September 7, 1969

Senate Everett McKinley Dirksen Dies

During the 11 years as his party's Senate floor leader, Illinois Republican Everett McKinley Dirksen became more closely identified in the public mind with the U.S. Senate than any other senator of his time. His physical appearance, his dramatic flair, his cathedral-organ voice—all these attributes made him the personification of radio entertainer Fred Allen's fictional 1940s "Senator Claghorn."

He was the grand marshal of the Tournament of Roses parade; he pioneered a televised weekly press conference with his House counterpart; and, with a narrative album entitled Gallant Men, he became a recording star. The hordes of admiring tourists who flocked to his leader's office in the Capitol forced him to remove his name from its door. Today, because a Senate office building honors him, his is one of the best-known names on Capitol Hill from his generation.

Everett Dirksen first came to Congress in 1933 as a House member. During World War II, he lobbied successfully for an expansion of congressional staff resources to eliminate the practice under which House and Senate committees borrowed executive branch personnel to accomplish legislative work. He gained national attention in 1950 when he unseated the Senate Democratic majority leader in a bitter Illinois contest. Enjoying the confidence of his party's conservative and moderate factions, he became assistant Republican leader in 1957 and minority leader two years later.

During 10 of his 11 years as party floor leader, the number of Senate Republicans never exceeded 36. Yet, as a supremely creative and resourceful legislator, Dirksen routinely influenced the agenda of the majority-party Democrats. His willingness to change position on issues earned him designations ranging from "statesman" to "Grand Old Chameleon."

On the subject of Senate leadership, it was Dirksen who said, "There are 100 diverse personalities in the U.S. Senate. Oh Great God. What an amazing and dissonant 100 personalities they are! What an amazing thing it is to harmonize them."

Researchers have been unable to track down the quotation most commonly associated with Dirksen. Perhaps he never said it, but the comment would have been entirely in character. Cautioning that federal spending had a way of getting out of control, Dirksen is said to have observed, "A billion here and a billion there, and pretty soon you're talking real money."

This singularly colorful Senate leader died at the age of 73 on September 7, 1969.

Everett McKinley Dirksen, senator from Illinois (1951-1969).

Further Reading

Dirksen, Everett McKinley. *The Education of a Senator.* Urbana: University of Illinois Press, 1998.

MacNeil, Neil. *Dirksen: Portrait of a Public Man.* New York: World Publishing Company, 1970.

May 14, 1971

First Female Pages Appointed

On May 14, 1971, Paulette Desell and Ellen McConnell made history. Thanks to the appointments of Senators Jacob Javits and Charles Percy, these two 16-year-olds became the first females to serve as Senate pages.

Senator Daniel Webster had selected the first male page nearly a century and a half earlier. Proving that personal connections counted in those days, he chose Grafton Hanson, the nine-year-old grandson of the Senate sergeant at arms. In 1831, the Senate added a second page—12-year-old Isaac Bassett. As the son of a Senate messenger, Bassett also benefited from family connections.

Beginning a tradition in which service as a page sometimes became the first step on a Senate career path, Hanson held a variety of increasingly responsible Senate jobs over the next ten years. Bassett, who is well known to students of 19th-century Senate folklore, remained in the Senate's employ for the rest of his long life. In 1861, he became assistant Senate doorkeeper—a post in which he earned the legendary distinction of being the official who stopped a Massachusetts soldier from bayoneting the Senate desk previously occupied by Mississippi Senator Jefferson Davis. In late-19th-century engrav-

Left to right, *Senators Charles Percy of Illinois (1967-1985) and Jacob Javits of New York (1957-1981), with pages Paulette Desell and Ellen McConnell.*

ings showing the Senate struggling to wrap up end-of-session legislation, former page Bassett appears as the elderly man in the long white beard moving the chamber clock's minute hand backwards from the twelve o'clock adjournment time to gain a few precious minutes to complete the Senate's work.

By the 1870s, the Senate required pages to be at least 12 and no older than 16, although those limits were occasionally ignored. Until the early 1900s, pages were responsible for arranging their formal schooling during Senate recesses. In various page memoirs, there runs a common theme that no classroom could offer the educational experience available on the floor of the Senate. At Vice President Thomas Marshall's 1919 Christmas dinner for pages, 17-year-old Mark Trice explained, "a Senate page studying history and shorthand has a better opportunity than a schoolboy of learning the same subjects, because we are constantly in touch with both. We boys have an opportunity to watch the official reporters write shorthand and they will always answer questions that we do not understand, thereby making a teacher almost useless." By May 1971, long after the Senate had established a professionally staffed page school, "we boys," had finally become, "we boys *and* girls."

Further Reading
U.S. Congress. Senate. *The Senate, 1789-1989*, Vol. 2, by Robert C. Byrd. 100th Congress, 1st sess., 1991. S. Doc.100-20. Chapter 17.

October 11, 1972

Senate Office Buildings Named

Long before e-mail guaranteed citizens instantaneous communication with their representatives in Washington, Senator Harry Truman jokingly informed his Missouri constituents that they could easily reach him by using the following simple address: "Truman, S.O.B., Washington." And, he was right. Even as an obscure first-year senator in 1935, Truman knew the post office would direct any envelope marked S.O.B. to a member of the United States Senate.

That abbreviation for "Senate Office Building" served nicely until 1958, when a second office building opened. After that, senators had to specify in their addresses whether they resided in the "Old S.O.B." or "New S.O.B."

In October 1972, the Senate passed legislation providing for a third office building. Although that structure would not open for another 10 years, its authorization doomed the practice of referring simply to the old and the new S.O.B.s. Recognizing this, West Virginia Senator Robert C. Byrd offered a resolution, which the Senate adopted on October 11, 1972, naming the old and new buildings, respectively, in honor of two recently deceased Senate leaders—Georgia Democrat Richard Russell and Illinois Republican Everett Dirksen. In 1976, shortly after ground-breaking for the third building, the Senate named that structure in honor of Michigan's then terminally ill senior senator, Philip Hart.

The practice of honoring illustrious members on the Senate side of Capitol Hill had begun two decades earlier with the 1955 authorization for a Capitol Hill bell tower in memory of former Republican Majority Leader Robert Taft. That same year, the Senate set up a committee, chaired by Massachusetts Senator John F. Kennedy, to select five outstanding former members, whose portraits would be permanently displayed in the Senate Reception Room. In 1964, the Senate provided for the placement of plaques in the Capitol rooms assigned to the two senators who formed the 1960 Democratic presidential ticket—John F. Kennedy and Lyndon B. Johnson.

Since then, other Capitol spaces have acquired names associated with former Senate leaders. They include Arthur Vandenberg, Styles Bridges, Hugh Scott, Mike Mansfield, Robert C. Byrd, Strom Thurmond, Howard Baker, and Bob Dole. In 1998, workers affixed a small plaque outside a second-floor office in the original S.O.B. that is currently assigned to Missouri Senator Christopher Bond. It reads, simply, "The Senate Office once occupied by Harry S. Truman."

Aerial view of the three Senate office buildings. In the foreground is the Hart Senate Office Building, the Dirksen Senate Office Building sits in the middle, and the Russell Senate Office Building is closest to the Capitol.

Further Reading

U.S. Congress. Senate. *History of the United States Capitol: A Chronicle of Design, Construction, and Politics*, by William C. Allen. 106th Congress, 2d sess., 2001. S. Doc. 106-29.

U.S. Congress. Senate. *Historical Almanac of the United States Senate*, by Bob Dole. 100th Congress, 2d sess., 1989. S. Doc. 100-35.

March 28, 1973

Watergate Leaks

A crowd of reporters strained against a barrier on the first floor of the Capitol hoping to question the six senators arriving for a politically charged closed-door committee hearing. That hearing had been called at the request of a single witness—a convicted burglar.

On March 28, 1973, the Senate held its first hearing on the Watergate break-in. That nearly five-hour meeting generated so many leaks to the media that committee leaders decided to conduct all future hearings in public session.

Senator Howard Baker of Tennessee (1967-1985), left, *with Senator Sam Ervin of North Carolina (1954-1974),* center, *during the Watergate hearings in 1973.*

Nine months earlier, five burglars and two accomplices had been arrested in the Democratic National Committee's Watergate offices. Their eventual connection to President Richard Nixon's 1972 reelection campaign, and their conviction in January 1973, led the Senate in February to create the Select Committee on Presidential Campaign Activities—the Watergate committee.

Working under committee chairman Sam Ervin of North Carolina, Democratic chief counsel Sam Dash assured concerned Republicans that the panel would probe wrongdoing by members of both political parties. Its goal, he said, would be to make recommendations for the reform of election laws.

The committee's single closed-door witness, James McCord, had been security coordinator for the Committee to Re-elect the President. Preparing to sentence McCord for his crime, Federal District Judge John Sirica advised him to cooperate fully with the Senate inquiry.

In a private meeting with committee counsel Dash, McCord confirmed rumors that Nixon aides John Dean and Jeb Magruder knew about the plot before it took place and he promised to name others. When Dash reported this to the media, the resulting furor led McCord to request the opportunity to address members of the committee in secret session.

In that session, McCord testified that his boss, G. Gordon Liddy, had told him that Attorney General John Mitchell had approved the specific burglary plans. McCord also revealed the involvement of Dean, Magruder, and former presidential counsel Charles Colson. McCord promised to provide documents that would substantiate his allegations.

Within minutes of the closed session's conclusion, details of McCord's disclosures reached the media. That evening, vice-chairman Howard Baker of Tennessee, in an address to the Washington Press Club, confirmed what the committee had learned about Dean and Magruder.

McCord's performance at that closed session initiated one of the most important investigations in Senate history and began the unraveling of the White House cover-up. As one journalist later observed, McCord "opened the road to havoc."

Further Reading
Olson, Keith W. *Watergate: The Presidential Scandal That Shook America.* Lawrence, Kans.: University Press of Kansas, 2003.

Church Committee Created

In 1973, CIA Director James Schlesinger told Senate Armed Services Chairman John Stennis that he wished to brief him on a major upcoming operation. "No, no my boy," responded Senator Stennis. "Don't tell me. Just go ahead and do it, but I don't want to know." Similarly, when Senate Foreign Relations Committee Chairman J.W. Fulbright was told of the CIA subversion of the Allende government in Chile, he responded, "I don't approve of intervention in other people's elections, but it has been a long-continued practice."

Late in 1974, investigative reporter Seymour Hersh revealed that the CIA was not only destabilizing foreign governments, but was also conducting illegal intelligence operations against thousands of American citizens.

On January 27, 1975, an aroused Senate voted overwhelmingly to establish a special 11-member investigating body along the lines of the recently concluded Watergate Committee. Under the chairmanship of Idaho Senator Frank Church, with Texas Senator John Tower as vice-chairman, the select committee was given nine months and 150 staffers to complete its work.

The so-called Church Committee ran into immediate resistance from the administration of President Gerald Ford, concerned about exposing American intelligence operations and suspicious of Church's budding presidential ambitions.

The committee interviewed 800 individuals, and conducted 250 executive and 21 public hearings. At the first televised hearing, staged in the Senate Caucus Room, Chairman Church dramatically displayed a CIA poison dart gun to highlight the committee's discovery that the CIA directly violated a presidential order by maintaining stocks of shellfish toxin sufficient to kill thousands.

Lacking focus and necessarily conducting much of its work behind closed doors, the panel soon lost any hope of becoming a second Watergate Committee. Critics, from singer-actor Bing Crosby to radio commentator Paul Harvey, accused it of treasonous activity. The December 1975 assassination of a CIA station chief in Greece intensified the public backlash against its mission.

The panel issued its two-foot-thick final report in May 1976 without the support of influential Republican members John Tower and Barry Goldwater. Despite its shortcomings, the inquiry demonstrated the need for perpetual surveillance of the intelligence community and resulted in the creation of the permanent Select Committee on Intelligence.

Historian Henry Steele Commager assessed the Committee's legacy. Referring to executive branch officials who seemed to consider themselves above the law, he said, "It is this indifference to constitutional restraints that is perhaps the most threatening of all the evidence that emerges from the findings of the Church Committee."

Frank Church, senator from Idaho (1957-1981).

Further Reading

Ashby, LeRoy and Rod Gramer. *Fighting the Odds: The Life of Senator Frank Church*. Pullman: Washington State University Press, 1994.

Johnson, Loch K. *A Season of Inquiry: The Senate Intelligence Investigation*. Lexington: University Press of Kentucky, 1985.

Senate Reform Commission

*John Culver,
senator from Iowa
(1975-1981).*

*Harold Hughes,
senator from Iowa
(1969-1975).*

Soon after he entered the Senate early in 1975, Iowa Democrat John Culver concluded that the upper house was in danger of becoming dysfunctional. Describing the Senate as a "sick patient," the former five-term House member said what was needed was not just a "quick physical examination," but "a careful and probing study of the whole central nervous system of the Senate and its institutional well-being."

On July 29, 1975, in response to Senator Culver's widely shared concerns, the Senate authorized the first-ever review of its administrative and legislative operations by an outside panel. The 11 members of the Commission on the Operation of the Senate included university administrators, former state governors, and long-time Senate observers.

Majority Leader Mike Mansfield explained that the panel would "look into conflicts in the programming of business, problems of office layouts and facilities, information resources and the internal management and supporting staff structures of the Senate." It would also examine "workload, lobbying, pay and increments, office allowances, possible conflicts of interest and whatever other matters are pertinent to the effective operation of the Senate."

With only a year to conduct its review, the Commission relied heavily on a 20-member staff, the Library of Congress, and outside experts. Chairman Harold Hughes, a former Iowa Democratic senator, acknowledged, "Much of the Commission's work has consisted of sifting through studies that we instructed the staff to prepare."

In December 1976, the Commission—known variously as the "Culver Commission" after its principal sponsor, or the "Hughes Commission" for its chairman—proposed several dozen reforms. The Senate subsequently adopted several, including greater use of computers for committee scheduling and floor status information. It also voted a pay raise tied to a ban on honoraria and full public financial disclosure by each senator. Ten years would pass, however, before the Senate agreed to the recommendation for televising its floor proceedings. Other commission proposals fared less well. These included creation of central administrator, appointment of a non-senator to preside over routine sessions, and a reduction in the size and visibility of the Capitol Police force.

Today, the Culver/Hughes Commission retains its status as the only outside body ever invited to review the Senate's internal operations. Its final report, *Toward a Modern Senate,* along with 11 detailed staff studies, offers rich insights about the Senate of the 1970s and reminds us of how significantly advances in computer technology have changed the institution's operations over the past 30 years.

Further Reading

U.S. Congress. Senate. *Toward a Modern Senate: Final Report of the Commission on the Operation of the Senate.* 94th Congress, 2d sess., 1976. S. Doc. 94-278.

September 16, 1975

Closest Election in Senate History

The closest election in Senate history was decided on September 16, 1975. The 1974 New Hampshire race for an open seat pitted Republican Louis Wyman against Democrat John Durkin.

Although Wyman enjoyed a lead during the campaign, the Watergate scandals and the August 1974 resignation of President Richard Nixon made it a tough year to run as a Republican. On election day, Wyman barely won with a margin of just 355 votes.

Durkin immediately demanded a recount. That recount shifted the victory to Durkin—but by only 10 votes. Reluctantly, the Republican governor awarded Durkin a provisional certificate of election.

Now, it was Wyman's turn to demand a recount. The state ballot commission tabulated the ballots in dispute and ruled that Republican Wyman had won—but by just two votes. The governor cancelled Durkin's certificate and awarded a new credential to Wyman.

As a last option, Durkin petitioned the Senate—with its 60-vote Democratic majority—to review the case. On January 13, 1975, the day before the new Congress convened, the Senate Committee on Rules and Administration tried unsuccessfully to resolve the matter. Composed of five Democrats and three Republicans, the Rules Committee deadlocked four-to-four on a proposal to seat Wyman pending further review. Alabama Democrat James Allen voted with the Republicans on grounds that Wyman had presented proper credentials.

The full Senate took up the case on January 14, with Wyman and Durkin seated at separate tables at the rear of the chamber. Soon, the matter returned to the Rules Committee, which created a special staff panel to examine 3,500 questionable ballots that had been shipped to Washington.

Following this review, the Rules Committee sent 35 disputed points to the full Senate, which spent the next six weeks debating the issue, and took an unprecedented six cloture votes, but resolved only one of the 35 items in question. Facing this deadlock, Durkin agreed to Wyman's proposal for a new election. The Senate declared the seat vacant and the governor appointed former Senator Norris Cotton to hold the seat for six weeks until the September 16 balloting.

A record-breaking turnout gave the election to Durkin by a 27,000-vote margin. The real winners, however, may have been the Senate's Republicans—since the late 1950s a dispirited and hopeless minority. This contest unified their ranks and, as some believed, gave them invaluable tactical experience in dealing with an overwhelming Democratic majority.

John Durkin, senator from New Hampshire (1975-1980).

Further Reading

Tibbetts, Donn. *The Closest U.S. Senate Race in History, Durkin v. Wyman.* [Manchester ?, N.H.]: J.W. Cummings Enterprises, 1976.

June 16, 1976

A Shrine Restored

The heroes of this story include a Senate subcommittee chairman and a former first lady. The villain—from the Senate's perspective—was the chairman of the House Appropriations Committee. The object of their attention: the historic room in the Capitol that served as the Senate's chamber between 1810 and 1859.

After the Senate moved to its current chamber in 1859, the Supreme Court took up residence in the old chamber until 1935, when it left the Capitol for its permanent building across the street. The Senate and House then agreed to restore the room to its 1850s elegance.

Despite this agreement, decades passed with no action. In an increasingly crowded Capitol, both houses wanted the room's convenient space for various meetings and functions. By 1960, countless luncheons and cocktail parties had rendered the old chamber grimy and threadbare. The odor of tobacco and alcohol overwhelmed the aroma of history.

In 1960, construction of a major extension to the east front of the Capitol neared completion. By providing several large meeting spaces, including today's Mike Mansfield and Sam Rayburn Rooms, the extension would relieve demands on the Old Senate Chamber.

The first hero of this story is Mississippi Senator John Stennis. As chairman of the Subcommittee on Legislative Branch Appropriations, he secured $400,000 to restore this room and an earlier Supreme Court chamber directly below it.

House appropriators failed to share the Senate's enthusiasm for this historical project. Although Senator Stennis gained the active support of Majority Leader Mike Mansfield and Senate Appropriations Chairman Carl Hayden, Representative George Mahon, who would soon chair the House Appropriations Committee, had a problem. He made it clear that his problem might be solved if the Senate dropped its opposition to a House-endorsed plan for another Capitol extension project—this one on the west front. No extension; no restored Senate Chamber. This stalemate continued for another 10 years.

Then, in 1972, Chairman Mahon received a phone call from a fellow Texan to whom he could not say "no." Lady Bird Johnson's gentle persuasion and Mansfield's promise to do what he could to ease Senate opposition to the west front project ended the House chairman's opposition.

The Old Senate Chamber restoration project concluded with a festive dedication ceremony on June 16, 1976. (The West Front extension project was later abandoned.)

Today, this "noble room," as Henry Clay once called it, serves as a reminder of the Senate's rich history and, perhaps less obviously, of its historically delicate relations with the House of Representatives.

The Old Senate Chamber restored to its 1850s appearance.

Further Reading
Goodwin, Stephen. "Safeguarding the Senate's Golden Age," *Historic Preservation* November/December 1983: 19-23.
Mitchell, Henry. "Lambs and Leopards Played Where Great Men Have Trod," *Washington Post,* June 17, 1976, C3.

November 22, 1982

Hart Building Opens Under Protest

During the 1970s, the number of Senate staff members working for senators and committees more than doubled. Rising demands for constituency services and the new prerogative that allowed senators to add one staffer to each of their assigned committees contributed to this dramatic increase. By 1979, with the two permanent office buildings densely packed, staff overflowed into nearby former hotels, apartment buildings, and expensive commercial office space.

Recognizing the looming need for more Senate working space, Congress in 1972 authorized construction of a third office building. In 1976, as workers broke ground for that facility, senators agreed to name it after Michigan's Philip A. Hart, a deeply respected colleague who was then in his final struggle with cancer.

To design a flexible, energy-efficient building that would accommodate both the expanded staff and the new technology of the modern Senate, Congress retained the San Francisco architectural firm of John Carl Warnecke & Associates. As construction proceeded in the late 1970s, spiraling inflation tripled the facility's anticipated cost. This caused frustrated lawmakers to impose a $137 million spending cap. These financial constraints forced elimination of a gymnasium and a rooftop restaurant, and delayed completion of the Central Hearing Facility (SH-216).

The building's starkly modern design and excessive costs prompted New York Senator Daniel Patrick Moynihan to introduce the following "Sense of the Senate" Resolution in May 1981:

Hart Senate Office Building under construction.

Whereas in the fall of 1980 the frame of the new Senate Office Building was covered with plastic sheathing in order that construction might continue during winter months; and Whereas the plastic cover has now been removed revealing, as feared, a building whose banality is exceeded only by its expense; and Whereas even in a democracy there are things it is well the people do not know about their government: Now, therefore, be it resolved, That it is the sense of the Senate that the plastic cover be put back.

When the building's office suites for 50 senators became ready in November 1982, only a bold few senators chose to risk public scorn by moving there. Consequently, in a not-soon-to-be repeated reversal of established seniority tradition, many junior senators were permitted to claim to some of Capitol Hill's most desirable quarters.

Further Reading

Bredemeier, Kenneth. "Offices in Hart Building Rejected by 25 Senators," *Washington Post*, November 23, 1982, A1.

"Senate's New Marble Monument," *Washington Post*, September 30, 1982, A1.

"The Ironies of the Hart Senate Office Building," *Washington Post*, November 27, 1982, D1.

Time, January 17, 1983.

November 7, 1983

Bomb Explodes in the Capitol's Senate Wing

The Senate had planned to work late into the evening of Monday, November 7, 1983. Deliberations proceeded more smoothly than expected, however, so the body adjourned at 7:02 p.m. A crowded reception, held near the Senate Chamber, broke up two hours later. Consequently, at 10:58 p.m., when a thunderous explosion tore through the second floor of the Capitol's north wing, the adjacent halls were virtually deserted. Many lives had been spared.

Minutes before the blast, a caller claiming to represent the "Armed Resistance Unit" had warned the Capitol switchboard that a bomb had been placed near the Chamber in retaliation for recent U.S. military involvement in Grenada and Lebanon.

The force of the device, hidden under a bench at the eastern end of the corridor outside the Chamber, blew off the door to the office of Democratic Leader Robert C. Byrd. The blast also punched a potentially lethal hole in a wall partition sending a shower of pulverized brick, plaster, and glass into the Republican cloakroom. Although the explosion caused no structural damage to the Capitol, it shattered mirrors, chandeliers, and furniture. Officials calculated damages of $250,000.

Bomb damage to the second floor of the Capitol, outside the Senate Chamber.

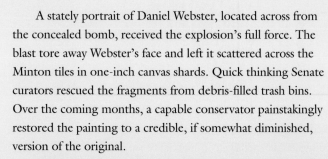

A stately portrait of Daniel Webster, located across from the concealed bomb, received the explosion's full force. The blast tore away Webster's face and left it scattered across the Minton tiles in one-inch canvas shards. Quick thinking Senate curators rescued the fragments from debris-filled trash bins. Over the coming months, a capable conservator painstakingly restored the painting to a credible, if somewhat diminished, version of the original.

Following a five-year investigation, federal agents arrested six members of the so-called Resistance Conspiracy in May 1988 and charged them with bombings of the Capitol, Ft. McNair, and the Washington Navy Yard. In 1990, a federal judge sentenced Marilyn Buck, Laura Whitehorn, and Linda Evans to lengthy prison terms for conspiracy and malicious destruction of government property. The court dropped charges against three codefendants, already serving extended prison sentences for related crimes.

The 1983 bombing marked the beginning of tightened security measures throughout the Capitol. The area outside the Senate Chamber, previously open to the public, was permanently closed. Congressional officials instituted a system of staff identification cards and added metal detectors to building entrances to supplement those placed at Chamber gallery doors following a 1971 Capitol bombing.

Further Reading

Burkhardt, Rich. "Bomb Blast Damages Senate Side of Capitol," *Roll Call*, November 10, 1983, 1.

Thompson, Tracy, "Two Are Sentenced in 1983 Capitol Bombing," *Washington Post*, December 7, 1990, B10.

"Woman Gets Ten Years In 1983 Bombing of US Capitol," *Roll Call*, November 26, 1990.

June 2, 1986

Live Television from the Senate Chamber

Few households in the United States owned television sets in November 1947 when the Senate, for the first time, allowed the televising of a committee hearing. From the 1950s through the 1970s, televised Senate hearings played a major part in shaping public opinion on topics ranging from organized crime and alleged communist infiltration of federal agencies to the war in Vietnam and the Watergate scandals.

Anticipating an impeachment trial for President Richard Nixon in 1974, the Senate quietly made provisions for the first live television coverage from its chamber. Several months after Nixon's resignation made a trial unnecessary, the Senate took advantage of those preparations to telecast Nelson Rockefeller's December 19 swearing-in as vice president.

In 1977, the Senate took a half-step toward television coverage by authorizing radio broadcasts of the 1978 debates on the Panama Canal Treaties. When the House of Representatives decided in 1979 to offer gavel-to-gavel coverage of its floor proceedings, pressure intensified on the Senate to do the same.

During his first week as majority leader in 1981, Tennessee Republican Howard Baker introduced legislation to permit permanent live gavel-to-gavel coverage of floor proceedings. He was aware, however, that influential senior senators firmly opposed such a move. Rhode Island Democrat Claiborne Pell feared that "the presence of television will lead to more, longer, and less relevant speeches, to more posturing by Senators and to even less useful debate and efficient legislating than we have today." Conceding that television in the House seemed to be operating smoothly, he cautioned that "the unique character of the Senate and its very different rules and methods of floor operation make such a venture in the Senate much less likely to be positive."

By early 1986, Majority Leader Bob Dole and Democratic Leader Robert C. Byrd worried that the lack of television coverage was transforming the Senate into the nation's forgotten legislative body. House members were becoming far more visible than senators to their constituents. The two leaders eventually engineered a vote in which the Senate agreed to a three-month trial period, with live national coverage to begin on June 2, 1986. Within weeks, the Senate voted to make this coverage permanent.

Not since the Senate had first voted nearly two centuries earlier to end its policy of conducting all sessions behind closed doors had the body made such a large stride towards improved public awareness of its procedures and activities.

Footage of Senator Bob Dole of Kansas (1969-1996) during the first live television broadcast from the Senate Chamber.

Further Reading

U.S. Congress. Senate. *The Senate, 1789-1989*, by Robert C. Byrd, Vol. 2. 100th Congress, 1st sess., 1991. S. Doc.100-20

U.S. Congress. Senate. *Television and Radio Coverage of Proceedings in the Senate Chamber*. 97th Congress, 1st sess., August 13, 1981. S. Rept. 97-178.

Mountains and Clouds Dedicated

People either love it or hate it. The monumental sculpture, entitled *Mountains and Clouds*, occupies the nine-story atrium of the Hart Senate Office Building. Rising 51 feet, the mountains are formed from 36 tons of sheet steel painted black. Suspended above this stabile is a 75-foot-wide black mobile, representing clouds. Constructed of aircraft aluminum, the mobile is designed to rotate in random patterns set by a computer-controlled motor.

In 1975, months before construction of the Hart Building began, Capitol officials invited five sculptors to submit designs for a work that would harmonize with the atrium's surrounding white marble architecture and yet stand apart from the cluttering distraction of adjacent doors, windows, and balconies. In April 1976, 77-year-old Alexander Calder won the design commission. Forty years earlier, Calder had invented the mobile and stabile as art forms. Although Calder had previously designed a mobile attached to a stabile, this was his first—and only—work to place them as separate units within a single sculptural composition.

On November 10, 1976, Calder presented his scaled model to congressional officials and the building's architect. To accommodate their comments, he made several on-the-spot adjustments with a borrowed pair of pliers and metal shears. Leaving all parties happy with his final design, he returned to New York City, where, later that evening, he died.

In 1979, midway through the building's construction, severe cost overruns led Congress to eliminate funding for Calder's sculpture. When the building opened in 1982, its empty atrium appeared unusually barren. To fill that void, former New Jersey Senator Nicholas Brady organized the Capitol Art Foundation, which raised $650,000 to pay for Calder's work and its installation. A team of fabricators devoted more than a year to assembling the clouds: painting, sanding, repainting in seemingly endless cycles.

In March 1986, the clouds rose to the heavens and construction of the mountains by another firm proceeded more rapidly. The Senate dedicated *Mountains and Clouds* on May 5, 1987.

Calder failed to anticipate two problems. The apparatus designed to rotate the clouds at 140 different speeds has been out of service for years. And, no one has found an easy way to remove the paper airplanes that passersby enjoy sailing from the upper floors onto the clouds' surface.

Mountains and Clouds *by Alexander Calder, located in the Hart Senate Office Building atrium.*

Further Reading

Swisher, Kara. "Calder's Capital Creation: Senate Dedicates 'Mountains, Clouds,'" *Washington Post*, May 6, 1987, B11.

U.S. Congress. Senate. *United States Senate Catalogue of Fine Art*, by William Kloss and Diane K. Skvarla. 107th Congress, 2d sess., 2002. S. Doc. 107-11.

April 6, 1989

The Senate Celebrates 200 Years

In the early 1980s, Senate leaders began to think ahead to the body's forthcoming 200th anniversary in 1989. Wishing to maximize this once-in-a-lifetime opportunity to focus national attention on the Senate's history, traditions, and constitutional role, floor leaders Howard Baker and Robert C. Byrd arranged for the establishment of a special 15-member Study Group on the Commemoration of the Senate Bicentenary. Chaired by former Senate Republican Leader Hugh Scott, the panel included current and former senators, the librarian of Congress, the archivist of the United States, and leading congressional scholars. In 1983, it issued detailed recommendations for a coordinated program of exhibits, symposia, ceremonial events, and publications.

Over the next six years, the recommended projects began to materialize. They included Senator Robert C. Byrd's four-volume history of the Senate, Senator Bob Dole's *Historical Almanac of the U.S. Senate,* the *Biographical Directory of the United States Congress,* the *Guide to the Records of the United States Senate at the National Archives,* an exhibition entitled *A Necessary Fence: The Senate's First Century,* a commemorative Senate postage stamp, and a series of gold and silver congressional bicentennial coins issued by the U.S. Mint.

The highlight of the Senate's bicentennial program began at 11 a.m. on April 6, 1989, as members convened in special legislative session in the Old Senate Chamber. Two former members, in an honor without precedent, were invited to address the Senate. Missouri's Thomas Eagleton counseled senators to appreciate the art of compromise. "It is the essence of our political existence—the grease for the skids of government. Without it, we screech to a halt, paralyzed by intransigence." Tennessee's Howard Baker, who had served as presidential chief of staff after leaving the Senate, urged members to strengthen their partnership with the presidency. "When the partnership has suffered, the nation has inevitably suffered; when [it] has prospered, so have we all."

The Senate then proceeded to its current chamber, festively decorated in red-white-and-blue bunting, to be greeted by the stirring music of a Marine band and soloist. For the next 90 minutes, six senior senators addressed topics related to the Senate's past, present, and future. The session concluded with the adoption of a resolution conveying the Senate's good wishes to the senators of the future. "It is our hope that they will strive ceaselessly to meet the aspiration of Daniel Webster that the Senate be a body to which the Nation may look, with confidence, 'for wise, moderate, patriotic, and healing counsels.'"

Former Senator Howard Baker of Tennessee (1967-1985) delivers remarks during the special session held in the Old Senate Chamber to commemorate the 200th anniversary of the Senate's first quorum.

Further Reading

U.S. Congress. *Congressional Record,* 101st Congress, 1st sess., pp. S3402-10.

U.S. Congress. Senate. F*inal Report of the Study Group on the Commemoration of the United States Senate Bicentenary.* 98th Congress, 1st sess., 1983. S. Doc. 98-13.

October 5-6, 1992

D'Amato Revives Old-time Filibuster

In Frank Capra's 1939 classic film, *Mr. Smith Goes to Washington*, the fictional Senator Jefferson Smith, played by Jimmy Stewart, tried to save a boys' camp. In a real-life imitation of that Hollywood classic, New York Senator Alfonse D'Amato tried to save a typewriter factory.

On October 5, 1992, for the first time since the Senate inaugurated gavel-to-gavel television coverage of its floor proceedings in 1986, television viewers had the opportunity to watch a senator conduct an old-fashioned filibuster—a dusk-to-dawn talkathon.

Those with long memories might have recalled the intense Senate debates over the 1964 Civil Rights Act, in which teams of filibustering senators consumed 57 days between March 26 and final passage on June 19.

The issue in 1992 involved Smith-Corona's plans to move 875 jobs from its Upstate New York typewriter factory to Mexico to save wage costs so that it could compete against low-priced Japanese imports. Senator D'Amato chose his time well. Historically, filibusters have been most effective in achieving the goals of those who conduct them when they occur in the hectic final days of a congressional session, particularly if those days fall on the eve of congressional and presidential elections, when members desire only to leave Washington for the campaign trail. Political observers noted that Senator D'Amato, facing his own tight reelection race, could expect to benefit from the media attention that a televised classic filibuster might produce.

So as not to interrupt other Senate business—a consideration that did not exist in the classic filibusters of the pre-1965 era—D'Amato began speaking around dinnertime on October 5 and continued his "gentleman's filibuster" for 15 hours and 14 minutes. His object was to amend a pending $27-billion tax bill. Hoarse and out of things to say—and to sing—he abandoned his quest at midday on October 6, after the House of Representatives had adjourned for the year, dooming any chances that his amendment would be included in the final legislation. If D'Amato had spoken for another 17 minutes, he would have broken the record Huey Long set in 1935, when he conducted the most notable filibuster in Senate history—the one that included his recipes for fried oysters and turnip-green potlikker.

Proclaiming that he had proudly stood up not only for the workers of New York but also for those of the entire nation, D'Amato went on to win reelection by a mere 90,000 votes out of six million cast.

Alfonse D'Amato, senator from New York (1981-1999).

Further Reading

Bradsher, Keith. "Windy but Proud, D'Amato Sings for Jobs," *New York Times*, October 7, 1992, B4.

U.S. Congress. *Congressional Record*, 102nd Congress, 2nd sess., pp. S16846-S16924 (Daily edition).

January 3, 1993

"Year of the Woman"

The hotly contested 1991 Senate confirmation hearings for Supreme Court nominee Clarence Thomas troubled many American women. Televised images of a committee, composed exclusively of white males, sharply questioning an opposing witness—African-American law professor Anita Hill—caused many to wonder where the women senators were.

In 1991, the Senate included two women members, but neither Nancy Kassebaum of Kansas nor Barbara Mikulski of Maryland served on the Judiciary Committee. Watching the hearings on the West Coast, Washington State senate member Patty Murray asked herself, "Who's saying what I would say if I was there?" Later, at a neighborhood party, as others expressed similar frustrations, Murray spontaneously announced to the group, "You know what? I'm going to run for the Senate."

While Murray set out to raise the necessary funds, two other women several hundred miles to the south in California began work on their own Senate campaigns. As a result of their activity, on January 3, 1993, for the first time in American history, California became the first state in the nation to be represented in the Senate by two women. In the 1992 elections, Dianne Feinstein, a former Democratic mayor of San Francisco, running for the balance of an uncompleted term, trounced her opponent with a margin of nearly two million votes. Barbara Boxer, a 10-year veteran of the U.S. House of Representatives who had joined six of her Democratic women colleagues in a march on the Senate to urge greater attention to Anita Hill's charges, solidly won a full term for that state's other seat.

A week after the election, a front-page *Washington Post* photograph told the story. Standing with exultant Democratic Majority Leader George Mitchell were not only Feinstein and Boxer, but also Carol Moseley Braun of Illinois and Patty Murray of Washington. Never before had four women been elected to the Senate in a single election year.

When the newcomers joined incumbents Kassebaum and Mikulski in January 1993, headline-writers hailed "The Year of the Woman." To this, Senator Mikulski responded, "Calling 1992 the Year of the Woman makes it sound like the Year of the Caribou or the Year of the Asparagus. We're not a fad, a fancy, or a year."

Over the following decade, as the number of women members more than doubled, the novelty of women senators—as Mikulski predicted—began to fade. There may no longer be a market for a revised edition of the popular book published in 2000, *Nine and Counting*.

In the 108th Congress (2003-2005), a record-setting 14 women served as United States senators. Back row, from left: *Olympia Snowe (ME), Mary Landrieu (LA), Hillary Rodham Clinton (NY), Elizabeth Dole (NC), Kay Bailey Hutchison (TX), Barbara Mikulski (MD), Lisa Murkowski (AK), Deborah Stabenow (MI), Maria Cantwell (WA), Patty Murray (WA);* Seated on sofa, from left: *Blanche Lincoln (AR), Barbara Boxer (CA), Susan Collins (ME) Dianne Feinstein (CA).*

Further Reading

Gugliotta, Guy. "'Year of the Woman' Becomes Reality as Record Number Win Seats," *Washington Post*, November 4, 1992, A30.

Mikulski, Barbara, et al. *Nine and Counting: The Women of the Senate*. New York: HarperCollins, 2000.

Senate Impeachment Trial Powers Upheld

Videotaped footage of Walter L. Nixon appearing on the Senate floor in his own defense.

What is the meaning of the verb "to try"? In 1992, justices of the U.S. Supreme Court consulted a shelf-full of dictionaries in search of a precise answer. They sought to settle a case initiated by a federal district judge, who in 1989 had been impeached by the House of Representatives and removed from office by the Senate. Imprisoned on a conviction for lying to a grand jury, Judge Walter Nixon disputed the Senate's interpretation of "try" as it exercised its exclusive constitutional power to "to try all impeachments."

The story began in 1986, when the House delivered to the Senate articles of impeachment against federal Judge Harry Claiborne, who had been imprisoned for tax fraud. As this was the first impeachment case to reach the Senate in half a century, members carefully reviewed the body's trial procedures. The Senate decided to create a special 12-member committee to receive the testimony of Claiborne—who had already been convicted in federal court—rather than tie up the full Senate busy with more pressing matters. On October 7, 1986, after the panel reported its findings, Claiborne appeared in the Senate Chamber for closing arguments. Two days later the Senate convicted and removed him from office.

In 1989, the House referred two more cases to the Senate. In both proceedings, the Senate employed a trial committee and allowed the defendant to participate in closing arguments before the full body. While considering articles against Federal Judge Alcee Hastings, the Senate received impeachment articles against Judge Nixon.

The Senate convicted Hastings in October 1989 and removed Nixon two weeks later. Both former jurists filed suit against the Senate for its use of the trial committee. Nixon argued that the Constitution's framers had used the word "try" to mean that the entire Senate must participate in taking evidence, rather than merely "scanning a cold record" created by a committee. Although lower courts refused to take Nixon's case, he took encouragement from a September 1992 decision in the Alcee Hastings case by Federal District Judge Stanley Sporkin. Finding the Senate's use of the trial committee to be improper, Judge Sporkin reversed Hastings' Senate conviction.

On January 13, 1993, Supreme Court Chief Justice William Rehnquist put his dictionaries away and settled any doubts about all three cases. On behalf of a unanimous court, he ruled that authority over impeachment trials "is reposed in the Senate and nowhere else."

Further Reading

Gerhardt, Michael J. *The Federal Impeachment Process: A Constitutional and Historical Analysis*. Princeton: Princeton University Press, 1996.

Walter L. Nixon, Petitioner v. United States et al. 506 U.S. 224 (1993)

Washington Post, September 18, 1992, and January 14, 1993.

March 24, 1998

Former Senator Mansfield Delivers Delayed Lecture

Minutes before 6 p.m., C-SPAN camera operators took up their assigned positions. In the cramped gallery of the historic Old Senate Chamber, a capacity audience struggled through the narrow aisles to reach its minimally comfortable seats. On the floor below, senators greeted former colleagues, preparing for what all knew would be a historic occasion. On schedule, three men—two in their 50s and one in his 90s—began their procession down the center aisle. At first, they passed unnoticed. Then, as if by signal, the audience erupted in boisterous applause.

Majority Leader Trent Lott, accompanied by Democratic Leader Tom Daschle, began the proceedings by explaining that this was to be the first in a series of "Senate Leader's Lectures." Designed to "foster a deeper appreciation of the Senate as an institution, and to show the way it continues both to adapt to circumstances and to master them," the series would present observations of nine former Senate party leaders and vice presidents of the United States.

Ninety-five-year-old Mike Mansfield then took the lectern to recall lessons learned during his record-setting tenure as leader, from 1961 to 1977. With the Montana Democrat's opening remarks, it became clear to the audience that the evening would bring an added historical treat.

Mansfield explained that he had originally drafted his remarks 35 years earlier, in November 1963. He had done this in response to the whispered criticism from some of his Democratic colleagues, blaming him for not moving more speedily to advance President John F. Kennedy's legislative agenda. "If some of my party colleagues believed that mine was not the style of leadership that suited them, they would be welcome to seek a change." But President Kennedy's assassination on the very afternoon Mansfield had planned to deliver his remarks caused him to shelve his address.

The 1998 lecture series presented an ideal opportunity for Mansfield to dust off his old speech to share its timeless observations about the nature of leadership in the Senate. An opening quotation from the Chinese philosopher Lao Tsu expressed his own leadership style. "A leader is best when the people hardly know he exists. And of that leader, the people will say when his work is done, 'We did this ourselves.'"

Over the next four years, the other speakers in the series carefully consulted the remarks of those who had preceded them, each thereby building a uniquely compelling record on the initial observations of the exemplary Mike Mansfield.

Former Majority Leader Mike Mansfield of Montana (1953-1977) speaks in the Old Senate Chamber.

Further Reading

U.S. Congress. Senate. *Leading the United States Senate*. 107th Congress, 2nd sess., 2002. S. Pub. 107-54.

http://www.senate.gov. Art & History _ People _ Leader's Lecture Series

The Capitol Building as a Target

In 1833, Massachusetts Representative Rufus Choate captured the grandeur and symbolism of the recently completed U.S. Capitol Building. He wrote, "We have built no national temples but the Capitol; we consult no common oracle but the Constitution."

In the years before and since Choate's time, enemies of the United States have repeatedly chosen this "national temple" as a target for their hostilities.

In 1814, while the United States was at war with Great Britain, invading British troops attacked the Capitol and used books from the Library of Congress to fuel the fires that badly damaged the then only partially completed structure. Nearly 50 years later, in 1861, hastily recruited Union troops rushed to Washington to protect the Capitol against Confederate armies in their unsuccessful drive to capture the city. Another half-century passed before the next major attack. In 1915, as the United States asserted its neutrality during the early months of World War I, a German sympathizer detonated a bomb in the Senate Reception Room to protest America's evident sympathies toward Great Britain. Again, in 1971 and 1983, protestors of American foreign policies set off explosives that caused significant damage to the Capitol.

View of the U.S. Capitol Building from the northeast corner.

On the morning of September 11, 2001, the Capitol once again became the target of foreign enemies. As two hijacked commercial airplanes thundered into the twin towers of New York City's World Trade Center, and another flew into the Pentagon, a fourth plane—through the heroic struggle of its passengers—missed its intended target and crashed into a Pennsylvania field southeast of Pittsburgh. All 40 passengers and crew members on United Airlines Flight 93 perished. Subsequent investigations by the National Commission on Terrorist Attacks discovered a high probability that the Capitol was the intended target of the Flight 93 hijackers.

News of the first strike against the World Trade Center reached the Capitol within minutes. In an unprecedented act, the Senate canceled its session moments before the appointed convening time. At 10:15 a.m., officials ordered evacuation of the Capitol and office buildings. While congressional leaders were taken to a secure facility, other members and staff were urged to leave the area amidst rumors that the Capitol was a bombing target.

Over the weeks and months that followed the terrors of September 11, despite unprecedented security enhancements, congressional leaders insisted that the Capitol remain open, continuing more than two centuries of service as the "national temple" of representative democracy.

Further Reading

Daschle, Tom. *Like No Other Time: The 107th Congress and the Two Years That Changed America Forever.* New York: Crown, 2003.

National Commission on Terrorist Attacks on the United States. *The 9/11 Commission Report.* New York: W.W. Norton, 2004.

New Senate Seniority Record Set

During the first 100 years of the Senate's existence, members who made it into their second six-year term were considered long-time veterans. During any Congress of that era, as many as half the senators failed to serve out a full six-year term. In fact, the early 19th century witnessed several complete turnovers of Senate membership within just 12 years.

Looking back to the Senate of the 19th century, when the average life expectancy of an American was slightly above the age of 40, few senators would have believed it possible to serve 30, let alone 40 years. Many hated the rigors of travel to the capital and back home several times a year. Travel by stagecoach, riverboat, or open railway cars extracted a great price in aches and pains. Lodging in rustic accommodations along the way often required senators to share a bed with one or more strangers.

Until the Civil War, up-and-coming politicians who aspired to roles as legislators usually focused their attention on their easier-to-reach state capitols. While they might serve a term or two in the U.S. Congress to gain broader name recognition within their states and to build out-of-state contacts, it was in state legislatures that members had the opportunity to have a direct impact on the daily lives of their constituents.

By the 1870s, however, the nation's capital had become the principal arena for major legislative activity, as evidenced by brutal battles in state legislatures over the election of U.S. senators.

The first person to approach a 30-year service record in the U.S. Senate was Missouri's Thomas Hart Benton, who reached this milestone in 1851. Another 40 years passed, however, before a second senator achieved the three-decade mark. Today, among the 1,885 who have ever served, 47 have logged at least 30 years.

In 2002, the Senate set a new record for member seniority. For the first time in history, as of November 7, the Senate included three incumbent members who had served 40 or more years—Senators Strom Thurmond, Robert C. Byrd, and Edward Kennedy. The start of the 108th Congress in 2003 also saw a Senate with three 40-year veterans: Senators Byrd, Kennedy, and Daniel Inouye.

Only two others among all who have ever served share this 40-year distinction: Arizona's Carl Hayden and Mississippi's John Stennis.

Thomas Hart Benton, senator from Missouri (1821-1851), was the first senator to achieve a 30-year service record in the Senate.

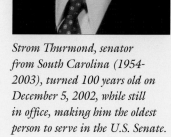

Strom Thurmond, senator from South Carolina (1954-2003), turned 100 years old on December 5, 2002, while still in office, making him the oldest person to serve in the U.S. Senate.

Further Reading
http://www.senate.gov

The Unforgettable 107th Congress

O ver the course of its 656 days in session, from January 3, 2001 to November 22, 2002, the 107th Congress proved to be, in the title of a 2003 memoir by Senate Majority Leader Tom Daschle, "Like No Other Time."

The story of the extraordinary 107th began on election day in November 2000, when—for the first time in history—voters knowingly elected a deceased candidate, Mel Carnahan of Missouri, to a Senate seat. Also on November 7, New York voters chose the First Lady of the United States, Hillary Rodham Clinton, as that state's first woman senator. With the appointment of Carnahan's widow, Jean, to his vacant seat, the number of incumbent women senators rose to a record-breaking 13.

The 2000 election also produced for the first time a Senate with 50 Republicans and 50 Democrats. This placed the Senate under Democratic control for the initial 17 days of the new Congress, with outgoing Vice President Al Gore providing the tie-breaking vote on organizational matters. On January 20, the majority shifted to the Republicans with the swearing-in of Vice President Dick Cheney.

U.S. Senate of the 107th Congress, photographed in the Senate Chamber on May 8, 2002.

On May 24, 2001, Vermont Republican James Jeffords shocked his colleagues and the nation by announcing that he would leave his party to become an Independent and would caucus with the Democratic Party. His action returned Democrats to the majority. Never before the 107th Congress had party control formally shifted within the course of a two-year congressional term.

The September 11, 2001, attacks on the World Trade Center and Pentagon forced a brief evacuation of the Capitol Building for the first time since the War of 1812. Discovery five weeks later of an envelope containing lethal anthrax spores in the Hart Senate Office Building mail room of Majority Leader Daschle resulted in that building's closure—and displacement of the 50 senators with offices there—for three months.

The November 2002 election produced the fourth party shift of the session as Missouri Republican Jim Talent defeated appointed Senator Jean Carnahan, thereby becoming eligible to take his oath of office in the waning days of the 107th.

This extraordinary session ended with the celebration of the 100th birthday of South Carolina's Strom Thurmond, the oldest member in Senate history, and the swearing-in of Alaska Senator Lisa Murkowski, the Senate's 14th woman member. Murkowski became the first senator appointed by her father, an incumbent governor and former senator whose resignation created the vacancy that he appointed her to fill.

Further Reading

Daschle, Tom. *Like No Other Time: The 107th Congress and the Two Years That Changed America Forever.* New York: Crown, 2003.

ACKNOWLEDGEMENTS

Since 1789, 31 secretaries of the Senate have successively guided the chamber's legislative, administrative, and financial operations. Over the past three decades, the Senate Historical Office has had the good fortune of working under the jurisdiction of 11 of these elected Senate officers. We have benefitted greatly from their support, beginning with Secretary of the Senate Francis R. Valeo, who helped establish the Historical Office in 1975. Secretary Valeo's successors include J. Stanley Kimmitt, William F. Hildenbrand, Jo-Anne L. Coe, Walter J. Stewart, Martha S. Pope, Sheila P. Burke, Kelly D. Johnston, Gary L. Sisco, Jeri Thomson, and Emily Reynolds. Secretary Reynolds read an early version of this work and offered incisive editorial and substantive comments, for which we are most grateful. Assistant Secretary Mary Suit Jones also read the entire text with her customary discernment and sensitivity.

Within the Historical Office, this book owes so much to the good humor and technical expertise of Historical Editor Beth Hahn, who balanced its gestation with that of her son, William. Photo Historian Heather Moore enlisted her mastery of the office's extensive photographic collections and those of suitable repositories elsewhere to produce the engaging images displayed within these pages. She also assumed and skillfully managed editorial responsibilities in the crucial weeks before this work went to press. My colleagues Betty K. Koed and Donald A. Ritchie constructively answered countless questions of substance and style.

One could not ask for a more proficient guide through the complex world of printing and graphics than Karen Moore, director of the Senate Office of Printing and Document Services. This volume testifies to the effectiveness of her partnership with talented and helpful staff within the Government Printing Office, including: Jerry Hammond, director of Congressional Publishing Services; Lyle Green, associate director; Joseph Benjamin and Sheron Minter, printing service specialists; Dean Gardei, designer; and Sarah Trucksis, technical specialist.

Finally, I wish to thank former Senate Democratic Leader Tom Daschle for inspiring an earlier series of historical vignettes designed to help busy senators learn more about the issues and personalities that collectively have shaped the Senate of our times.

Richard A. Baker, Senate Historian

CREDITS FOR ILLUSTRATIONS

June 7, 1787: *Scene at the Signing of the Constitution of the United States* by Howard Chandler Christy, Architect of the Capitol

June 19, 1787: *Philadelphia, 1775* by Allyn Cox, Architect of the Capitol

July 16, 1787: National Archives and Records Administration

September 30, 1788: Maclay, U.S. Senate Historical Office; Morris, Library of Congress, LC-USZ62-48942

March 4, 1789: Library of Congress, LC-USZC4-1799

April 7, 1789: National Archives and Records Administration

April 8, 1789: *Samuel Alleyne Otis* by Gilbert Stuart, National Gallery of Art, Washington

April 27, 1789: Library of Congress, LC-USZC2-2645

May 15, 1789: U.S. Capitol Historical Society

July 17, 1789: U.S. Senate Historical Office

August 5, 1789: National Archives and Records Administration

September 11, 1789: U.S. Senate Historical Office

August 12, 1790: Library of Congress, LC-USZC4-4547

December 6, 1790: *Philadelphia in 1858* by Ferdinand Richardt, White House Historical Association, White House Collection

February 20, 1792: National Archives and Records Administration

December 2, 1793: Independence National Historical Park

June 24, 1795: Library of Congress, LC-USZ62-50375

October 24, 1795: U.S. Senate Historical Office

December 9, 1795: Library of Congress, LC-USZ61-1290

December 15, 1795: Library of Congress, LC-USZ62-91143

February 15, 1797: *John Adams* by Eliphalet Andrews, U.S. Senate Collection

February 5, 1798: Independence National Historical Park

June 25, 1798: National Archives and Records Administration

March 27, 1800: *William Duane* by Charles Balthazar Julien Févret de Saint-Mémin, 1802, National Portrait Gallery

November 17, 1800: Watercolor by William Birch, Library of Congress, LC-USZC4-247

February 27, 1801: *Thomas Jefferson* by Thomas Sully, U.S. Senate Collection

October 17, 1803: U.S. Senate Historical Office

November 30, 1804: *Samuel Chase* by Charles Willson Peale, Maryland Historical Society

March 2, 1805: Library of Congress, LC-USZ62-16737

July 19, 1807: Library of Congress, LC-USZ62-83310

April 25, 1808: National Archives and Records Administration

September 19, 1814: Library of Congress, LC-USZC4-11489

October 10, 1814: *View of Congress Library, Capitol, Washington* by Alexander Jackson Davis and Stephen H. Gimber, 1832, I.N. Phelps Stokes Collection of American Historical Prints, Miriam and Ira D. Wallach Division of Art, Prints and Photographs, New York Public Library

October 11, 1814: Library of Congress, LC-USZC4-4555

March 19, 1816: U.S. Senate Historical Office

December 10, 1816: *Plan of the Attic Story of the North Wing of the Capitol U.S. as authorized to be built*, by B. Henry Latrobe, drawn by Frederick C. DeKrafft, 1817, Library of Congress, LC-USZC4-203

November 16, 1818: U.S. Senate Historical Office

March 4, 1825: *J. C. Calhoun*, from a miniature by Blanchard, engraved by A. L. Dick, Library of Congress, LC-USZ62-102297

January 26, 1830: Boston Art Commission

December 13, 1831: Library of Congress, LC-USZC2-2494

June 24, 1834: Library of Congress, LC-USZ6-1538

March 16, 1836: National Archives and Records Administration, Records of the U.S. House of Representatives

January 16, 1837: Library of Congress, LC-USZC4-2386

February 8, 1837: Library of Congress, LC-USZ62-42311

March 14, 1841: *Henry Clay* by Henry F. Darby, U.S. Senate Collection

July 31, 1841: Architect of the Capitol

March 26, 1848: Library of Congress, LC-USZ62-16011

March 4, 1849: Library of Congress, LC-USZ62-109952

March 7, 1850: U.S. Senate Collection

April 3, 1850: Library of Congress, LC-USZ62-4835

July 4, 1851: *Illustrated News*, New York, January 8, 1853, Architect of the Capitol

June 5, 1852: Library of Congress, LC-USZC2-3179

June 29, 1852: Library of Congress, LC-USZ62-14031

May 22, 1856: *The Assault in the U.S. Senate Chamber on Senator Sumner*, in *Frank Leslie's Illustrated Newspaper*, June 7, 1856, U.S. Senate Collection

January 4, 1859: Architect of the Capitol

September 13, 1859: Library of Congress, LC-DIG-cwpbh-02513

January 21, 1861: Library of Congress, LC-USZ62-129742

March 4, 1861: Library of Congress, LC-USZC4-7996

April 19, 1861: Architect of the Capitol

July 11, 1861: *The Cambridge Modern History Atlas*, 1912, University of Texas Libraries

October 21, 1861: *Death of Col. Edward D. Baker, At the Battle of Ball's Bluff near Leesburg Va.*, Currier & Ives print, Library of Congress, LC-USZC2-2229

February 5, 1862: *Expulsion of Senator Bright from the United States Senate for Disloyalty*, wood engraving after M. Lumley, in *Pictorial Battles of the Civil War*, 1885, U.S. Senate Collection

February 18, 1862: Library of Congress, LC-B8171-3360

February 22, 1862: U.S. Senate Historical Office

January 29, 1864: Library of Congress, LC-BH824-5296

March 6, 1867: *History of the United States Capitol* by Glenn Brown, 1900

May 16, 1868: *The Senate as a Court of Impeachment for the Trial of Andrew Johnson*, wood engraving after T. R. Davis, in *Harper's Weekly*, v. 12, 1868, p.232-3, Library of Congress, LC-USZ61-269

September 8, 1869: Library of Congress, LC-USZ62-68701

February 25, 1870: National Archives and Records Administration

January 17, 1871: Willard Saulsbury, Library of Congress, LC-BH83-3539; Eli Saulsbury, Library of Congress, LC-BH826-29268

January 31, 1873: *Harper's Weekly*, March 10, 1860, Library of Congress

March 11, 1874: Library of Congress, LC-USZC2-2228

March 2, 1876: *The Committee-Room of the War Department in the Capitol—General W.W. Belknap, Secretary of War, Appearing Before the Committee on Expenditures*, in *Frank Leslie's Illustrated Newspaper*, March 18, 1876, U.S. Senate Collection

February 5, 1877: U.S. Senate Collection

January 22, 1879: Library of Congress, LC-BH832-176

February 14, 1879: *Blanche Kelso Bruce* by Simmie Knox, U.S. Senate Collection

March 18, 1881: Library of Congress, LC-USZ62-13021

May 16, 1881: *The Scene in the Senate Chamber on the Announcement of the Resignation of Senators Conkling and Platt, of New York, May 16th*, in *Frank Leslie's Illustrated Newspaper*, June 4, 1881, U.S. Senate Collection

September 2, 1884: Library of Congress, LC-BH832-1229

May 13, 1886: *Henry Wilson* by Daniel Chester French, U.S. Senate Collection

August 7, 1893: U.S. Senate Historical Office

June 17, 1894: Library of Congress, LC-BH832-804

November 6, 1898: Architect of the Capitol

December 28, 1898: *Justin Morrill* by Jonathan Eastman Johnson, U.S. Senate Collection

February 22, 1902: Library of Congress, LC-USZ62-9901

March 6, 1903: *Arthur P. Gorman* by Louis P. Dieterich, U.S. Senate Collection

April 28, 1904: Architect of the Capitol

February 17, 1906: U.S. Senate Historical Office

April 19, 1906: Library of Congress, LC-USZ62-106669

May 21, 1906: U.S. Senate Historical Office

July 31, 1906: Architect of the Capitol

April 12, 1907: Library of Congress, LC-USZ62-64181

August 4, 1908: U.S. Senate Historical Office

April 27, 1911: Library of Congress, LC-USZ62-109649

May 11, 1911: Gallinger, Library of Congress, LC-USZ62-134633;
Bacon, U.S. Senate Historical Office

July 14, 1911: U.S. Senate Historical Office

July 13, 1912: Library of Congress

January 28, 1913: Library of Congress, LC-USZ61-1230

March 15, 1913: U.S. Senate Historical Office

May 28, 1913: *J.Hamilton Lewis* by Louis Betts, U.S. Senate Collection

June 2, 1913: Library of Congress, LC-USZ62-105111

March 9, 1914: Library of Congress, LC-USZ62-39672

July 2, 1915: Architect of the Capitol

March 8, 1917: U.S. Senate Historical Office

April 2, 1917: Library of Congress, LC-USZ62-36185

October 6, 1917: Library of Congress, LC-USZ62-39145

September 30, 1918: Library of Congress, LC-USZ62-38965

November 5, 1918: Library of Congress, LC-USZ62-8422

November 19, 1919: Library of Congress, LC-USZ62-8828

January 15, 1920: Underwood, Library of Congress, LC-G39-T01-0088;
Hitchcock, Library of Congress, LC-USZ62-39184

May 12, 1920: Library of Congress, LC-USZ61-1227

May 27, 1920: Architect of the Capitol

November 2, 1920: Library of Congress, LC-USZ62-70724

January 12, 1922: Library of Congress, LC-USZ62-104398

April 15, 1922: Library of Congress, LC-USZ62-61491

November 21, 1922: Library of Congress, LC-USZ62-67895

January 9, 1924: Library of Congress, LC-USZ62-99925

May 2, 1924: Library of Congress, LC-USZ62-98143

January 28, 1925: Library of Congress, LC-USZ62-102581

June 1, 1926: Clifford Berryman cartoon, Library of Congress

May 11, 1928: Library of Congress, LC-USZ62-98148

November 4, 1929: Library of Congress, LC-USZ62-22753

November 24, 1929: Library of Congress, LC-USZ62-119271

May 7, 1930: Library of Congress, LC-USZ62-119996

June 25, 1930: U.S. Senate Historical Office

April 26, 1932: Library of Congress, LC-USZ62-130059

June 17, 1932: Library of Congress, LC-USZ6-525

February 7, 1933: Library of Congress, LC-USZ62-98138

September 4, 1934: La Follette Collection, Manuscript Division, Library
of Congress

June 12-13, 1935: Library of Congress, LC-USZ62-111006

July 1, 1935: Office of the Senate Parliamentarian

July 11, 1935: U.S. Senate Historical Office

January 5, 1937: *Charles L. McNary* by Henrique Medina, U.S. Senate
Collection

March 25, 1937: U.S. Senate Historical Office

July 14, 1937: U.S. Senate Historical Office

October 17, 1939: Library of Congress, LC-USZ62-123288

January 22, 1940: Architect of the Capitol

March 1, 1941: Library of Congress, LC-USZ62-104407

December 26, 1941: Library of Congress, LC-USZ62-51496

October 10, 1942: U.S. Senate Historical Office

November 14, 1942: U.S. Senate Historical Office

July 25, 1943: National Archives and Records Administration

October 19, 1943: U.S. Senate Historical Office

February 24, 1944: National Archives and Records Administration,
Franklin D. Roosevelt Library

September 2, 1944: U.S. Senate Historical Office

May 28, 1945: U.S. Senate Historical Office

September 18, 1945: Library of Congress, LC-USZ62-90080

July 18, 1947: U.S. Senate Historical Office

August 21, 1947: U.S. Senate Historical Office

July 15, 1948: Library of Congress, LC-USZ62-86087

September 13, 1948: U.S. Senate Historical Office

October 1, 1949: Collection of the Supreme Court of the United States

February 9, 1950: Library of Congress, LC-USZ62-105449

May 3, 1950: Library of Congress, LC-USZ62-104405

June 1, 1950: Library of Congress, LC-USZ62-98230

September 22, 1950: University of Kentucky Libraries

February 3, 1951: Library of Congress, LC-USZ62-135260

April 18, 1951: U.S. Senate Historical Office

May 3, 1951: Clifford Berryman cartoon, U.S. Senate Historical Office

April 24-25, 1953: Library of Congress, LC-USZ62-83735

June 9, 1954: U.S. Senate Historical Office

November 2, 1954: Library of Congress, LC-USZ62-127669

November 17, 1954: U.S. Senate Collection

April 30, 1956: Library of Congress, LC-USZ62-46202

July 13, 1956: Architect of the Capitol

July 27, 1956: Library of Congress, LC-USZ62-87410

January 10, 1957: U.S. Senate Historical Office

March 12, 1959: Dirksen Congressional Center

April 14, 1959: Architect of the Capitol

June 19, 1959: Library of Congress, LC-USZ62-77095

November 8, 1959: U.S. Senate Historical Office

October 1, 1960: U.S. Senate Historical Office

March 20, 1962: U.S. Senate Historical Office

April 2, 1962: U.S. Senate Historical Office

September 24, 1963: National Geographic and U.S. Capitol Historical Society

May 8, 1964: U.S. Senate Historical Office

June 10, 1964: National Archives and Records Administration, Lyndon B. Johnson Library

June 25, 1964: Library of Congress, LC-USZ62-106242

July 9, 1964: Associated Press

October 1, 1968: Collection of the Supreme Court of the United States

September 7, 1969: *Everett McKinley Dirksen* by Richard Hood Harryman, U.S. Senate Collection

May 14, 1971: U.S. Senate Historical Office

October 11, 1972: U.S. Senate Historical Office

March 28, 1973: U.S. Senate Historical Office

January 27, 1975: U.S. Senate Historical Office

July 29, 1975: Culver, U.S. Senate Historical Office; Hughes, U.S. Senate Historical Office

September 16, 1975: U.S. Senate Historical Office

June 16, 1976: U.S. Senate Commission on Art

November 22, 1982: U.S. Senate Historical Office

November 7, 1983: U.S. Senate Historical Office

June 2, 1986: C-SPAN

May 5, 1987: Architect of the Capitol

April 6, 1989: U.S. Senate Historical Office

October 5-6, 1992: U.S. Senate Historical Office

January 3, 1993: Office of Senator Barbara Mikulski

January 13, 1993: U.S. Senate Recording Studio

March 24, 1998: U.S. Senate Photo Studio

September 11, 2001: U.S. Senate Photo Studio

November 7, 2002: U.S. Senate Historical Office

November 22, 2002: U.S. Senate Photo Studio